Caledonian Craftsmanship:
The Scottish Latin Tradition

DAVID HOWLETT

In *Caledonian Craftsmanship: The Scottish Latin Tradition* David Howlett presents a documented account of the origins of a brilliant Scottish Latin literature from the end of the 11th century and the 12th. Editions of thirty texts from original manuscripts – liturgical, diplomatic, poetic, hagiographic, historical, genealogical, and theological – many translated here for the first time, illustrate both links with earlier English, Irish, and Welsh Latin traditions and links within the emerging class of Scottish Latin writers. One purpose of this literature was to provide in a common acquired language cultural monuments for a 'Regnum Scottorum', a kingdom of the Scots, embracing Gaels, Britons, Picts, Norsemen, Englishmen, and Normans, independent of both Anglo-Norman kings and English archbishops, in a stylish act of self-definition that has few parallels in European history.

David Howlett is the author of the *The Book of Letters of Saint Patrick the Bishop* (1994), *The Celtic Latin Tradition of Biblical Style* (1995), *The English Origins of Old French Literature* (1996), *British Books in Biblical Style* (1997), *Cambro-Latin Compositions: Their Competence and Craftsmanship* (1998), and *Sealed from Within: Self-Authenticating Insular Charters* (1999). Forthcoming is *Pillars of Wisdom: Irishmen, Englishmen, Liberal Arts*.

Caledonian Craftsmanship
The Scottish Latin Tradition

DAVID HOWLETT

FOUR COURTS PRESS

Typeset in 10.5 pt on 12 pt Bembo by
Carrigboy Typesetting Services, County Cork for
FOUR COURTS PRESS LTD
Fumbally Court, Fumbally Lane, Dublin 8, Ireland
e-mail: info@four-courts-press.ie
and in North America for
FOUR COURTS PRESS
c/o ISBS, 5804 N.E. Hassalo Street, Portland, OR 97213.

© David Howlett 2000

A catalogue record for this title is available
from the British Library.

ISBN 1–85182–485–5

The blocking device on the case of this book incorporates
an eighteenth-century drawing of the seal Thor Logus, used
by permission of the dean & chapter of Durham.

Printed in Great Britain
by MPG Books, Bodmin, Cornwall

For Martin Kauffmann and David Ganz

I owe much to two men, a successor to Richard Hunt in the Bodleian Library, Oxford, and a successor to Julian Brown at King's College, London, both successors to Tilly de la Mare. At a time in which many academics suffer from loss of conviction and purpose both these men sustain the finest traditions of their illustrious predecessors, sharing their learning with those who want it.[1]

1   I owe thanks for helpful criticism to Professor Archibald Duncan, Professor Robert Bartlett, Dr Dauvit Broun, Mr Theodore Christchev, Professor David Dumville, Dr Leofranc Holford-Strevens, Dr Tom O'Loughlin, Mr Roger Norris, Dr Jacques Paviot, and Mr Alan Piper.

CONTENTS

A PRAYER IN THE BOOK OF DEER

The oldest extant Scottish Latin prayer is an *Oratio ante Dominicam Orationem* from the service for Commemoration of the Sick in the Book of Deer.[1] The prayer may have been composed as early as the seventh century, though the copy in this manuscript was written early in the twelfth century. Capital letters and punctuation marks in boldface represent features of Cambridge, University Library, MS Ii.6.32, folios 28v–29r. I have arranged the text in lines, supplied complete texts where the manuscript records only the first few words, and marked the clausular and cursus rhythms.

1   **ITEM ORATIO ANTE DOMINICAM ORATIONEM .**   5

I

2   **C**reator naturarum omnium Deus et parens uniuersarum in celo
       et in térrạ oríginum   13
     has trementis populi tui religiosas preces ex illo inaccessibilis lucis
       throno tŭo súscipē   13
     et inter hiruphin et zaraphin indefessas circumstantium laudes
       exaudi spei non ambigue précatiōnes .   13

II

5   **P**ater noster qui es [in celis
     sanctificetur nomen tuum
     ueniat regnum tuum
     fiat uoluntas tua
     sicut in celo et in terra
10   panem nostrum supersubstantialem da nobis hodie
     et dimitte nobis debita nostra
     sicut et nos dimisimus debitoribus nostris
     et ne inducas nos in temptationem
     sed libera nos a malo. Amen] .   50

1   Michael Lapidge and Richard Sharpe, *A Bibliography of Celtic-Latin Literature 400–1200*, Dictionary of Medieval Latin from Celtic Sources, Ancillary Publications 1 (Dublin: Royal Irish Academy, 1985) [hereafter *BCLL*], no. 1032 p. 287. *The Book of Deer*, ed. J. Stuart, Spalding Club (Edinburgh: Robert Clark, 1869), pp. 89–91, pls X–XI. *Councils and Ecclesiastical Documents Relating to Great Britian and Ireland*, ed. A.W. Haddan and W. Stubbs, 3 vols (Oxford: Clarendon Press, 1869–78), vol. II pt I p. 275. I owe thanks for helpful criticism to Dr Tom O'Loughlin.

III
15 Libera nos Dómine a málo
    Dómine Xpìste Iésu
    custodi nos semper in omni ópere bóno
    Fons et auctor ómnium bonórum
    Deus euacua nos uitiis . et reple nos uirtútibus bónis .
20 per té Xpiste Iésu ∴ —   33

    Hisund dubar sacorfaicc dau . 7   4
IIII
    Corpus cum sanguine Domini nostri Iesu Xpisti sanitas sit tibi in
        uitam perpétuam èt salútem .   15
    Refecti Xpisti corpore et sanguine tibi sémper dicàmus Dómine .
        Alleluia Alleluia .   11
    Quia satiauit animam inanem et animam essurientem sátiauit
        bónis . Alleluia Alleluia .   11
25 ET sacrificent sacrificium laudis et [adnuntient opera eius in]
        éxultatióne . Alleluia Alleluia .   12
    Calicem salutaris accipiam et nomen Dómini ìnuocábo . Alleluia
        Alleluia .   9
    Refecti Xpisti corpore [et sanguine tibi sémper dicàmus Dómine] .
        Alleluia Alleluia .   11
    Laudate Dóminum òmnes géntes . Alleluia Alleluia .   6
V
    Gloria [Patri et Filio et Spiritui Sancto . Sicut erat in principio]   11
30 Refecti Xpisti [corpore et sanguine tibi sémper dicàmus Dómine] .
        Alleluia Alleluia .   11
    et nunc . Et semper [et in secula seculorum Amen] .   9
    Refecti [Xpisti corpore et sanguine tibi sémper dicàmus Dómine .
        Alleluia Alleluia .]   11
    Sacrificate sacrificium iustitie et speráte in Dómino .   7
VI
    Deus tibi grátias ágimus
35 per quem misteria sancta célebráuimus
    et a te sanctitatis dóna depóscimus
    miserere nobis Domine saluator mundi .
    Qui regnas in sécula sèculórum Amen .   26
39 Finit .   I

2 Crętor. cl'o. 3 relegiosas. inaccessibileis. trono. 5 qui es. usque in finem. 17 bona.
22 sangine. perpetua. 23 Reffecti. 25 usque exultatione. 27, 30, 32 Reffecti.
33 iustitię.

24 Psalm CVI 9. 25 Psalm CVI 22. 26 Psalm CXV 13. Psalm CXVI 1. 33 Psalm
IV 16.

I   IN THE SAME MANNER A PRAYER BEFORE THE LORD'S
        PRAYER.

I

     Creator of all natures, God, and progenitor of all beginnings in heaven
         and on earth, these religious prayers of Your trembling people
         receive from that Your throne of inaccessible light,
     and among the unwearied praises of cherubim and seraphim standing
         round hear out the prayings of a not ambiguous hope.

II

5   Our Father, Who are [in the heavens,
     may Your name be sanctified,
     may Your kingdom come,
     may Your will be done
     just as in heaven so also on earth;
10   our more-than-substantial bread give us today,
     and forgive to us our debts
     just as we have forgiven our debtors,
     and may you not lead us into trial,
     but free us from evil. Amen].

III

15   Free us, Lord, from evil,
     Lord, Christ Jesus,
     guard us always in all good work,
     Fountain and author of all good things,
     God, empty us from vices and refill us with good virtues,
20   through You, Christ Jesus.

     Here give the sacrifice to him.

IIII

     May the body with the blood of Our Lord Jesus Christ be health for
         you to perpetual life and salvation.
     Fed[2] with the body and blood of Christ, let us say always to You, Lord,
         Alleluia, Alleluia,
     because He has satisfied the empty soul and satisfied the starving soul
         with good things, Alleluia, Alleluia,
25   and let them sacrifice the sacrifice of praise and [they will announce His
         works in] exultation, Alleluia, Alleluia.
     I will accept the chalice of salvation and I will invoke the name of the
         Lord, Alleluia, Alleluia.
     Fed with the body [and blood] of Christ [let us say always to You, Lord],
         Alleluia, Alleluia.
     Praise the Lord, all peoples, Alleluia, Alleluia.

---

2   Understand the implication of *reficere* as *re-* + *facere* 'to remake', 'to create anew'.

V

    Glory [to the Father and to the Son and to the Holy Spirit. As it was in
        the beginning,]

30   Fed [with the body and blood] of Christ [let us say always to You, Lord],
        Alleluia, Alleluia,
    and now and always [and to ages of ages, Amen.]
    Fed [with the body and blood of Christ let us say always to You, Lord,
        Alleluia, Alleluia].
    Sacrifice the sacrifice of justice and hope in the Lord.

VI

    God, we give thanks to You,

35   through Whom we have celebrated holy mysteries,
    and from You we ask gifts of holiness.
    Be merciful to us, Lord, Saviour of the world,
    Who reign for ages of ages, Amen.

39   It ends.

Let us consider first indications that discrete units of the composition exhibit
their original form intact.

In Part III the thirty-third letter is the first of *Iesu* 17, and the thirty-third
word is *Iesu* 20, Who lived on earth for thirty-three years.

In Part IIII the thirty-third letter is the last of *Iesu* 22.

The shape of the entire composition emerges after restoration of complete
texts of which the manuscript records only the first few words.

The title contains five words and one punctuation mark, together six units.
From the space before *Item* to the space after the punctuation point there are
thirty-two letters and one punctuation point and six spaces, together thirty-nine,
a number that suggests the shape of the entire composition of six sections and
thirty-nine lines.

In section I there are thirteen words in each of the three lines, together
thirty-nine words. From the space before *Creator* to the space after *precationes*
there are 272 letters and spaces between words. Excluding the title and the four
Gaelic words of line 21 and the concluding *Finit* there are in the prayer proper
from *Creator* to *Amen* inclusive 272 words.[3]

Including *Finit* there are 273 words (39 x 7).

Including the title and the four Gaelic words there are 282 words in the
entire composition, which divides into thirds of ninety-four words each. The

3   For other examples of infixed elements that define incrementally the numbers of
    units of composition see below pp. 51, 85, 89, 96, 102, 115, 141, 150, 152, 155, 186–7,
    and David Howlett, 'Insular Acrostics, Celtic Latin Colophons', *Cambrian Medieval
    Celtic Studies* XXXV (1998), pp. 27–44, 'Synodus Prima Sancti Patricii: An Exercise in
    Textual Reconstruction', *Peritia* XII (1998), pp. 238–53, 'The Structure of the Liber
    Angeli', *Ibid.*, pp. 254–70, 'Enigma variations', *Ad Familiares: The Journal of Friends of
    Classics* XVI (1999), pp. xi–xii.

three mentions of the name *Iesu* begin in Part III, before which there are ninety-four words. The 282 words divide by sesquitertian ratio 4:3 at 161 and 121, at *Xpiste | Iesu* 20.

From | *Corpus cum sanguine Domini nostri Iesu* to *saluator mundi qui regnas in secula seculorum* | inclusive there are 888 letters, coincident with the numerical value of the name IHCOYC in Greek alphabetical notation, 10+8+200+70+ 400+200 or 888.[4]

Four features suggest that this prayer is an Insular composition. Survival in a Scottish manuscript and the inclusion of a sentence in Gaelic prove use and transmission among Insular scholars. The correct clausular rhythms of the first few lines indicate a high literary register in the tradition of the fifth-century Romano-British writers Pelagius (*ob. a*430), Patrick (*ob.* 461), and Faustus of Riez (*ob. c*490), the Briton Gildas Sapiens (*fl.* 540), the note about Mo-Sinu maccu Min (*ob.* 610), Columban of Bangor (*ob.* 615), and the Cambro-, Hiberno-, and Anglo-Latin writers who succeeded them.[5] As insertion of spaces between words is an Insular invention of the late sixth or early seventh century, the reckoning of spaces between words indicates that this text is an Insular composition, as distinct from a copy of an earlier Mediterranean or Continental text written in *scriptura continua*. This prayer may be as old as the seventh century. But even if it is only a little older than the twelfth-century Book of Deer in which it survives, it is an appropriate text with which to begin study of the Caledonian tradition. Addressed to the *Creator naturarum omnium Deus*, it exhibits in finely wrought Latin the mathematical art by which the author believed that God *omnia mensura et numero et pondere disposuit.*

4   For other examples of this feature see below pp. 6–9, 159–60, and David Howlett, 'Five Experiments in Textual Reconstruction and Analysis', *Peritia* IX (1995), pp. 1–50 at 30, *The Celtic Latin Tradition of Biblical Style* (Dublin: Four Courts, 1995), p. 151, *The English Origins of Old French Literature* (Dublin: Four Courts, 1996), pp. 131–2, *British Books in Biblical Style* (Dublin: Four Courts, 1997), pp. 119–21, 539–40, *Cambro-Latin Compositions: Their Competence and Craftsmanship* (Dublin: Four Courts, 1998), p. 82, *Sealed from Within: Self-Authenticating Insular Charters* (Dublin: Four Courts, 1999), pp. 89–91.

5   David Howlett, 'Insular Latin Writers' Rhythms', *Peritia* XI (1997), pp. 53–116. The clausulae do not prove that the composition is early. For clausular composition from the fifth century to the eleventh see Howlett, *Celtic Latin Tradition*, pp. 56–72, 79–80, 262–4, *Cambro-Latin Compositions*, pp. 2–14, 40, 113–16, and *Sealed from Within*, pp. 11–50.

A CHARTER OF DUNCAN II
TO THE COMMUNITY OF SAINT CUTHBERT

Let us consider the oldest extant royal Scottish charter of a grant of land that has any claim to authenticity.[1] Although it offers to the diplomatic scholar some apparent difficulties because of the form of the seal, the style of the figure on it, and the manner of its attachment to the charter, Archibald Duncan has presented convincing explanations for all of these. The grant is likely to have been made after the death of Fothad II Bishop of Saint Andrews in A.D. 1093. The charter was written between the death of Malcolm III, Mael Coluim Ceann Mór, Malcolm Canmore, on 13 November 1093 and the death of Duncan II, Donnchad, on 12 November 1094, probably before the end of the first reign of Donaldbane, Domnall Bán, in May 1094, probably at the instigation of Turgot Prior of Durham. For present purposes the reality of the grant and the authenticity of the charter matter less than its existence as a literary artefact.

In the text that follows capital letters and punctuation marks in boldface represent features of Durham, Dean and Chapter, Miscellaneous Charter 554. I have arranged the text in sentences and marked the rhythms of the cursus.

I   **Ego** Dunecanus filius regis **M**alcolumb constans hereditárie rex Scótiae : dedi in elemosina **S**ancto **C**uthberto et suis seruitoribus **T**ininge ham . **A**lde ham . **S**cuc hale . **C**nolle . **H**ather uuich . et de **B**rocces muthe omne seruitium quod inde habuit **F**ódanus epíscopus . et haec dedi in tali quitantia cum sáca et sóca . qualem unquam meliorem habuit Sánctus Cuthbértus . ab illis de quibus tenet suas élemósinas .

II   **Et** hoc dédi pro me ípso . et pro ánima pàtris méi . et pro frátribus méis . et pró uxore méa . et pro infántibus méis .

1   *BCLL*, no. 1049 p. 292. J. Anderson, *Selectus Diplomatum et Numismatum Scotiae Thesaurus* (Edinburgh: Thomas and Walter Ruddiman, 1739), pl. IV. J. Raine, *The History and Antiquities of North Durham* (London: John Bowyer Nichols and Son, 1852), app. no. I p. 1, facsimile opp. p. 373. Cosmo Innes and Sir Henry James, *Facsimiles of the National Manuscripts of Scotland*, 3 vols (Southampton: Ordnance Survey 1867–71), vol. I no. II. *Early Scottish Charters Prior to A.D. 1153*, ed. Sir Archibald C. Lawrie (Glasgow: James MacLehose and Sons, 1905), no. XII pp. 10, 240–3. P. Hume Brown, *History of Scotland to the Present Time*, 3 vols (Cambridge University Press, 1911), vol. I pl. XIV. A.A.M. Duncan, 'The Earliest Scottish Charters', *The Scottish Historical Review* XXXVII (1958), pp. 103–35.

III   Et quoniam uolui quod istud donum stábile ésset . Sáncto Cuthbérto :
           feci quod fratres méi concessérunt .

IIII   Qui autem istud uolúerit destrúere . uel ministris Sancti Cuthberti
           aliquid índe auférre : maledíctionem Déi . et Sáncti Cuthbérti . et méam :
           hábeat . Amen .

           Crux Dun + ecani Regis Scribtoris Gr + entonis Ace + ard Ul + f
               Malcolumb Eadgari
                      +   +
           Vui + get Her + mer Hem + ming Ælf + ric Teo + dbold Ea + rnulf

I   I, Duncan, son of King Malcolm, established King of Scotland by heredity,
           have given in alms to Saint Cuthbert and his own servants Tyningham,
           Aldeham, Scuchale, Cnolle, Hatherwick, and of Broxmouth all the service
           that Bishop Fothad had from that place, and I have given these in such
           quittance with sake and soke [i.e. jurisdiction and the profits that accrue
           from jurisdiction] as better than Saint Cuthbert ever had from those
           [lands] from which he holds his own alms.

II   And I have given this for myself and for the soul of my father and for my
           brothers and for my wife and for my infants.

III   And as I have wished that that gift to Saint Cuthbert be stable I have
           made that my brothers have conceded.

IIII   Who, however, might wish to destroy that or to take away anything from
           that place from the ministers of Saint Cuthbert should have the curse of
           God and Saint Cuthbert and mine. Amen.

           The Cross of Dun+can the king, of the scribe Gr+ento, Ace+ard, Ul+f,
           Malcolm +, of Edgar +, Vui+get, Her+mer, Hem+ming, Ælf+ric,
           Teo+dbold, A+rnulf.

     The scribe of the original charter signed himself as Grento. The scribe of this
copy of the charter 'is also to be found at work in one writ of Rufus and two
literary manuscripts, and … his name was William. He certainly worked at
Durham, and was probably a monk-chaplain.'[2] He may have been William the
cantor, a Norman brought to Durham in or soon after 1091 by Bishop William
of Saint Calais.[3]

2   Duncan, 'Charters', p. 122.
3   Michael Gullick, 'The Hand of Symeon of Durham: Further Observations on the
     Durham Martyrology Scribe', Symeon of Durham: Historian of Durham and the North,

The point of the charter is stated in the central word *elemosinas* at the end of the first sentence, the sixtieth of 119 words of the charter proper. The charter contains four sentences, the first two beginning *Ego … dedi … et haec dedi* and *Et hoc dedi*, the last two beginning *Et quoniam uolui* and *Qui autem uoluerit*. The entire text is composed on multiples of the number 4.[4] From the beginning of the charter to | *Sancto Cuthberto* there are twelve words (4 x 3). From | *Cuthberto* to *Cuthbertus* | inclusive there are forty words (4 x 10), and from *Sanctus Cuthbertus* | to *Sancto Cuthberto* | there are also forty words. From | *Sancto Cuthberto* to *Sancti Cuthberti* | there are sixteen words (4 x 4). From *Sancti Cuthberti* | to *Sancti Cuthberti* | there are eight words (4 x 2), after which there are four words (4 x 1) to the end of the text. From *regis* | to *rex* | there are four words (4 x 1). From *istud* | to | *istud* there are twelve words (4 x 3). From | *seruitoribus* to *seruitium* | there are sixteen words (4 x 4). From *uolui* | to *uoluisset* | there are sixteen words. From *elemosina* | to *elemosinas* | there are forty-eight words (4 x 12). Between the first *dedi* and the third *dedi* there are fifty-two words (4 x 13), and from the first *dedi* to the second *dedi* inclusive there are twenty-four words (4 x 6). There are twelve witnesses (4 x 3) to the charter.

Reckoning letters as numbers, $A=1$, $B=2$, $C=3$ … $X=21$, $Y=22$, $Z=23$, the numerical value of the name *DUNECANUS* is $4+20+13+5+3+1+13+20+18$ or 97 and the value of the name *CUTHBERTUS* is $3+20+19+8+2+5+17+19+20+18$ or 131.[5] From the space before *Ego Dunecanus* to the space before *Cuthberto* inclusive there are ninety-seven letters and punctuation mark and spaces between words. In sentence 1 apart from the four syllables of *Dunecanus* there are 131 syllables.

Reckoning the elements of the place-names and separated personal names separately, there are 144 words in the entire composition, 144 being the square of 12 and the twelfth number in the Fibonacci series 1–1–2–3–5–8–13–21–34–55–89–144, the number of cubits in the walls of the heavenly Jerusalem and part of the number of the elect.[6] As a device for fixing the date this might suggest the 144th day of the year, 24 May, which fell in the year 1094 on the

ed. David Rollason, Studies in North-Eastern History I (Stamford: Shaun Tyas, 1998), pp. 14–31 at 21; A.J. Piper, 'The Early Lists and Obits of the Durham Monks', *Ibid.*, pp. 161–201 at 161, 174, 178, pl. 6d.

4   For other examples of composition on multiples of 4 see below pp. 10–14, 49, 90, and Howlett, *Sealed from Within*, pp. 89–91.

5   See above p. 5 and below pp. 22, 35, 58–61, 84, 89, 95, 141, 159–60, 174, 184.

6   Apocalypse VII 4 and XXI 12. For other examples of play with the number 144 see below pp. 75, 96, 150, 174, and David Howlett, *Liber Epistolarum Sancti Patricii Episcopi: The Book of Letters of Saint Patrick the Bishop* (Dublin: Four Courts, 1994), pp. 43, 46, 'Five Experiments', pp. 17, 47, 'Seven Studies in Seventh-Century Texts', *Peritia* X, pp. 1–70 at 53, *Celtic Latin Tradition*, pp. 21, 25, 71, 264, *British Books in Biblical Style*, pp. 19, 26, *Cambro-Latin Compositions*, pp. 133–4, 137, *Sealed from Within*, pp. 19, 36, 56, 66, 91.

Wednesday before Whitsun, consistent with 'the period before the end of the first "usurpation" of Donaldbane in May'.[7] There are 888 characters and spaces between words, the value of the name IHCOYC in Greek alphabetical notation being 10+8+200+70+400+200 or 888.[8]

Composition with so many infixed features that authenticate the text, if not the grant,[9] is hardly to be expected in the first monument of a tradition. But there is no reason to suppose that this was the first such monument.[10] It stands rather as the oldest extant Scottish document in a long tradition of distinctively English diplomatic compositions that stretch back to a charter from Hlothhere King of the dwellers in Kent to Abbot Beorhtwald of Reculver on a single sheet of A.D. 679,[11] 415 years before this charter. Regardless of the reality of the grant described in this document, the text illustrates a form of Latinity considered by scholars of the late eleventh century suitable for expression of claims to the ownership of land.

7 For other examples of infixed dates see below pp. 23, 36, 59, 61, 74, 83–5, 89, 96, 110, 142, 150, 160, 174, 182–4, and Howlett, *Celtic Latin Tradition*, pp. 101–2, 124–9, 152, 187–93, 222–3, 268–73, 332–3, 'Five Experiments', pp. 29–30, 'Seven Studies', pp. 1–6, 20, 68–9, 'A Possible Date for Aldhelm's Letter to Heahfrith', *Archivum Latinitatis Medii Aevi* LIV (1996), pp. 99–103, 'Arithmetic Rhythms in Latin Letters', *Ibid.* LVI (1998), pp. 193–225, 'Numerical Play in Wulfstan's Verse and Prose', *Mittellateinisches Jahrbuch* XXXI (1996), pp. 61–7, *Cambro-Latin Compositions*, pp. 42–3, 67–8, 80–3, 93–4, 107, 126, 140–1, 149, 152, *Sealed from Within*, pp. 21, 35, 47, 55, 77.

8 For other examples of play with the number 888 by Insular authors see above pp. 5–9 and below pp. 159–60.

9 'The lands granted were part of the endowment of the see of S. Andrew's, to which they again reverted; probably when Duncan's usurpation of the Scottish throne came to an end.' Haddan and Stubbs, *Councils*, vol. II pt. I p. 165. According to Lawrie, *Charters*, p. 242, 'This grant ... was inoperative; the monks of St. Cuthbert at Durham never possessed these lands'.

10 For analysis of other early Scottish charters, including a memorandum of agreement between Malcolm III and Queen Margaret and the monks of Durham in 1093, see Howlett, *Sealed from Within*, pp. 87–94.

11 Howlett, 'Insular Latin Writers' Rhythms', pp. 98–104, *Sealed from Within*, pp. 13–22. Analysis of compositions in *Sealed from Within* reveals the utter distinctness of Welsh and Cornish and Irish from English charters and the great similarity between Scottish and English charters.

A CHARTER OF THOR LONGUS
TO THE COMMUNITY OF SAINT CUTHBERT

Here follow three texts about a grant of land from a layman named Thor Longus, who after improving land given by King Eadgar, son of Malcolm Canmore, presented it to the community of Saint Cuthbert,[1] then appealed to Eadgar's brother Earl David to confirm the grant. Thor must have received the land before the death of Eadgar on (?) 8 January 1107 and directed his appeal after the death of Eadgar but before the accession of David on 25 April 1124. Capital letters and punctuation marks in boldface represent features of a charter of Durham, Dean and Chapter, now lost but represented by a facsimile in Anderson's *Diplomata* and by a copy in *Cartularium Vetus*, folio 114v. I have arranged the text in sentences and clauses and marked the rhythms of the cursus.

OMNIBUS SANCTAE MATRIS ECCLÉSIAE FÍLIIS .
THOR LONGUS IN DÓMINO SALÚTEM .

I   **S**ciatis quod **Æ**dgarus dominus meus Rex Scottorum dedit mihi
       Ædnaham desértam .
     quam ego suo auxilio et mea propria pecunia ínhabitáui .
     et ecclesiam in honorem Sancti **C**uthbérti fabricáui .
     Quam ecclesiam cum una cárrucata térrae
     Deo et Sancto **C**uthberto et mónachis eíus   5
     in perpetuum póssidendam dédi .

II   **H**anc igitur donationem feci pro anima domini mei Régis **Æ**dgari .
     et pro animabus patris et mátris illíus .
     et pro salute fratrum et sorórum ipsíus .
     et pro redemptione Lefwini fratris mei dílectíssimi .   10
     et pro meimet ipsi tam corporis quam ánimae salúte .

III   **E**t si quis hanc meam donationem Sancto praedicto et monachis
       sibi séruiéntíbus
     aliqua ui uel ingenio auférre praesúmpserit .

---

1   Anderson, *Diplomata*, pl. LXIX (upper). Lawrie, *Charters*, no. XXIV p. 19.

auferat ab eo Deus Omnipotens uitam régni caeléstis .
et cum diabolo et angelis eius penas sustíneat aetérnas . Amen .   15

3 honore. 7 Hane.

TO ALL SONS OF HOLY MOTHER CHURCH
LONG THOR IN THE LORD GREETING.

I   You should know that Eadgar my lord, King of the Scots, gave to me
      Ednam derelict,
which I with his aid and my own proper money inhabited,
and I built a church in honour of Saint Cuthbert,
which church with one carrucate of land
to God and Saint Cuthbert and his monks   5
I gave to be possessed in perpetuity.

II   This donation therefore I have made for the soul of my lord, King
      Eadgar,
and for the souls of the father and mother of that man,
and for the salvation of the brothers and sisters of the same man,
and for the redemption of Leofwine my most beloved brother,   10
and for my very self for the salvation as much of body as of soul.

III And if anyone this my donation to the foresaid saint and the monks
      serving him
should presume to take away by any force or ruse,
may God Almighty take away from him the life of the celestial realm,
and may he sustain eternal punishments with the devil and his
      angels. Amen.   15

    The Salutation contains ten words, in the central of which, fifth from the beginning and fifth from the end, the donor mentions his beneficiaries, *filiis*, and names himself, *Thor*. The ten words divide by extreme and mean ratio at 6 and 4, between his name and his soubriquet, *Thor | Longus*.

    The text of the charter is composed on multiples of the number 4.[2] After the Salutation there are six lines in the first sentence, five in the second, and four in the third, together sixteen lines (4 x 4).[3] There are forty-four words (4 x 11) in the first sentence, forty (4 x 10) in the second, thirty-six (4 x 9) in the third.

2   For another example of composition on multiples of 4 see above pp. 6–9.
3   For other examples of serial composition see below p. 83 and Howlett, *Celtic Latin Tradition*, pp. 152–6, 338–42, 355–8. For composition specifically on the series 3–4–5 see below pp. 14, 176.

There are four words (4 x 1) between *Domino* | and | *dominus*. There are eight words (4 x 2) from | *ecclesiam* to *ecclesiam* | inclusive, as there are from | *anima* to *animabus* | inclusive. After *fratrum fratris* is the eighth word. There are twelve words (4 x 3) from | *Sancti* to *Sancto* | inclusive, as there are from | *Cuthberti* to *Cuthberto* | inclusive. After *salute salute* is the twentieth word (4 x 5). There are twenty-four words (4 x 6) from *sciatis* to *honorem* before | *Sancti Cuthberti*. After *ecclesiae ecclesiam* is the twenty-eighth word (4 x 7). Between *anima* | and | *animae* there are thirty-two words (4 x 8). From | *sanctae* to *sancti* | inclusive there are thirty-six words (4 x 9). After *dedit dedi* is the thirty-sixth word. From | *donationem* to *donationem* | inclusive there are forty-four words (4 x 11). From | *dominus* to *domini* | inclusive there are forty-eight words (4 x 12), as there are from | *rex* to *regis* | inclusive. From | *Ædgarus* to *Ædgari* | inclusive there are fifty-two words (4 x 13). From | *Sancto* to *Sancto* | inclusive there are fifty-six words (4 x 14). From | *monachis* to *monachis* | inclusive there are fifty-six words (4 x 14). Between *matris* | and | *matris* there are sixty-eight words (4 x 17). After *Deo Deus* is the seventy-second word (4 x 18). After *salutem salute* is the eighty-fourth word (4 x 21).

Among the pronouns with which Thor refers to himself there are four words before *meus*, after which the fourth word is *mihi*, after which the fourth word is *ego*, after which the fourth word is *mea*. From | *mea* to *mei* | inclusive there are thirty-six words. After *mei* the fourth word is *meimet*. From | *meimet* to *meam* | inclusive there are twelve words. *Meam* is the thirty-second word from the end of the charter.

As noted above the numerical value of the name *CUTHBERTUS* is 131. From | *Sciatis* to | *Sancti Cuthberti* there are 131 letters. The name *THOR* bears a numerical value of 19+8+14+17 or 58. Between *ego* | and | *Lefwini fratris mei* there are fifty-eight words. The name *LEFWINUS* bears a numerical value of 11+5+6+40+9+13+20+18 or 122. From | *pro redemptione Lefwini* to *Amen* | inclusive there are 122 syllables.

The 130 words of the complete charter divide by extreme and mean ratio at 80 and 50. Between *Ædgarus* | and | *Ædgari* there are fifty words.

Thor subsequently wrote between 1107 and 1117 to Earl David seeking confirmation of the grant. The brief survives in Durham as Miscellaneous Charter 722, with a seal that reads *THOR ME MITTIT AMICO*.[4]

DOMINO SUO KARISSIMO .DAVIDI. COMITI .
THOR OMNINO SUUS . SALUTEM .

I   Sciatis domine mi quod Eadgarus Rex frater uester dedit mihi
        Édnaham desértam .
     quam ego suo auxilio et mea pecunia ínhabitáui .

4   Anderson, *Diplomata*, pl. LXIX (lower). Lawrie, *Charters*, no. XXXIII pp. 25–6.

et ecclesiam **a** fundaméntis fabricáui .
quam frater uester rex in honorem **S**ancti **C**uthberti fécit dedicári .
et una carrucata terrae éam dotáuit .   5

II   **H**anc eandem ecclesiam pro **a**nima eiusdem domini mei **R**égis **E**ádgari
        et pátris et màtris uéstri .
        et pro salute uestra et **R**egis **A**lexandri et **M**athíldis **R**egínae
        Sancto praedicto et **M**ónachis eìus dédi .

III   **U**nde uos precor sicut dominum méum karíssimum .   10
        ut pro animabus parentum uestrorum et pro salúte uiuórum
        hanc donationem **S**ancto **C**uthberto et **M**onachis sibi in perpetuum
            seruitúris concedátis .

7 urę.

TO HIS OWN DEAREST LORD DAVID THE EARL THOR, ENTIRELY HIS OWN, GREETING.

I   You should know, my lord, that King Eadgar your brother gave to me
            Ednam derelict,
        which I with his aid and my money inhabited,
        and I built a church from the foundations,
        which your brother the king made to be dedicated in honour of Saint
            Cuthbert,
        and with one carrucate of land he endowed it.   5

II   This same church for the soul of the same lord, my King Eadgar,
        and your father's and mother's,
        and for your salvation and King Alexander's and Queen Mathilda's
        to the foresaid saint and his monks I gave.

III   Whence I pray you as my dearest lord   10
        that for the souls of your parents and for the salvation of living men
        this donation to Saint Cuthbert and his monks bound to serve in
            perpetuity you concede.

Earl David replied with the following confirmation, which survives in Durham,
Cartularium Vetus, folio 114v.[5]

5   Lawrie, *Charters*, no. XXXIV p. 26.

DAVID COMES
IOHANNI EPISCOPO ET OMNIBUS SUIS FIDELIBUS
ET LODONEO SALUTEM

Sciatis quod ego do et concedo Deo et Sancto Cuthberto et monachis eius ecclesiam de Edenham et unam carrucatam terrae sicut Thor Longus dedit liberam et quietam pro anima patris mei et pro ... animae meae et coniugis meae et fratrum meorum et sororum.

DAVID THE EARL
TO JOHN THE BISHOP AND ALL HIS FAITHFUL MEN
AND TO LOTHIAN GREETING.

You should know that I give and concede to God and Saint Cuthbert and his monks the Church of Ednam and one carrucate of land just as Long Thor gave, free and quit, for the soul of my father and for [the salvation] of my soul and my wife's and my brothers' and sisters'.

Thor's letter exhibits structural features similar to those of his charter, but different numbers. There are three sentences, containing five, four, and three lines respectively. The words of Thor's Salutation are arranged in a little chiasmus: *suo – Dauidi – Comiti – Thor – suus*. There are nine words in the Salutation and ninety-nine words in the rest of the letter, the whole being composed on multiples of the number 11. Between *regis* | and | *regis* there are eleven words (11 x 1). After *ecclesiam ecclesiam* is the twenty-second word (11 x 2). *Cuthberti* is the thirty-third word (11 x 3), and between *Sancti Cuthberti* | and | *sancto praedicto* there are thirty-three words. Between *domine mi* | and | *domini mei* there are forty-four words (11 x 4). After *rex regis* is the forty-fourth word. Before *dedit* there are seventeen words, and after *dedi* there are twenty-seven words, together forty-four. The central word, fifty-fifth from the beginning of the Salutation (11 x 5), is *anima*. From | *domine mi* to *dominum meum* | inclusive there are seventy-seven words (11 x 7). From *salutem* to *salute* | *uiuorum* there are eighty-eight words (11 x 8), and from | *domino meo carissimo* to *dominum meum carissimum* | inclusive there are also eighty-eight words.[6]

Whether Thor Longus drafted his own prose matters less than the fact that both his grant and the request for confirmation of it are recorded in craftsmanly Latin, composed with many infixed and mutually corroborative devices that make the text proof against change by any tamperer who does not understand the coherence of the original structure.

6   For other examples of composition on multiples of 11, 111, 1111 see below pp. 17, 102, 174, 183–4, 186–7, and Howlett, 'Five Experiments', p. 15, 'Seven Studies', pp. 6–20, 'Vita I Sanctae Brigitae', *Peritia* XII (1998), pp. 1–23, *The English Origins of Old French Literature*, pp. 125–6, 130–1, 142–5, *Cambro-Latin Compositions*, pp. 135–7, *Sealed from Within*, p. 88.

VERSES IN SAINT MARGARET'S GOSPEL BOOK

The oldest extant Scottish Latin verses, written in script from about the year 1100, relate an episode in the history of the Gospel Book that belonged to Saint Margaret,[1] granddaughter of Eadmund Ironside, daughter of Eadweard the Exile, sister of Eadgar the Ætheling, and from about 1069 queen of Malcolm III. She was the mother of Kings Eadgar and David mentioned in the texts of charters and brief considered above, mother of Kings Alexander and David mentioned in texts to be considered below.[2] In the text that follows capital letters and punctuation marks in boldface represent features of Oxford, Bodleian Library, MS Lat. Liturg. F.5, folio 2r.

> **X**piste tibi semper grates persoluimus omnes .
> **T**empore qui nostro nobis miracula pandis ;
> **H**unc librum quidam inter se iurare uolentes ;
> **S**umpserunt nudum sine tegmine neque ligatum
> **P**rebuit accipie**ns** ponit sinuamine uestis .   5
> **F**lumine tran**s**misso codex est mersus in amnem ;
> **P**ortitor ignorat librum penetrasse profundum ;
> **S**ed miles quidam cerne**ns** post multa momenta ;
> **T**ollere iam uoluit librum de flumi**ne** mersum ;
> **S**ed titubat subito librum dum uidit apertum ;   10
> **C**rede**ns** quod codex ex toto perditus esset ;
> **A**ttamen inmitte**ns** undis corpus cum uertice summo ;
> **H**oc euangelium profert de gurgite apertum ;
> **O** uirtus clara cunctis o gloria magna ;

---

1   *BCLL*, no. 1023 p. 284. *The Gospel Book of St. Margaret, Being a Facsimile reproduction of St. Margaret's Copy of the Gospels preserved in the Bodleian Library Oxford*, ed. W. Forbes-Smith (Edinburgh: David Douglas, 1896), p. 11. R. Gameson, 'The Gospels of Margaret of Scotland and the Literacy of an Eleventh-Century Queen', *Women and the Book, Assessing the Visual Evidence*, ed. L. Smith and J.H.M. Taylor (British Library and University of Toronto Press, 1996), pp. 148–71, facsimile p. 148, text and transl. pp. 165–6. Gameson's statement 'that line 14 does not scan' wants adjustment. The verse can be scanned with one false quantity in *clara*.

2   See above pp. 6–14 and below pp. 19–24, 66–7, 124–6, 146–7, 151–4.

Inuiolatus enim codex permansit ubique ;   15
Exceptis foliis binis que cernis utrinque ;
In quibus ex undis paret contractio quedam ;
Que testantur opus Xpisti pro codice sancto ;
Hoc opus ut nobis maius mirabile constet
De medio libri pannum lini abtulit unda ;   20
Saluati semper sint rex reginaque sancta ;
Quorum codex erat nuper saluatus ab undis .
Gloria magna Deo librum qui saluat eundem ;   23

O Christ, we always give all thanks to you,
Who in our time show miracles to us.
Men wishing to swear oaths among themselves
Took this book without cover and unbound.
The carrier tucked it folded in his clothes,   5
And when he crossed a stream the book slipped out.
He did not know that it had sunk below.
A soldier, after looking for some while,
Wished from the stream to take the sunken book,
But staggered when he saw it lying open,   10
For he believed it would be wholly lost.
Yet, leaping where the deepest whirlpool was,
He brought this open Gospel from the swirl.
O glory great and power clear to all!
The book remained undamaged everywhere,   15
Except for these two pages that you see,
On which some shrinking from the water shows,
Which proves the care of Christ for this His book.
To make a greater miracle for us
The wave brought from the book a flaxen cloth.   20
Unharmed be the king and holy queen
Whose manuscript unharmed came from the flood.
And glory be to God, Who saved the book.   23

This is a versified account of a story related by Turgot in chapter XI of his *Vita Margaritae Reginae*.[3]

The soldier retrieved the book by putting his body into the waves of the river in the deepest whirlpool, *uertice summo*. That is the 'deepest', 'inmost', part of the poem, at the end of the longest, seven-footed, line 12.[4] The poet

3 See below pp. 111–15.
4 For an earlier Celtic Latin example of the weighting of a central verse see line 14 of the *Praefatio Vitae Uuinualoei* by Uurdisten of Landévennec, about A.D. 880, in Howlett, *Celtic Latin Tradition*, p. 265: *Conquatiat. Neque enim huic operi inuitum attraho quemquam.*

composed twenty-three verses, arranged 11–1–11.[5] In this central line there are eleven syllables before *uertice summo*, the first words of the second half of the poem, after the central seventy-fifth of 149 words.

The poet refers to the book eleven times as *librum* 3, *codex* 6, *librum* 7, *librum* 9, *librum* 10, *codex* 11, *codex* 15, *codice* 18, *libri* 20, *codex* 22, *librum* 23, and important words recur at multiples of 11. From | *saluati* 21 to *saluatus* | 22 there are eleven words (11 x 1). From | *mersus* 6 to *mersum* | 9 there are twenty-two words (11 x 2). The last of *de medio libri* | 20 is the 'middle' eleventh of twenty-two words between *codice* 18 and *codex* 22. From | *codice sancto* 18 to *reginaque sancta* | 21 there are twenty-two words. After *Xpisti* | 18 *Deo* | 23 is the thirty-third word, 33 being the age of Jesus Christ when He ascended to God (11 x 3). From | *undis* 12 to *undis* | 17 there are thirty-three words. After *undis* | 17 there are forty-four words (11 x 4) to the end of the poem. From | *cernens* 8 to *cernis* | 16 there are fifty-five words (11 x 5). From | *gloria* 14 to *gloria* | 23 there are also fifty-five words. From *miracula* | 2, the eleventh word, to *mirabile* | 19 there are 110 words (11 x 10). From *Xpiste* | 1 to | *Xpisti* 18 there are 110 words, or reckoned another way, from | *Xpiste* 1 to | *Xpisti* 18 there are 111 words.

The poet plays with the ratios of cosmic and musical theory. The 149 words of the poem divide by duple ratio 2:1 at 99 and 50, at *binis* | 16, before which there are two words in the line. They divide by extreme and mean ratio at 92 and 57, at | *codex* 15. They divide by sesquialter ratio 3:2 at 89 and 60, at *librum* | 10. They divide by sesquioctave ratio 9:8 at 79 and 70, at *euangelium* | 13.

The poet arranged words and ideas in a chiastic pattern.

14	1	o gloria magna
15	2a	inuiolatus
15	2b	codex
16	3	undis
20	4	| de medio libri
20	3'	unda
21	2'a	saluati
22	2'b	codex
23	1'	gloria magna

The 149 words of the entire poem divide by extreme and mean ratio at 92 and 57. The passage from | *o gloria magna* to *gloria magna* | inclusive contains exactly fifty-seven words, which divide in turn by extreme and mean ratio at 35 and 22, at the crux of the chiasmus, | *de medio libri*. The poet has made the word *medio* illustrate the sense 'middle' in that the last of *de medio libri* | 20 is the central eleventh word of twenty-two between *codice* 18 and *codex* 22. But he has made the same word also illustrate the sense 'mean' in that the first of | *de medio libri*

---

5 For other examples of composition on multiples of 11 see above p. 14 and below pp. 102, 174, 183–4, 186–7.

stands at the golden mean of the passage.[6] In the major part of the golden
section the thirty-five words divide by duple ratio 2:1 at 23.3 and 11.7, at *exceptis
foliis binis qu|e cernis utrinque*. We have noted above that the poet made the duple
ratio of the words of the entire poem fall at *binis* |.

Observing a widespread convention of reference to himself or his patrons at
one-ninth and eight-ninths of a composition,[7] the poet divided the twenty-
three lines at 20.4 and 2.6 and the 149 words at 132 and 17, at *saluati semper sint
| rex reginaque sancta* at the centre of line 21.

There is much to be said for the architectonic standards of both composition
and reading in a tradition that begins with such a work. We shall see hereafter
many indications that other Scottish Latin writers of both prose and verse shared
a deep understanding of the art exhibited here.

6   For other examples of this device see below p. 123, Howlett, '*Vita I Sanctae Brigitae*',
     pp. 1–23, *Celtic Latin Tradition*, pp. 379–81, and *Sealed from Within*, p. 100.
7   For other examples of authorial self-reference at places determined by sesquioctave
     ratio and one-ninth and eight-ninths see below pp. 22, 90, 95, 106, 160, 184, and
     D.R. Howlett, 'Some Criteria for Editing Abaelard', *Archivum Latinitatis Medii Aevi*
     LI (1993), pp. 195–202 at 198–9, 'Aldhelm and Irish Learning', *Ibid*. LII (1994), pp.
     37–75 at 70, 'Two Works of Saint Columban', *Mittellateinisches Jahrbuch* XXVIII (1994
     for 1993), pp. 27–46 at 29, 'Numerical Play in Wulfstan's Verse and Prose', *Ibid*. XXXI
     (1996), pp. 61–7 at 63–4, 'Busnois' Motet *In hydraulis*: An Exercise in Textual
     Reconstruction and Analysis', *Plainsong and Medieval Music* IV (1995), pp. 185–91 at
     189–90, 'Five Experiments', pp. 5, 15–17, 28–30, 'The Polyphonic Colophon to
     Cormac's Psalter', *Peritia* IX (1995), pp. 81–90 at 83, 'Seven Studies', pp. 36, 46,
     '*Rubisca*: An Edition, Translation, and Commentary', *Peritia* X (1996) pp. 71–90 at 89,
     'Insular Latin Writers' Rhythms', pp. 83, 87, 'Insular Acrostics, Celtic Latin Colophons',
     pp. 27–44 at 30, 33–4, 43, *Book of Letters*, p. 46, *Celtic Latin Tradition*, pp. 84, 115, 119,
     129, 132, 181, 215, 222, 227–8, 259, 267, 272, 354, 371–2, 378, 384, 394, *English Origins*,
     pp. 25, 45, 61, 66, 73, 88–90, 95, 98, 104, 109, 117–8, 122–3, 127, 142, 145–6, *British
     Books in Biblical Style*, pp. 240, 246, 540, 611–12, *Cambro-Latin Compositions*, pp. 42–3,
     62–3, 67, 74, 107, 112–13, 137, 140, 152.

SIMEON:
'VERSUS IN SANCTUM COLUMBAM'

The verses about Saint Columba that follow were written by a poet named Simeon to accompany a text of Adomnán's *Vita Sancti Columbae*, at the command of King Alexander I, son of Malcolm III and Queen Margaret, and under the direction of William, identified as Bishop William of Man.[1] Although the verses survive in a manuscript of the end of the twelfth century or the beginning of the thirteenth, they must have been written during the reign of Alexander, between 8 January 1107 and 25 April 1124. The terminal dates can be narrowed further. The reference in line 17 to Queen Sybilla implies composition before her death in 1122. As William was succeeded by Bishop Wymund A.D. 1109X1114, the verses must have been composed during the period between 1107 and 1114. Capital letters and punctuation marks in boldface represent features of London, British Library, MS Cotton Tiberius D.III, folio 217ra. Italics mark rhymes between the caesura and the end of a verse. Solid underlining marks alliteration within a line. Dotted underlining marks alliteration between adjacent lines. Text within square brackets derives from an edition by Ussher, who had access to the manuscript before it was damaged in the library fire of 1731. Letters within angle brackets are my insertions on the basis of rhyme and chiastic arrangement of diction.

<SIMEONIS POETAE VERSUS IN SANCTUM COLUMBAM>

> **S**ancte Columb*a* p*ater* quem fudit [Hiberni*a* m*at*]*er* **.**
> **Q**u*em* **X**p*i*sti nu*men* dedit [ecclesie for]e lu*men* **.**
> **Q**u*e* tibi scripta d[amus tibi si]nt accepta rogamus **.**
> **N**a[m licet indig]ne tua scripsimus acta [benigne .]
> [**S**cr]ipsimus et uitam uirtu[tis ab arce po]litam **.**   5
> **T**e petimus per eum <**D**eo prece>s dante per euum **.**
> **I**n tua de[uotos ser]uitia protege totos **.**
> [**A** Bono creat]us pro cunctis funde precatus **.**

---

1   BCLL, no. 1024 pp. 284–5. R. Sharpe, *A Handlist of the Latin Writers of Great Britain and Ireland Before 1540*, Publications of the Journal of Medieval Latin I (Turnhout: Brepols, 1997) [hereafter *Latin Writers*], no. 1624 p. 607. Haddan and Stubbs, *Councils*, vol. II pt I pp. 276–7.

Auge uirt*utem* fer opem ṣeruaque ṣal*utem*
R̲egis Al*exandri* qui causa te uen*erandi* .   10
I̲usserat ecce *tuos* pingi scribendo tri*umpho*s .
H̲uic assiste *pater* quem spiritus <in>uolat *ater* .
U̲t nichil in *peius* temptatio transferat *eius* .
U̲t bon*us accedat* cui se Rex et *sua* cr*edat* .
R̲ex actus R*egis* fac formet ab ordine l*egis* .   15
M̲alo *seruatur* cum Rex a lege *regatur* .
P̲rotege *Reginam* ne sentiat ipsa *ruinam* .
I̲nsula pontif*icum* sibi te cognoscat am*icum* .
P̲lebem cum cl*ero* Rege Xpisto principe u*ero* .
O̲mnes sancte i*uua* pater et patrone Col*umb*a .   20
E̲nsis Scott*orum* sis et munimen e*orum* .
A̲uxiliumqu*e b*oni* prece fer seruo Sim*eoni* .
H̲ec qui u*erb*a pr*ecum* tibi scribere dux*erat eq*uum* .
W̲illelmoque I*ona* sacer affer celica *dona* .
H̲unc librum cl*are* qui dignum duxit ar*are* .   25

7 *after* seruitia tatum *interlined.* 12 quos. *Beneath the hole before* uolat *there is no descender
for* per *in* peruolat *printed by Haddan and Stubbs.*

VERSES OF SIMEON THE POET ON SAINT COLUMBA

Saint Columba, father whom mother Ireland gave birth to
     [lit. 'poured out'],
whom the divine power of Christ gave to be a light to the Church,
we request that the written things which we give to you may be
     accepted by you,
for we have written about your acts kindlily, though unworthily,
and we have written about your life refined from the citadel of virtue.   5
We ask you through Him, God granting prayers through the age,
protect all those devoted to your services.
Created by Good [God], pour prayers for all,
increase virtue, bring power, guard the health
of King Alexander, who for the sake of venerating you   10
had commanded, lo, your triumphs to be depicted in writing.
Assist this man, father, whom a black spirit flies at,
so that his temptation bring nothing into a worse state,
so that a good man may approach him and the king may trust
     himself and his own.
O King [*i.e.* God], make that he form the acts of a king from
     the order of the law.   15
He is saved from evil when the king is ruled by law.
Protect the queen lest she experience ruin.

Let the island of bishops [*i.e.* Iona] know you as a friend to it.
The people with the clergy by Christ the King, the true prince,
aid all, holy father and patron Columba.   20
May you be the sword of Scotsmen and their fortification.
Bring aid by the prayer of a good man to the servant Simeon,
he [*i.e.* William] who had ordered a just man [*i.e.* Simeon] to
    write these words of prayers for you,
to William also, holy dove [*i.e.* Columba], bring heavenly gifts,
who ordered a worthy man [*i.e.* Simeon] to write [lit. 'plough']
    this book clearly.   25

Let us note first the chiastic statement and restatement of words and ideas.

1	A1	Sancte Columba
2–3	A2	dedit ... d[amus]
4–5	B	scripsimus ... scripsimus
6	C	te
6	D	<prece>s
6	E	deuotos
7	F	seruitia
8	G1	<bono>
8	G2	precatus
9	H	auge
10	I	regis
10–11	J	te ... tuos
12	K	huic
12	L	assiste
15	M	rex actus regis fac formet ab ordine legis
16	M'	malo seruatur cum rex a lege regatur
17	L'	protege
17	K'	reginam
18	J'	te
19	I'	rege
21	H'	auxilium
22	G'1	boni
22	G'2	prece
22	F'	seruo
22	E'	Simeoni
23	D'	prece
23	C'	tibi
23	B'	scribere
24	A'1	Iona sacer
24	A'2	dona

The chiastic balance of A2 and A'2 confirms *dona* and restored *damus*, as that of D and D' confirms restored *preces* and *prece* and that of G1 and G'1 confirms restored *bono* and *boni*. The twenty-five lines of the poem divide by extreme and mean ratio at 15 and 10, between lines 15 and 16, at the crux of the chiasmus. One may therefore proceed from the known toward the unknown, inferring that as the ten complete lines originally comprised 0.38197 of the whole, twenty-five lines, so the sixty-six complete words in those lines originally comprised 0.38197 of the whole, which would have been 173 words.

After noting that the twenty-five lines and 173 words of the poem divide by extreme and mean ratio at 107 and 66 at the crux of the chiasmus, at the fifteenth line and the 107th word, one observes further that the major part of the golden section, the first fifteen lines and 107 words, divides in turn by extreme and mean ratio, the lines at 9 and 6, the words at 66 and 41, at *Regis Alexandri* |, who commanded the poem to be written, and that the minor part of the golden section, the last ten lines and sixty-six words, divides in turn by extreme and mean ratio, the lines at 6 and 4, the words at 41 and 25, at *auxiliumque boni* | *prece fer seruo Simeoni*, that is Columba, who aided Simeon to write the poem. The last twenty-five words divide by extreme and mean ratio at 15 and 10, at *tibi scribere | duxerat equum*, another reference to Simeon. The last fifteen words divide by extreme and mean ratio at 9 and 6, at *hunc | librum*, a reference to Simeon's work.

Reckoning letters as numerals, $A=1$, $B=2$, $C=3$ ... $X=21$, $Y=22$, $Z=23$, the name *SIMEON* bears a numerical value of $18+9+12+5+14+13$ or 71.[2] In lines 22–3 the words from | *auxilium* to *duxerat* | inclusive

> | Auxiliumque boni prece fer seruo Simeoni
> Hec qui uerba precum tibi scribere duxerat | equum

contain seventy-one letters. The word *equum* refers to Simeon. From the space after *equum* inclusive to the space after *dignum* inclusive, *dignum* referring also to Simeon, there are in lines 24–5

> Willelmoque Iona sacer affer celica dona
> Hunc librum clare qui dignum | duxit arare

seventy-one letters and spaces between words.

The poem divides by one-ninth and eight-ninths at 19 and 154, at | *tibi* 3, that is Columba, and at *hec qui | uerba precum tibi scribere duxerat equum*, that is William's order and Simeon's words.[3]

One notes further the seven recurrences of *regis* 10, *rex* 14, *rex* 15, *regis* 15, *rex* 16, *reginam* 17, *rege* 19. Between the first and the second there are thirty words

2   For other examples of this feature see above pp. 5–8, and below pp. 35, 58–61, 84, 89, 95, 141, 159–60, 174, 184, and Howlett, *Sealed from Within*, pp. 21, 25, 32, 41, 62, 66, 73, 77–8, 85–6, 91, 94, 99.

3   See above p. 18 and below pp. 90, 95, 106, 160, 184.

(3 x 10). Between the second and the third there are three words (3 x 1). From the third to the fourth inclusive there are three words (3 x 1). After the fourth the fifth is the ninth word (3 x 3). From the fifth to the sixth inclusive there are six words (3 x 2). From the sixth to the seventh inclusive there are fifteen words (3 x 5). From the first to the seventh inclusive there are sixty-six words (3 x 22), another minor part of the golden section of the whole poem.

There are from *protege* 7 to *protege* 17 inclusive sixty-six words, another minor part of the golden section of the whole poem.

The first three words of the poem are *Sancte Columba pater* 1. After *pater et patrone Columba* 20 there are thirty-three words to the end of the poem. Of this the first third marks the poet's name *seruo* | *Simeoni* at the end of line 22, the twenty-second word from the end of the poem. The last third marks the third reference to the patron's name *Iona* | *sacer* 24.

Including the reconstructed title there are 1112 letters and spaces between words in the entire text, an indication, perhaps, of composition A.D. 1112.[4]

4   For other examples of infixed dates see above pp. 8–9 and below pp. 36, 59, 61, 74, 83–5, 89, 96, 110, 142, 150, 160, 174, 182–4.

WILLIAM OF GLASGOW: 'CARMEN DE MORTE SUMERLEDI'

Some time after the death of King David in 1153, during the episcopate of Herbert, 1147–64, Sumerled, Shomhairle, attacked Glasgow, an event commemorated by William of Glasgow in his *Carmen de Morte Sumerledi*.[1] In the edition that follows capital letters and punctuation marks in boldface represent features of Cambridge, Corpus Christi College, MS 139, folio 135rb-vb, written about 1166, perhaps at Durham for Sawley.[2]

QUO MODO A PAUCISSIMIS INTERFECTUS SIT SUMERLEDUS SITE BI ÞE KING . CUM SUO IMMENSO EXERCITU ;

Dauid rege mortis lege clauso in sarcofago
Fraus Scottorum infestorum propalatur illico
Galienses . Argaidenses freti ui Albanica
Seuiebant . et cedebant iustos manu impia
Iusti ruunt atque luunt impiorum furias   5
Seuientes . destruentes urbes et ecclesias
Pace fracta . ui redacta . fortes trudunt debiles
Hostes cedunt . atque ledunt igne . ferro flebiles
Debachantur et uastantur orti . campi . aratra
Dominatur et minatur mites manus barbara   10
Glasguensis ictus ensis Iesus fugit populus
Marcus uero sparso clero solus sistit querulus
Infra duros templi muros casus ferens asperos
Ibi flebat et lugebat dies olim prosperos

1   *BCLL*, no. 1010 p. 281. *Latin Writers*, no. 2062 p. 771. *Symeonis Monachi Opera Omnia*, ed. T. Arnold, 2 vols, Rolls Series LXXV (London: Longman, 1882–5), vol. II pp. 386–8. For a charter of Reginald son of Sumerled see Howlett, *Sealed from Within*, pp. 95–100.
2   David N. Dumville, '"Nennius" and the *Historia Brittonum*', *Studia Celtica* X–XI (1975–6), pp. 78–95 at 78–9. J.E. Story, 'Symeon as Annalist, *Symeon of Durham: Historian of Durham and the North*, ed. David Rollason, Studies in North-Eastern History I (Stamford: Shaun Tyas, 1998), pp. 202–13.

Sed modestus et honestus Herbertus episcopus   15
Condolebat et merebat secum longe positus
Kentegernum ut supernum regem oret obsecrat
Pro suorum captiuorum spe . ac hostes execrat
Cum oraret et spiraret precum in discrimina
Et effectu non defectu carerent precamina   20
Cepit sanctos Scotticanos uerbo paruipendere
Et beatum Kentegernum pie reprehendere
His sopitis et oblitis pene contumeliis
Kentegernus non oblitus est clamorem presulis
Nam post multum tempus ultum reuocat episcopum   25
Ut sanctorum Scotticorum deleret obprobrium
Venerandus et laudandus senex mox episcopus
Iam perfecto spreto lecto perrexit quantotius
Et nocturnum et diurnum iter quasi iuuenis
Diligenter et libenter carpebat cum famulis   30
Sed cum iret et nesciret cur tam erat auidus
Ire . quia cum Helia inspiratur celitus
Quod probauit qui rogauit illum cito regredi
Liberare et saluare se a manu inuidi
Sumerledi fraude fedi . hostis atrocissimi   35
Conspirantis anhelantis in ministros Domini
Qui repente cum ingente classium satellite
Applicatur et minatur regnum totum perdere
Hec cum iret et audiret spiritu ingemuit
Quis nec ire aut redire inquiens me arguit   40
Salomonem at tyronem bellicosum aduocat
Et Heliam qui per uiam illum sepe adiuuat
Festinemus adiuuemus desolatos patrie
Et oremus et obstemus illorum miserie
Debet doctor atque rector pugnare pro patria .   45
Prosperemus et pugnemus nostra est uictoria .
Quia Deus semper meus non hasta nec gladio
Suum gregem atque plebem tuetur in prelio
Resistentes audientes aduentum episcopi
Ut dracones et leones fiunt audacissimi   50
Quinque ille atque mille Sumerledus hostium
Contra centum innocentum promti sunt ad prelium
Accurrerunt et fecerunt in falanges impetum
Perfidorum Argaidorum infaustorum militum
Audi mira quia dira diris erant prelia   55
Miriceta et spineta uerticem mouentia
Tymus usta et arbusta . rubi atque filices
Timebantur et rebantur hostibus ut milites

In hac uita non audita erant hec miracula
Umbre tymi atque fimi extant propugnacula   60
Sed in prima belli rima dux funestus cecidit
Telo lesus . ense cesus Sumerledus obiit
Atque unda furibunda eius sorbet filium
Ac multorum fugatorum uulneratos milium
Nam hoc truce strato duce fugam petunt impii   65
Tam in terris quam in aquis trucidantur plurimi
Cum in undis sanguibundis naues uellent scandere
Cateruatim alternatim suffocantur reumate
Facta strage atque clade perfidorum milium
Nullus lesus neque cesus erat expugnantium   70
Sic detrusis et delusis hostium agminibus
Kentegernum omne regnum laudat altis uocibus
Caput ducis infelicis Sumerledi clericus
Amputauit et donauit pontificis manibus
Ut sueuit pie fleuit uiso hostis capite   75
Dicens Sancti Scotticani sunt laudandi utique
Et beato Kentegerno tradidit uictoriam
Cuius semper et decenter habete memoriam
Hoc quod uidit et audiuit Willelmus composuit
Et honori et decori Kentegerni tribuit   80

IN WHAT MANNER SUMERLED WHO SITS BY THE KING WITH HIS OWN IMMENSE ARMY WAS KILLED BY A FEW MEN.

With David the King by the law of death enclosed in a sarcophagus
the fraud of the offensive Scots is displayed on the spot.
The men of Galloway, the men of Argyll, relying on the power of Alba,
were raging and smiting just men with an impious hand.
Just men are rushing headlong and suffering the furies of impious men. 5
Raging, destroying cities and churches,
with peace broken, with power reduced, the strong compel the weak,
enemies smite and wound those weeping by fire, by sword.
They debauch and lay waste the ploughs of garden, of field.
A barbarous hand dominates and threatens meek men.   10
The wounded people of Glasgow flees the blows of the sword.
Mark, in truth, with the clergy scattered, remains alone, querulous,
within the hard walls of the temple bearing harsh accidents.
There he was weeping and lamenting days formerly prosperous.
But the modest and honest Bishop Herbert,   15
situated far away, was grieving and mourning together with him.
He beseeches Kentigern that he might pray to the supernal King
for hope of his own captives, and he curses the enemies.

When he prays and hopes for judgements of the prayers,
that the prayers might be lacking in defect, not in effect,   20
he began to vilify in word the Scottish saints
and piously to reprehend blessed Kentigern.
With these insults quieted [lit. 'put to sleep'] and almost forgotten,
Kentigern did not forget the clamour of the bishop,
for after a long time he reminds the avenged bishop   25
that he should wipe out the opprobrium of the Scottish saints.
Immediately the venerable and praiseworthy old bishop,
now fully mature, with his bed spurned, proceeded as quickly as possible
and pressed on in a night-time and day-time journey, as if he were a
     youth,
diligently and willingly with servants.   30
But though he went he did not know why he was so eager
to go, since he is inspired from heaven by Elias,
which he who asked proved him to go back quickly
to free and save himself from the hand of the hated
Sumerled, from the fraud of the fiercest foul enemy,   35
conspiring, breathing fire against the servants of the Lord,
who suddenly with a huge escort of fleets [by hypallage 'a huge
     fleet of escorts']
is landed at and threatens to destroy the whole kingdom.
And when he heard these things, he groaned in spirit that he should go,
saying, 'Who accuses me that I do not go or come back?'   40
But he invokes a warlike novice Solomon
and Elias, who along the way often helps him.
'Let us hasten, let us aid the desolate men of the fatherland,
let us both pray and make a stand against their misery.
A teacher and ruler ought to fight for the fatherland.   45
May we prosper, and let us fight; victory is ours,
because my God always, not with spear nor sword,
will look over His own flock and people in battle.'
Those resisting, hearing of the advent of the bishop,
become like dragons and the boldest lions.   50
That Sumerled and one thousand five enemies
are brought out to battle against one hundred innocents.
They ran to attack, and they made phalanxes against the onrush
of the ill-starred soldiers of the perfidious men of Argyll.
Hear the wondrous things, for the battles against the dire men were dire. 55
Thickets of broom and thickets of thorn bushes moving to a peak,
thyme and burned shrubs, brambles and bracken,
were feared and imagined by the enemies as soldiers.
In this life these miracles were not heard of.
Empty forms of thyme and dung serve as bulwarks.   60

But in the first lightning crack of battle the murderous leader fell.
Wounded by a weapon, smitten by a sword, Sumerled died,
and a raging wave swallows his son,
and the wounded among many thousands put to flight,
for with this pitiless leader laid low the impious men seek flight.   65
Very many are killed, as many on lands as in the waters.
When the ships wish to ascend on the blood-bound waves
they are squeezed by the current alternately, in throngs.
With destruction and disaster of the perfidious thousands effected,
no one of the fighters was left wounded or smitten.   70
Thus with the throngs of enemies thrust down and deluded,
the whole kingdom praises Kentigern with raised voices.
The head of the unhappy leader a clerk of Sumerled
cut off and gave to the hands of the bishop.
As he was accustomed, he wept piously once the head of the enemy
    was seen,   75
saying that the Scottish saints are to be praised everywhere,
and he handed victory to blessed Kentigern,
whose memory keep always and fittingly.
This which he saw and heard William composed,
attributed both to the honour and for the adornment of Kentigern.   80

61 *rimia* with the second *i* subpuncted for deletion.

The poet places himself in the Insular Latin tradition, partly in the choice of metre, pentadecasyllabic like the oldest extant Latin poem composed in these islands.[3] Line 71 of this pentadecasyllabic poem is based upon line 8, *hoste truso ac deluso*, of a seventh-century Hiberno-Latin poem, *Christum peto Christum preco*, which ends with a pentadecasyllabic line.[4] The words of the title *site bi þe king* mark the poet as a speaker and writer of English.

This text survives in almost, if not exactly, the form in which it issued from the poet's pen. William mentions *Salomonem* as the first word of a central line of the poem. William signs his work in the last couplet, of which the thirteen words divide by extreme and mean ratio at 8 and 5, at | *Willelmus composuit*. The thirty syllables divide by the same ratio at 19 and 11, at *Willelmus | composuit*. After fifty lines of verse the first word is *quinque* 'five'. In the first five words of line 51 William tells us that with Sumerled were 1005 opponents. From | *mille* to *memoriam* | 78, the last word before the last couplet, in which William signs his work, there are exactly 1005 letters. The point is to imply a large claim for William's work by comparing it with the poetry of Solomon: *et fuerunt carmina eius quinque et mille* (III Kings IV 32).

3 'Saint Sechnall's Hymn' *Audite Omnes Amantes Deum*, in Howlett, *Celtic Latin Tradition*, pp. 138–52.
4 Howlett, 'Seven Studies', p. 28.

'DE SITU ALBANIE'

During the fourth quarter of the twelfth century, about 1184, perhaps in 1189, someone not yet identified composed a tract about mytho-historical topography, *De Situ Albanie*, that survives in a unique manuscript, now Paris, Bibliothèque Nationale de France, MS latin 4126, folios 26va–27rb, compiled and written at York by Robert of Poppleton in the West Riding of Yorkshire.[1] This Carmelite friar became prior of the convent at Hulne near Alnwick in 1364 and died in 1368. In the edition that follows, as in the four succeeding texts, capital letters and punctuation marks in boldface represent features of the Poppleton manuscript. For fourteenth-century spellings of *c* before *e* or *i* I have silently restored *t* appropriate to the twelfth century. I have divided the text into units, putatively authorial, sections numbered in upper case Roman numerals, and sentences numbered in Arabic numerals, and parts of sections numbered in lower case Roman numerals to the left, and lines numbered in Arabic numerals to the right. I have suggested alliteration with underline and rhymes with italics, and marked the rhythms of the cursus.

I

I   **DE SITU ALBANIE QUE IN SE FIGURAM HÓMIN*IS* HÁBET
QUOMODO FUIT PRIMITUS IN SEPTEM REGIÓNIBUS D*IU*ÍS*A*
QUIBUSQUE NOMINIBUS ANTÍQUITUS SÌT UOC*ÁTA*
ET A QUIBUS ÍNHABIT*ÁTA* .**   I

II

2   **O**pere pretium puto mandáre memórie
qualiter Albania et a quibus habitatoribus fuit primitus ínhabitáta
quibus nomínibus nùncupáta
et in quot pártibus partíta .   5

III

3   **L**egimus in historiis et in cronicis antiquórum Brítonum
et in gestis et annalibus antiquis Scottórum et Pictórum
quod illa regio que nunc corrupte uocátur Scótia

I   *BCLL*, no. 1042 p. 290. *Chronicles of the Picts, Chronicles of the Scots*, ed. W.F. Skene (Edinburgh: H.M. General Register House, 1867), pp. 135–7. M.O. Anderson, *Kings and Kingship in Early Scotland* (Edinburgh and London: Scottish Academic Press, 1980), pp. 240–3. I owe thanks to Dr Jacques Paviot for collation of the manuscript and to Professor David Dumville for loan of a microfilm of the manuscript.

antiquitus appellabatur Albania áb Albanécto
iuniore filio Bruti primi regis Britannorum maióris Británnie .   10
Et post multum interuallum temporis a Píctis Pictáuia
qui regnauerunt in ea per circulum mille septuagínta annórum .
Secundum quosdam mille trecénti sexagínta .

4   Scotti autem regnauerunt per spatium trecenti quíndecim annórum
anno illo quo Willélmus rex Rúfus   15
frater Malcolmi uiri honeste uite et uirtutis régnum suscépit .

IIII

5   Regio enim ista formam et figuram hóminis in sé habet .
6 i   Pars namque principalis eius id est caput est ín Arregaíthel
in occidentali parte Scotie supra máre Hibérnie .
7 ii Pedes autem eius sunt supra máre Northwágie .   20
8 iii Montes uero et deserta de Arregaithel capiti et collo hominis
       ássimilántur .
9 iiii Corpus uero ipsius est mons qui Moúnid uocátur
qui a mari occidentali usque ad mare orientále exténditur .
10 v Brachia autem eius sunt ipsi montes qui diuidunt Scotiam áb
       Arregaíthel .
latus dextere partis ex Muref et Rós et Marr et Búchen .   25
11 vi Crura enim illius sunt illa duo principalia et preclára flúmina
que descendunt de monte predícto id est Moúnid
que uocántur Taé et Spe .
quorum unum flúit citra móntem .
alterum uero ultra in máre Norwegále   30
12 vii Inter crura huius hominis sunt Enegus et Moérne citra móntem
et ultra montem alie terre ínter Spe et móntem .

V

13 i Hec uero terra a septem fratribus diuisa fuit antiquitus ín septem
       pártes .
quarum pars principalis est Énegus cum Moérne
ab Enegus primogenito fratrum síc nomináta .   35
14 ii Secunda autem pars est Ádtheodle et Góuerin .
15 iii Pars enim tertia est Sradéern cum Méneted .
16 iiii Quarta pars partium est Fíf cum Fóthreue .
17 v Quinta uero párs est Marr cum Búchen .
18 vi Sexta autem est Muref et Ros .   40
19 vii Septima enim pars est Cathanesia citra móntem et ùltra móntem
       quia mons Mounid diuidit | Cathanésiam per médium

VI

20   Quelibet igitur istarum partium regio túnc uocabátur
et erat quia unaqueque earum subregionem ín se habébat .
21   Inde est ut hii septem fratres predicti pro septem régibus hàbebántur 45
septem regulos súb se habéntes .

22   Isti septem fratres regnum Albanie in septem régna diuisérunt
        et unusquisque in tempore suo in suo régno regnáuit .

23 i   Primum regnum fuit sicut mihi uerus relator | retulit Andreas
          uidelicet et uir uénerábilis
          Cathanensis episcopus natione Scottus et Dunférmelis mónachus   50
          ab illa aqua optima que Scottice uocata est Froch
          Británnice Wérid
          Románe uero Scóttewatre
          id est áqua Scottórum
          quia regna Scottorum et Anglórum diuídit[2]   55
          et currit iuxta oppidum de Striuelin usque ad flumen áliud nóbile
          quod uocatum est Tae .

24 ii Secundum régnum ad Hílef
          sicut mare circuit usque ad montem aquilonali plaga de
            Striuelin quí uocatur Áthran .

25 iii Tertium regnum ab Hilef usque ad De .   60

26 iiii Quartum regnum ex De usque ad magnum et mirabile flúmen
          quod uocátur Spe
          maiorem et meliorem totíus Scótie .

27 v   Quintum regnum de Spe usque ad móntem Drumálban .

28 vi Sextum regnum fuit Muref et Ros .

29 vii Septimum regnum érat Arregaíthel .   65
    i   Arregaithel dicitur quasi margo Scottorum seu Híbernénsium
    ii   quia omnes Hibernenses et Scotti generaliter Gaítheli dicúntur
    iii   a quodam eorum primeuo duce Gaíthelglas uocáto .

30 iiii Ibi enim semper Hibernenses applicari solebant ad damna
          faciénda Británnis .
    v   uel idcirco quia Scotti Picti ibi habitabant primitus post redditum
          súum de Hibérnia   70
    vi   uel quia Hibernenses illas partes occupauére super Píctos .
    vii   uel quod certius est quia illa pars regionis Scotie affinitima est
          regióni Hibérnie

VII

31   Fergus filius Erc ipse fuit primus qui de semine Chonare suscépit
          regnum Álban
          id est a monte Drumalban usque ad mare Hibérnie èt ad Ínchegal

32   Deinde reges de semine Fergus regnauerunt et Drumalban
          siue Drumheren   75
          usque ad Alpinum fílium Éochaid .

33   Kined filius huius Alpini primus Scottorum annis sedecim in
          Pictauia felíciter regnáuit .   77

---

2   This is consistent with the usage of the *Anglo-Saxon Chronicle*, which records *s.a.* 1091
    that *ferde se cyng Melcom of Scotlande hider in to Englum…. se cyng Melcolm … for mid his*
    fyrde ut of Scotlande into Loðene on Engla land 7 þær abad.

1 inse. hominis hominis . quibus que. 3 primus. 8 corupte. 10 iuniori. 11 ac. 12 M.lxx.
13 M.ccc.lx. 14 Nunc uero corupte uocatur scocia. 14 Scoti. ccc.xv. 15 ruffus. 16
malcolíní. 18 capud. arregarchel. 21 arregarchel. 22 mo¹nid. 24 arregaichel. 25 mari.
27 m/tiund. 29 c¹ca. 32 et ultra montem alie terre inter spe et montem et ultra
montem. 42 moinid. katanesiam. 44 inse. 50 katanensis. 56 opidum. 63 brumalban.
64 mures. 65 aᵗregaᶦchil. 66 arregathel. 67 gattheli. 68 garthelglas. 69 hibernienses.
dampna. 70 iccirco. 71 hibernienses. 72 scoctie. 73 fergius. eric. 74 brumalban.
75 brumalban. brumherc. 76 alpium. eochal. 77 alpi i. .xvi. pictiuia.

I

I   ON THE SITE OF ALBANY WHICH HAS WITHIN ITSELF THE FIGURE
          OF A MAN,
      HOW IT WAS FIRST DIVIDED IN SEVEN REGIONS,
      BY WHAT NAMES IT WAS CALLED IN ANTIQUITY,
      AND BY WHOM INHABITED.   I

II

2   I think it worthwhile to record [lit. 'commit to the memory']
      how Albany was first inhabited and by what inhabitants,
      by what names named,
      and in how many parts parted.   5

III

3   We read in histories and in chronicles of the ancient Britons
      and in the recorded deeds and ancient annals of the Scots and Picts
      that that region which now corruptly is called Scotland
      in antiquity was referred to as Albany from Albanect,
      younger son of Brutus, the first king of the Britons of
          Greater Britain,   10
      and after a great interval of time Pictland from the Picts,
      who reigned in it through a cycle of one thousand seventy years,
      according to certain men one thousand three hundred sixty.
4   The Scots, however, reigned through the space of three hundred
          fifteen years
      in that year in which King William the Ruddy,   15
      brother of Malcolm, a man of honest life and virtue,
          received the realm.[3]

IIII

5   The region, then, has within itself the form and figure of a man.
6 i   For its principal part, that is the head, is in Argyll,
        in the western part of Scotland above the sea of Ireland.
7 ii   Its feet, however, are above the sea of Norway.   20
8 iii The mountains, in truth, and deserted parts of Argyll are likened
        to the head and neck of a man.

3   Malcolm died on 9 December and William was inaugurated on 24 December 1165.

9 iiii Its body, in truth, is the mountain which is called the Mounth,
      which is extended from the western sea as far as the eastern sea.
10 v Its arms, however, are the same mountains which divide Scotland
      from Argyll, the side of the right [*i.e.* 'southern'] part from
      Moray and Ross and Mar and Buchan [the northern part]. 25
11 vi Its thighs, then, are those two principal and excellent rivers
      which descend from the foresaid mountain, that is the Mounth,
      which are called Tay and Spey,
      of which one flows on this side of the mountain,
      the other, in truth, beyond into the Norwegian sea. 30
12 vii Between the thighs of the man are Angus and the Mearns on this
      side of the mountain,
      and beyond the mountain other lands between Spey and
      the mountain.

V

13 i This land, in truth, was divided in antiquity into seven parts by
      seven brothers,
      of which the principal part is Angus with the Mearns,
      so named from Angus, the first-born of the brothers. 35
14 ii The second part, however, is Atholl with Gowrie.
15 iii The third part, then, is Strathearn with Menteith.
16 iiii The fourth part of the parts is Fife with Fothriff.
17 v The fifth part, in truth, is Mar with Buchan.
18 vi The sixth, however, is Moray and Ross. 40
19 vii The seventh part, then, is Caithness on this side of the mountain
      and beyond the mountain,
      because the mountain the Mound divides | Caithness
      through the middle.

VI

20 Each of these parts, therefore, was called a region,
      and that was because each one of them had within itself a sub-region.
21 Thence it is that these seven foresaid brothers were had for seven
      kings, 45
      having under themselves seven sub-kings.
22 These seven brothers divided the realm of Albany into seven realms,
      and each one reigned in his own time in his own realm.
23 i The first realm was, just as a true relator | related to me, Andrew,
      that is, and a venerable man,
      Bishop of Caithness, a Scot by nation and a monk of Dunfermline, 50
      from that best water which is called in Scottish [Gaelic] Froch,
      in British Werid,
      in Romance, in truth, Scot Water,
      that is Water of the Scots,
      because it divides the realms of the Scots and the English, 55

> and it runs alongside the town of Stirling as far as that other
>   noble river
>   that is called Tay.

24 ii   The second realm is to the river Isla,
>   just as the sea goes about as far as the mountain on the northern
>   territory of Stirling, which is called Athran.[4]

25 iii   The third realm from Isla as far as the Dee.   60

26 iiii The fourth realm from the Dee as far as the great and wonderful river
>   which is called Spey,
>   the greatest and best of the whole of Scotland.

27 v   The fifth realm from the Spey as far as the mountain Druimm–nAlban.

28 vi   The sixth realm was Moray and Ross.

29 vii   The seventh realm was Argyll.   65

   i   Argyll is said as if the margin of the Scots or the Irish,

   ii   because all Irish and Scots generally are called Gaels,

   iii   from a certain primeval leader of them called Gaidel Glass.

30 *iiii* There, then, always the Irish were accustomed to land for doing harms
>   to the British,

   v   either because the Scots Picts dwelt there first after their return from
>   Ireland,   70

   vi   or because the Irish occupied those parts over the Picts,

   vii   or because it is quite certain that that part of the region of
>   Scotland is nearest to the region of Ireland.

VII

31   Fergus son of Erc himself was first of the seed of Conaire who
>   received the realm of Alba,
>   that is from the mountain Druimm–nAlban as far as the sea of
>   Ireland and as far as Inchgal [*i.e.* the Hebrides].

32   Then kings of the seed of Fergus reigned also in Druimm–nAlban
>   or Druimm–nErenn   75
>   until Alpin the son of Eochaid.

33   Kenneth son of this Alpin first of the Scots reigned happily in
>   Pictland for sixteen years.   77

Let us consider ways in which the author has fixed the text of this composition, first in discrete sentences.

In the title the twenty-five words 'divide' by extreme and mean ratio and sesquialter ratio at 15 and 10, at | *diuisa*. They divide by the 'seven-part' sesquitertian ratio 4:3 at 14 and 11, at *septem* |.

In sentence 3 the sixtieth word is *sexaginta* 13.

---

4   This name is preserved in 'Airthrey Castle', Logie Parish STL, three kilometres
    northeast of Stirling.

In sentence 11 in the clause *Crura enim illius sunt illa duo principalia et preclara flumina* the ten words divide into two equal halves at | *duo*. The twenty-four syllables divide into two equal halves at *duo* |. There are thirty-one letters and spaces from | *crura* to *duo* | and thirty-one from | *principalia* to *flumina* |.

In sentence 13 the twenty-five words divide by the 'seven-part' sesquitertian ratio at 14 and 11, at *septem* | *partes*. The first eleven words divide by the same ratio at 6 and 5, at *septem* | *fratribus*. The last fourteen words divide by the same ratio at 8 and 6, at *Enegus* |. The last eight words divide by the same ratio at 5 and 3, at | *Enegus*.

In sentence 21 the sixteen words divide by sesquitertian ratio at 9 and 7, at *septem* | *regibus*. The first nine words divide by the same ratio at 5 and 4, at *septem* | *fratres*. The last seven words divide by the same ratio at 4 and 3, at *septem* | *regulos*.

In sentence 22 the eighteen words divide by sesquitertian ratio at 10 and 8. There are ten words from | *regna* to *regno* | *regnauit*. The first eight words, of which the eighth is *regna*, divide by the same ratio at 5 and 3, at | *regnum*. The seventh word is *septem*.

In sentence 23, reckoning letters as numerals, $A=1$, $B=2$, $C=3$ ... $X=21$, $Y=22$, $Z=23$, the name *ANDREAS* bears a numerical value of $1+13+4+17+5+1+18$ or 59.[5] From the beginning of the sentence to *Andreas* | inclusive there are fifty-nine letters and spaces between words.

Now let us consider ways in which the author linked discrete parts. After the title the word *septem* occurs seven times: 13 twice, 21 thrice, 22 twice. From | *septem* 13 to *septem* | 13 inclusive there are seven words and forty-nine letters and spaces (7×7). After the second *septem* 13 *septima* 19 is the forty-ninth word. From the space before | *septem fratres* 21 to the space after *septem* | *fratres* 22 there are fourteen words and ninety-eight letters and spaces (7×14).

Now let us consider ways in which the author fixed the integrity of the entire composition. There are seven parts, of which parts IIII, V, and VI contain seven subdivisions each, the seventh of VI with seven subdivisions, and seventy-seven lines in the entire composition.[6]

There are thirty-three sentences, in the third of which the thirty-third word from the end names the author's country, *Albania*, and the thirty-third word from the beginning names the eponymous hero of the author's island, *Bruti*, there being thirty-three letters from | *Bruti* to *maioris* | *Britannie*, and thirty-three syllables from | *Albania* to *Britannie* |. From the space before *Fergus filius Erc* to the space after *feliciter regnauit* inclusive there are in part VII 333 letters and spaces between words.[7]

5   For other examples of this feature see above pp. 5, 8, 22 and below pp. 58–61, 84, 89, 95, 141, 159–60, 174, 184.

6   Compare the seven parts of the *Cronica de Origine Antiquorum Pictorum* and the 777 words of 'Chronicle of the Kings of Alba' and *Vita Sancti Reguli* below, pp. 44–51, 61–2, 85.

7   See below pp. 61, 75, 83, 102.

There are several ways to confirm that 630 is the authorially intended number of words in the entire composition. First, one can be certain that the text is correct from the beginning as far as *duo* 11, considered above, as it is the 220th word, that is 'two twice', 220 or CCXX, not 222 or CCXXII. Second, half of the number 630 is 315, the length of time the Scots ruled, *Scotti autem regnauerunt per spatium trecenti quindecim annorum* 4. From the space before | *post multum interuallum temporis* to the space after *regnum suscepit* | there are 315 letters and spaces. Third, from the length of time of Scots rule | *trecenti quindecim annorum* 4 to the space that divides the Scots from the English, *Scottewatre* | *id est aqua Scottorum quia regna Scottorum et Anglorum diuidit* 23, there are 315 words. Fourth, from *Opere pretium* 2 to *diuidit* | *Cathanesiam per medium* 19 'divides | Caithness through the middle' there are 315 words. Fifth, the 605 words from *Opere* to the end divide by extreme and mean ratio at 374 and 231, at the author's reference to himself and his source, *mihi uerus relator* | *retulit Andreas*. From this one infers that our author understood a feature of the account of Creation in Genesis I 1 – II 4, in which the only immediately repeated word בְּצַלְמוֹ בְּצֶלֶם 'in His image, in the image' occurs at the golden section.[8] This allows us to date the text. The author refers to the accession of William the Ruddy, inaugurated on 24 December after the death of his brother Malcolm on 9 December 1165, and attributes his knowledge to Andrew, who was Bishop of Caithness from 1146 to 29/30 December 1184. From the end of Andrew's title *Andreas uidelicet et uir uenerabilis Cathanensis episcopus natione Scottus et Dunfermelis monachus* | to the end of the composition there are 1189 letters, representing perhaps the year of composition. From the year 1165 inclusive, in which William the Ruddy became king, 315 years take one back to A.D. 850, our author's date for the accession of Kenneth son of Alpin. Allowing one year for each of the twenty-five words of the title, twenty-five years from 1165 inclusive bring one forward to 1189, perhaps the year of composition.[9]

Now we may see a reason for the apparently puzzling statements about the length of Pictish rule in lines 12 and 13. If our author reckoned A.D. 850 as the beginning of rule by the Scots, preceded *per circulum mille septuaginta annorum*, Pictish history in 220 B.C. would be synchronized with Antiochus III in the Seleucid kingdom, Philip V in Macedon, Ptolemy IV in Egypt, and Hannibal in Carthage. With a past of *secundum quosdam mille trecenti sexaginta*, Pictish history in 510 B.C. would be synchronized with the foundation of the Roman Republic. This synchronizing of Pictish with Mediterranean history reproduces a feature of *Versus de Annis a Principio*, a Hiberno-Latin occasional poem of A.D. 645,[10] and of the *Historia Brittonum* of 829/830:[11]

---

8 Howlett, *Celtic Latin Tradition*, pp. 33–45 at 35 and 41, *British Books in Biblical Style*, pp. 37–50 at 40 and 46.
9 See above pp. 8, 23 and below pp. 59, 61, 74, 83–5, 89, 96, 110, 142, 150, 160, 174, 182–4.
10 Howlett, 'Seven Studies', pp. 1–6.
11 Howlett, *Cambro-Latin Compositions*, pp. 69–72.

Quando regnabat Britto in Brittannia Heli sacerdos iudicabat in Israel.
Et tunc arca testamenti ab alienigenis possidebatur.
Postumus frater eius apud Latinos regnabat.

Our author was thinking clearly in large terms and writing, if in a short tract, on a grand scale.

Four passages afford clues to our author's orientation. In lines 28–9 the *Tae ... fluit citra montem [Mounid].* In lines 31–2 *sunt Enegus et Moerne citra montem et ultra montem alie terre inter Spe et montem.* In lines 34–5 *Pars principalis est Enegus cum Moerne ab Enegus primogenito fratrum sic nominata.* The authority for this information was *Cathanensis episcopus natione Scottus et Dunfermelis monachus* 50. One reason for including a reference to the earlier career of the Bishop of Caithness may be that the author acquired the information in Dunfermline.

The idea that the land exhibits the shape of a man is ancient, at least as old as the Babylonian epic of Creation, the *Enuma Elish,* in which Marduk made the universe from the body of Tiamat; as old as Protagoras, who affirmed that man is the measure of all things; as old as Vitruvius, who stated that a beautiful building should exhibit extensions of the measure of the human body.[12] But the immediate sources were probably Gildas *De Excidio Britanniae,* published in A.D. 540, and the *Historia Brittonum,* published in 829/830. The statement in line 6, *Legimus in historiis et in cronicis antiquorum Britonum,* suggests that our author had read the *Historia Brittonum,* which states in line 6 of that work, *Et in ea [Brittannia insula] habitant quattuor gentes, Scotti, Picti, Saxones, Brittones.*[13] The only part of the island of Britain of which that statement is true is our author's subject. In writing that Albany exhibits the shape of a man and in relating the topography to the inhabitants our author suggests in an equally subtle way that he had read Gildas *De Excidio Britanniae* and the *Historia Brittonum,* in which the measurements of the land are related to the numbers of ancestors and generations and cities of the inhabitants.[14] The text of lines 8–10 suggests that he had read Geoffrey of Monmouth's *Historia Regum Britannie* II 1.

Description of the thighs of the Man of Alba as the rivers Tay and Spey may issue from the idea that the *crura,* as *flumina,* must *currere* 'run'. Description of the Firth of Forth as *Romane uero Scottewatre,* 'in Romance', that is 'in French', is as easily explicable as the name of the *Maison Française,* which is in Oxford in English 'Maison Française'. Our author is telling us clearly that in the twelfth century the Francophones he knew called the Firth of Forth *Scottewatre.* In his pun on *crura* and *currere,* at once anatomical, topographical, and etymological, and in his deliberate inclusion of languages other than Pictish — providing names

---

12 For a map of the Man of Alba see below p. 202.

13 Howlett, *Cambro-Latin Compositions,* p. 69. For another example of this device see below p. 121.

14 For relation of physical description of the land to numbers of generations of its inhabitants and their compositions see Howlett, *Cambro-Latin Compositions,* pp. 33–56, 69–83.

Scottice, *Britannice*, and *Romane*, but in this last case giving the form *Anglice* — he reveals himself as an imaginative philologist with a politically inclusive agenda.

Reckoning of the length of Pictish history as 1070 years and coincidence of division of the country into seven parts connect this text with seven parts of the Pictish king list in *Cronica de Origine Antiquorum Pictorum*.[15] The last line of this text, *Kined filius huius Alpini primus Scottorum annis sedecim in Pictauia feliciter regnauit*, connects with the first line of the 'Chronicle of the Kings of Alba', *Cinadius igitur filius Alpini primus Scottorum rexit feliciter istam annis sedecim Pictauiam*.[16] The first sentence of part VII of this text is repeated as the first sentence of the *Cronica Regum Scottorum*. Description of King William as *Rufus* and coincidental reckoning of the reign of the Scots as 315 years connect this text further with the *Cronica Regum Scottorum*.[17] Reckoning of A.D. 850 as the year of accession of Kenneth son of Alpin connects this text with the 'Chronicle of the Kings of Alba' and the *Cronica Regum Scottorum*.[18] Association with that text suggests something important about the reason for composition of *De Situ Albanie*, which our author's usage illuminates. A reading of lines 19 and 24 might suggest at first confusion or inconsistency, *caput est in Arregaithel in occidentali parte Scotie* implying that Argyll is within *Scotia*, and *montes qui diuidunt Scotiam ab Arregaithel* implying that Argyll is outwith *Scotia*. Because of the signs of punctilious order already observed let us assume that our author was neither inconsistent nor confused. His preferred locution for *illa regio que nunc* **corrupte** *uocatur Scotia* 8 is *Albania*. Let us infer from his condemnation of a usage as 'corrupt' that he avoids describing *Albania* as *Scotia*. By *in annalibus antiquis Scottorum* 7 he means 'in the ancient annals of Irishmen'. So the *Scotti Picti* of line 70 are those who formerly lived in Ireland, as he implies in *post redditum suum de Hibernia*. The Gaelic relatives and descendants of Irishmen are called *Scotti* 14, *Scottewatre, id est aqua Scottorum quia regna Scottorum et Anglorum diuidit* 53–5, *Scottorum seu Hibernensium* 66, *Hibernenses et Scotti generaliter Gaitheli dicuntur* 67, and *Scottorum* 77. The parts of Britain these people occupy and rule are called *Scotia, in occidentali parte Scotie supra mare Hibernie* 19, *montes qui diuidunt Scotiam ab Arregaithel* 24, *pars regionis Scotie affinitima regioni Hibernie* 72. One might without special pleading easily construe in the first of these phrases *in* as 'bordering on', understanding the entire phrase in apposition to *Arregaithel*, consistent with the usage of line 66, *Arregaithel dicitur quasi margo Scottorum seu Hibernensium*. When our author refers to a word in the Scottish Gaelic spoken by these people he writes *Scottice uocata est Froch* 51. The realm of Picts and Scots over which *Kined filius huius Alpini feliciter regnauit* is *Albania*.[19] But *Willelmus Rex Rufus* was great grandson of

15 See below p. 51.
16 See below p. 52.
17 See below p. 64. The epithet is elsewhere attested only in Higden's *Polychronicon*, deriving from these sources.
18 See below pp. 52, 61–2, 64.
19 For a reference to Pictland as *Scotia*, as if this were a usage requiring special notice, see *Vita Sancti Reguli* below p. 76.

English Margaret, grandson of half-English David and English Mathilda eldest daughter of Earl Waltheof of Northumberland, son of Henry, and the *regnum Scottorum* he ruled is that in which our author's informant *Andreas Cathanensis episcopus natione Scottus* 50 lived, in which he mentions the River Spey as *maiorem et meliorem totius Scotie* 62, the *regnum totius Scotie* including by this time the territories south of the Forth, the *regna Anglorum*, and men within them like Adam of Dryburgh who described himself as *essemus a quibus etiam nunc in regno Scottorum positi*.[20] Having declined to describe *Albania* 'corruptly' as *Scotia*, our author uses three locutions in two senses, *Scottus* and *Scotia* and *Scottice* referring with etymological correctness to Gaels and their homelands in Ireland and Dalriada and their language in the historic past, *Scottus* and *tota Scotia* referring with political correctness to the inclusive kingdom of Scotland in the present.

In attempting to understand *De Situ Albanie* one accumulates a great debt to Mrs Anderson, whose edition has done much to advance study of the text. The present writer, who began with her work and could not have begun without it, hesitates to disagree with so remarkable a lady and so sound a scholar, but the preceding analysis allows one to affirm that *De Situ Albanie* is not 'ill-composed and imperfectly digested'. Considering the punctilio with which our author represents features of the Creation story in Genesis 1 and topographical composition in the *Historia Brittonum*, and noting his consistent architectonic structure, and his lexically precise uses of *Scottus, Scotia, Scottice*, and his infixed dates that synchronize the history of the twelfth-century *Regnum Scottorum* with foundation of the Roman Republic, one may admire instead a perfectly finished work of mytho-historical topography, conceived and executed as a coherent prolegomenon to a tradition of Scottish historiography that is in its own terms faultless.

20 See below p. 157. Compare the reference to Melrose as part of the *totum Scotie regnum*, which may further connect this text with the *Cronica Regum Scottorum*, below p. 66–7, and the reference to *partem totius Scotie*, which may connect this text further with the *Vita Sancti Reguli*, below p. 78. Compare also the usage *Willelmus hominibus totius terre sue* in the grant of a Bishop of Aberdeen below p. 154. Contrast the old Cambro-Latin usage of Ieuan ap Sulien, *Albania*, with the new Anglo-Latin usage of Lifris of Llancarfan, *Albaniam quam uulgo Scotiam uocant*, and Caradog of Llancarfan, *rex Scotie*, in Howlett, *Celtic Latin Traditon*, pp. 236, 346, and *Vita Sancti Cadoci* § 26.

'CRONICA DE ORIGINE ANTIQUORUM PICTORUM'

Directly after *De Situ Albanie* in the Poppleton manuscript follows a text entitled *Cronica de Origine Antiquorum Pictorum* on folios 27rb–28va.[1] The first part of the *Cronica* is sometimes directly quoted and sometimes slightly revised from Isidore of Seville's *Etymologiae* IX II 27, 65, 89–90, 103, XIV III 31–2, IV 3, and *Historia Brittonum* 15.[2] The numbers of the sentences to the left of the text are mine and putatively the compiler's.

1   **CRONICA DE ORIGINE ANTIQUORUM PICTORUM .**

2   **Pi**cti propria lingua nomen habent a picto corp*o*re
     eo quod aculeis ferreis cum atramento uariarum figurarum stigmate annot*an*t*u*r .

3   Scotti qui nunc corrupte uocantur Hibernienses quasi S*citi*
     quia a Scithia regione *uenerunt*

4   Et inde originem duxerunt siue a Scotta filia Pharaonis regis E*gypti*
     que fuit ut fertur regina Scotie [uel Scottorum] .

5   **S**ciendum uero est quod Britones in tertia mundi etate ad Britanniam *uenerunt*

6   Sciti autem id est Scotti in quarta etate Scotiam siue Hiberniam obtin*uerunt*

7   Gentes Scithie *albo crine nascuntur ab assiduis niuibus*

8   Et ipsius capilli color genti nomen ded*it*

9   Et inde dicuntur Albani de quibus originem duxerunt Scoti et P*icti*

10   Horum glauca oculis id est picta inest pupilla adeo ut nocte plus quam die
     cern*ant*

11   Albani autem uicini Amazonibus *fuerunt*

12   **G**othi a Magog filio Iapheth nominati putantur de similitudine ultime sillab*e*
     quod ueteres Greci magis Gethas quam Gothos uoc*auerunt*
     gens fortis et potentissima corporum mole ardua : armorum genere terribil*is* .

13   De quibus Lucanus . '**H**inc Dacus premat inde Gethes incurrat [uel occurrat]
     Hiber*is*' .

---

1   *BCLL*, no. 1039 p. 289. Skene, *Chronicles*, pp. 3–8 with facsimiles opposite p. 3. Anderson, *Kings and Kingship*, pp. 243–9.

2   Mrs Anderson has distinguished departures from printed texts of the sources with larger type on pages 243–5 of her edition, though without access to our author's own text and his copies of the sources one cannot be certain about precise details. For her references to *Etymologiae* XIX read XIV. For other use of Isidore's *Etymologiae* in the *Vita Sancti Reguli* and the *Vita Sancti Seruani* see below, pp. 85, 88.

14 Daci autem Gothorum soboles *fuerunt*
15 Et dictos putant Dacos quasi Dagos quia de Gothorum stirpe creati *sunt* .
16 De quibus ille 'Ibis arctoos procul usque Dacos' .
17 Scithi et Gothi a Magog originem trax*erunt*
18 Scithia quoque et Gothia ab eodem Magog filio Iapheth fertur cognominat*a* :
cuius terra olim ingens fu*it* .
19 Nam ab oriente Indie a septentri*one* : per paludes Meotidas inter Danubium et
oceanum usque ad Germanie fines porrigeb*atur*
20 Post ea minor effecta est a dextra orientis parte qua oceanus Sericus tend*itur*
usque ad mare Caspium quod est a*d occasu*m
21 De hinc a meridie usque ad Caucasi iugum deducta est cui subiacet Hircania
ab occasu .
habens pariter gentes multas propter terrarum infecunditatem late uagant*es* .
ex quibus quedam agros incol*unt*
quedam portentuose ac truces carnibus humanis et eorum sanguine uiu*unt*
22 Scithie plures terre sunt locupletes inhabitabiles tamen plur*es* .
23 Namque in plerisque locis auro et gemmis afflu*ant*
24 Griphorum immanitate accessus hominum rarus *est*
25 Smaragdis autem optimis hec patria *est*
26 Cianeus quoque lapis et cristallus purissimus Scithie *est* .
27 Habet et flumina magna Oscorum Fasiden et Araxe*n*
28 Prima Europe regio Scithia inferior que a Meotidis paludibus incipi*ens*
inter Danubium et oceanum septentrionalem usque ad Germaniam porr*igitur*
que terra generaliter propter barbaras gentes quibus inhabitatur Barbarica d*icitur* .
29 Huius pars prima Alania est que ad Meotidas paludes pertin*git* .
30 Post hanc Dacia ubi et Gothi*a* .
31 Deinde Germania : ubi plurimam partem Sueui incol*uerunt*
32 In partes Asiatice Scithie sunt gentes que posteros se Iasonis cred*unt*
33 *Albo crine nascuntur ab assiduis niuibus* .
34 De hiis ista suffici*unt*

2 stingmate. 4 scocie uel [sco]torum. 5 etati a. 6 scite. 7 scitie. assidius. 11 amazonibus
above i rum. 12 gochi et. silabe. ueteris. gechas. gotos. 13 gethi incurrat uel oc[currat].
14 gottorum. 15 gottorum. 16 arcos. 17 Scithe. 18 Iaphet. 9gnominata. 19 occeanum.
porigebatur. 20 qui occeanus siricus 9ditur. 28 occeanum.

1 A CHRONICLE ABOUT THE ORIGIN OF THE ANCIENT PICTS.

2 Picts in their proper language have the name from a painted body,
because they are distinguished by marks with a tattoo of various shapes [made]
by iron barbs with ink.
3 Irishmen, who are now corruptly called Scots, as if Scits, because they came from
the region Scythia.
4 And they drew their origin thence, or from Scotta, who was a daughter of
Pharaoh king of Egypt, as is said, a queen of Scotland [or of the Scots].
5 It is to be known, in truth, that the Britons came to Britain in the third age of
the world.

6   The Scits, however, that is the Scots, obtained Scotland or Ireland in the fourth
     age.

7   The peoples of Scythia are born with white hair from the incessant snows.

8   And the colour of the same hair gave a name to the people.

9   And thence they are called men of Alba ['white men'], from whom the Scots and
     Picts drew their origin.

10   A grey, that is a painted, pupil is in their eyes so that they see better by night than
     by day.

11   The men of Alba, however, were neighbours to the Amazonians.

12   The Goths are supposed named from Magog son of Japheth from the similitude
     of the last syllable, because the ancient Greeks called them rather Geths than
     Goths,
     a people strong and most powerful in hardy bulk of body and terrible in the
     character of their arms [i.e. warfare].

13   About whom Lucan: 'On this side let the Dacian press, on that side let the Geth
     rush at [or counter] the Iberians'.[3]

14   The Dacians, however, were the offspring of Goths.

15   And they suppose the said Dacians, as if Dagoans [with play on de Go-], because
     they were created 'from' the stock of 'Goths'.

16   About whom that man [Paulinus wrote]: 'You will go to the northern Dacians'.

17   The Scythians and Goths drew their origin from Magog.

18   Scythia and also Gothia is said named from the same Magog son of Japheth,
     whose land was once immense.

19   For from the east of India, from the north through the Maeotian swamps,
     between the Danube and the ocean, as far as the bounds of Germany it was
     spread out.

20   Afterwards it was made less, from the right-hand [i.e. southern] part of the east,
     where the Chinese Sea stretches,
     as far as the Caspian Sea, which is toward the west.

21   On this side from the south as far as the ridge of the Caucasus, under which
     Hyrcania lies, it is stretched out from the west,
     having equally many peoples wandering far and wide on account of the
     infertility of the lands,
     from among which some cultivate fields,
     some monstrous and savage live on flesh of humans and their blood.

22   Many Scythian lands are rich, many nonetheless habitable.

23   For in many places they flow with gold and gems.

24   The attack on men by the savagery of griffins is rare.

25   This is the fatherland for the best emeralds.

26   Also blue stone [i.e. lapis lazuli] and the purest crystal is of Scythia.

27   It has also the great rivers Oxus, Phasis, and Aras.

28   The first region of Europe is lower Scythia, which, beginning from the Maeotian
     swamps,
     between the Danube and the northern ocean is spread out as far as Germany,

3   Our author may have understood Dacus as 'Dane', Gethes as 'Geat', and Hiberi as
     'Hibernians' or 'Irishmen'.

which land generally on account of the barbarous peoples by which it is inhabited is called Barbary.

29 The first part of it is Alania, which belongs to the Maeotian swamps.

30 After this Dacia, where also Gothia.

31 Thence Germany, where the Swabians dwell in the greatest part.

32 Among parts of Asiatic Scythia there are peoples who believe themselves descendants of Jason.

33 They are born with white hair from the incessant snows.

34 These things suffice about these matters.

These extracts form parallel and chiastic patterns of statement and restatement.

1	A	Cronica
4	B1	Et inde originem duxerunt siue a Scotta filia Pharaonis regis Egypti,
		que fuit ut fertur regina Scotie
7	B2	Gentes Scithie albo crine nascuntur ab assiduis niuibus
12	C1	Gothi a Magog filio Iapheth nominati putantur
13	C2	De quibus Lucanus 'Hinc Dacus premat inde Gethes incurrat Hiberis'
14	C3	Daci autem Gothorum soboles fuerunt.
15	C3'	Et dictos putant Dacos quasi Dagos quia de Gothorum stirpe creati sunt
16	C2'	De quibus ille 'Ibis arctoos procul usque Dacos'
18	C1'	Gothia ab eodem Magog filio Iapheth fertur cognominata
19	D	per paludes Meotidas inter Danubium et oceanum usque ad Germanie fines porrigebatur
22	E	Scithie … sunt …
23	F	Namque in plerisque locis … gemmis affluant
24	G	Griphorum immanitate accessus hominum rarus est
25	F'	Smaragdis autem optimis hec patria est
26		Cianeus quoque lapis et cristallus purissimus
	E'	Scithie est
28	D'	a Meotidis paludibus incipiens inter Danubium et oceanum … usque ad Germaniam porrigitur
30	C'	Post hanc Dacia ubi et Gothia.
32	B'1	In partes Asiatice Scithie sunt gentes que posteros se Iasonis credunt
33	B'2	Albo crine nascuntur ab assiduis niuibus.
34	A'	De hiis ista sufficiunt.

Compare the statements about ancestors in B1 and B'1, about hair in B2 and B'2, *Magog filio Iapheth* in C1 and C1', quotation from Lucan in C2 and quotation from Paulinus in C2', references to *Dacos* and *Gothia* in C and *Dacia* and *Gothia* in C', Maeotian swamps, Danube, ocean, and Germany in D and D',

Scythia in E and E', precious stones in F and F', round the crux about griffins in G, the seventh part of the chiasmus. One might suppose *Griphorum immanitate accessus hominum rarus est* to be odd as the crux of a chiastic structure unless he had seen the griffin on the most famous Pictish sculpture, the Saint Andrews Sarcophagus.[4]

References to white hair may connect this text with the 'Chronicle of the Kings of Alba'.[5] References to Scythia and the Scythians in 3, 6–7, 17–18, 22, 28, and 32 may connect this text with the *Vita Sancti Reguli*.[6] Reference *a dextra orientis parte* 20 may also connect this text with the *Vita Sancti Reguli*.[7] The second part of the *Cronica* is a list of Pictish kings, divided into seven parts, each of which exhibits multiples of seven.

I

    CRuidne filius Cinge pater Pictorum habitantium in hac insula .c. annis regnauit

.vij. filios habuit .

    Hec sunt nomina eorum . Fib . Fidach . Floclaid . Fortrenn . Got . Ce[.] Circinn .

I	**C**ircin .lx. regnauit .	
2	Fidaich [.]xl.	5
3	Fortrenn .lxx.	
4	Floclaid .xxx.	
5	Got [.]xij.	
6	Ce .xv.	
7	Fibaid [.]xxiiij.	10
II		
8	Gede Olgudach .lxxx.	
9	Oenbecan .c.	
10	Olfinecta .lx[.]	
11	Guidid Gaedbrechach .l.	
12	Gest Gurcich .xl.	15
13	Wur Gest [.]xxx.	
14	**B**rude Bont a quo [.]xxx. Brude regnauerunt Hiberniam et Albaniam per [.]c.l. annorum spatium .xl.viij annis regnauit id est	

4   *The St Andrews Sarcophagus: A Pictish masterpiece and its International Connections*, ed. Sally M. Foster (Dublin: Four Courts, 1998), pp. 28, 116–17, 145–6, 152, and pls 2–5, 10.

5   See below pp. 59–60.

6   See below p. 76.

7   See below p. 77.

III–IIII

1	Brude Pant.	Brude Ur Pant.	
2	Brude Leo.	Brude Ur Leo.	
3	Brude Gant.	Brude Ur Gant.	20
4	Brude Gnith.	Brude Ur Gnith.	
5	Brude Fecir.	Brude Ur Fecir.	
6	Brude Cal.	Brude Ur Cal.	
7	Brude Ciut.	Brude Ur Ciut.	
8	Brude Fec.	Brude Ur Fec.	25
9	Brude Ru.	Brude Ur Ru.	
10	Brude Gart[.]	[Brude] et Ur Gart.	
11	Brude Cinid[.]	Brude Ur Cinid.	
12	Brude Uip.	Brude et Ur Uip.	
13	Brude Grid[.]	Brude Ur Grid.	30
14	Brude Mund.	Brude Ur Mund.	

V–VI

1	**GI**l Gidi .c.l. annis regnauit	
2	Tharain [.]c.	
3	Mor Leo .xv.	
4	Deo Cilinion [.]xl.	35
5	Cinioiod filius Arcois .vij.	
6	Deo Ord .l.	
7	Blieiblituth .v.	
8	Dectotr'ic. frater Diu .xl[.]	
9	Usconbuts .xxx[.]	40
10	Caruorst [.]xl.	
11	Deo Artiuois .xx.	
12	Vist .l.	
13	Ru .c[.]	
14	**G**art Naith Loc a quo Gart Naith .iiij[.] regnauere	
	.ix[.] annis. regnauit .	45

VII

1	**B**reth filius Buthut .vij[. annis regnauit.]	
2	Vipoig Namet .xxx[.] annis regnauit[.]	
3	Canutulachama .iiij. annis regnauit.	
4	**W**r Adech Uecla .ij. annis regnauit.	
5	**G**art Naith Diu Berr .lx[.] annis regnauit.	50
6	**T**alorc filius Achiuir .lxxv[.] annis regnauit.	
7	Drust filius Erp .c. annis regnauit. et [.]c. bella peregit.	
	Nono decimo anno regni eius Patricius episcopus sanctus ad Hiberniam peruenit insulam.	
8	**T**alorc filius Aniel .iiij. annis regnauit.	

9	Necton Morbet filius Erip [.]xxiiij. [annis] regnauit .	55
	Tertio anno regni eius Dar Lugdach abbatissa Cille Dara de	
	Hibernia exulat pro Xpisto ad Britanniam	56
	Secundo anno aduentus sui immolauit Nectonius Apur Nethige	
	Deo et Sancte Brigide presente Dar Lugdach que cantauit	
	alleluia super istam hostiam	57
	Obtulit igitur Nectonius magnus filius Wirp rex omnium	
	prouinciarum Pictorum Apur Nethige Sancte Brigide usque	
	ad diem iudicii cum suis finibus	
	que posite sunt a lapide in Apur Feirc	
	usque ad lapidem iuxta Cair Fuill id est Leth Foss	
	et inde in altum usque ad Athan	58
	Causa autem oblationis hec est.	59
	Nectonius in uita exilii uiuens fratre suo Drusto expulsante se	
	usque ad Hiberniam Brigidam Sanctam petiuit ut	
	postulasset Deum pro se	60
	Orans autem pro illo dixit.	61
	"Si peruenies ad patriam tuam Dominus miserebitur tui	
	regnum Pictorum in pace possidebis"	62
10	Drest Gurthinmoch .xxx[.] annis regnauit.	
11	Galanan Erilich [.]xij. annis regnauit.	
12–3	Da Drest id est Drest filius Gyrom id est Drest filius W[r] Drost	
	.v. annis conregnauerunt.	65
	Drest filius Girom solus [.]v. annis regnauit.	
14	Gart Naith filius Girom [.]vij. annis regnauit.	
15	Cailtram filius Girom j anno regnauit.	
16	Talorg filius Muir Cholaich .xj. annis regnauit.	
17	Drest filius Munait j anno regnauit.	70
18–9	Galam Cennaleph j anno regnauit. cum Briduo .j. anno	
20	Bridei filius Mailcon [.]xxx[.] annis regnauit.	
	In octauo anno regni eius baptizatus est Sancto a Columba	
21	Gart Naith. filius Domelch .xj. annis regnauit.	
22	Nectu nepos Uerd .xx. annis regnauit.	75
23	Cinioch. filius Lutrin .xix. annis regnauit.	
24	Garnard. filius Wid .iiij. annis regnauit.	
25	Breidei. filius Wid .v. annis regnauit.	
26	Talorc frater eorum .xij. annis regnauit.	
27	Talorcen filius Enfret .iiij. annis regnauit.	80
28	Gart Naith filius Dounel .vj. annis regnauit. et dimidium[.]	
29	Drest frater eius .vij. annis regnauit.	
30	Bredei filius Bili .xxj. annis regnauit.	
31	Taran filius Enti Fidich .iiij. annis regnauit.	
32	Bredei filius Derelei .xj. annis regnauit.	85
33	Necthon filius Derelei .xv. annis regnauit.	

34–5 Drest et Elpin conregnauerunt .v. annis.
36 Oniust filius Vr Guist .xxx. [annis] regnauit.
37 Bredei filius Wir Guist .ij. annis regnauit.
38 Ciniod. filius Wr Edech .xij. annis regnauit. 90
39 Elpin filius Wr Oid .iiij. annis regnauit. et dimidium[.]
40 Drest filius Talorgen .iiij. uel [.]v. annis regnauit.
41 Talorgen. filius Onuist .ij. annis et dimidium regnauit.
42 Canaul. filius Tarl'a [.]v. annis regnauit.
43 Castantin. filius Wr Guist [.]xxx.v[.] annis regnauit. 95
44 Vnuist. filius Wr Guist [.]xij. annis regnauit.
45–6 Drest filius Constantini et Talorgen filius W[r] Thoil .iij. annis autem
    conregnauerunt.
47 Vuen. filius Vnuist .iij. annis regnauit.
48 Wr Ad. filius Bargoit [.]iij. [annis regnauit.]
49 et Bred j anno regnauit. 100

    1 emge. 6 fortenn. 12 denbecan. 13 olfinecta *with* i *corrected from* e. 17 hibernia.
centum. 19 B. leo. b. leo. b. uleo. 26 ru.b eru. 28 Burenid. 45 Gar^tnaithloc.
gartnait. regna.uere. 50 Gartnaichdi uberr. 51 Talore. 53 ix decimo. s̅p̅c. 54 Talore.
57 anno aduentus anno. aburnethige. dairlugdach. 58 Optulit. cum cum. 60 iulie.
67 Garthnach. 68 uno. 70 uno. 71 uno. 73 sancto a. 74 Gartnart. 79 Talore.
81 Gartnait. 87 congregauerunt. 93 diuidium. 97 congregauerunt. 98 V.nuist.
100 uno.

I   Cruidne son of Cinge father of the Picts dwelling in this island
      reigned one hundred years   I
    He had seven sons.   2
    These are their names. ...   3
II   Brude Bont, from whom thirty Brudes ruled Ireland and Albany
      through the space of 150 years, reigned forty-eight years   17
VI   Gart Naith Loc, from whom four Gart Naiths reigned, reigned
      nine years.   45
VII Breth son of Buthut [reigned] 7 [years].
2   Vipoig Namet reigned 30 years.
3   Canutulachama reigned 4 years.
4   Wr Adech Uecla reigned 2 years.
5   Gart Naith Diu Berr reigned 60 years.   50
6   Talorc son of Achiuir reigned 75 years.
7   Drust son of Erp reigned 100 years and completed 100 battles.
      In the nineteenth year of his reign Saint Patrick the bishop came
      through to the island of Ireland.
8   Talorc son of Aniel reigned 4 years.
9   Nechtan Morbet son of Erip reigned 24 [years].   55
      In the third year of his reign Darlugdach Abbess of Kildare
      came in exile from Ireland for Christ to Britain.   56

In the second year of her arrival Nechtan sacrificed Abernethy
to God and Saint Brigit, with Darlugdach present, who
sang Alleluia over that host.   57
Nechtan the great, son of Wirp, king of all provinces of the
Picts, offered to Saint Brigit until the day of judgement
Abernethy with its bounds,
which are set from the stone in Aberfarg
up to the stone next to Cairfuill, that is Lethfoss,
and thence upwards as far as Athan.   58
The cause, however, of the offering is this.   59
Nechtan, living in a life of exile, his own brother Drust
expelling him as far as Ireland, besought Saint Brigit
that she might ask God for him.   60
Praying for him, she said,   61
"If you come through to your fatherland the Lord will have
mercy on you; you will possess the realm of the Picts
in peace."   62

10   Drust Gurthinmoch reigned 30 years.
11   Galanan Erilich reigned 12 years.
12–3 Two Drusts, that is Drust son of Girom, that is Drust son of
      W[r] Drost, reigned together 5 years.   65
      Drust son of Girom alone reigned 5 years.
14   Gart Naith son of Girom reigned 7 years.
15   Cailtram son of Girom reigned 1 year.
16   Talorc son of Muir Cholach reigned 11 years.
17   Drust son of Munait reigned 1 year.   70
18–9 Galam Cennaleph reigned 1 year with Brude 1 year.
20   Brude son of Maelchon reigned 30 years.
      In the eighth year of his reign he was baptized by Saint Columba.
21   Gart Naith son of Domelch reigned 11 years.
22   Nechtan grandson of Uerd reigned 20 years.   75
23   Kenneth son of Luchtren reigned 19 years.
24   Gart Naith son of Foith reigned 4 years.
25   Brude son of Foith reigned 5 years.
26   Talorc their brother reigned 12 years.
27   Talorcan son of Eanfrith reigned 4 years.   80
28   Gart Naith son of Donald reigned 6½ years.
29   Drust his brother reigned 7 years.
30   Brude son of Bili reigned 21 years.
31   Tarain son of Ainftech reigned 4 years.
32   Brude son of Derile reigned 11 years.   85
33   Nechtan son of Derile reigned 15 years.
34–5 Drust and Alpin reigned together 5 years.

36   Angus son of Fergus reigned 30 years.
37   Brude son of Fergus reigned 2 years.
38   Kenneth son of Feredach reigned 12 years.   90
39   Alpin son of Wr Oid reigned 3½ years.
40   Drust son of Talorcan reigned 4 or 5 years.
41   Talorcan son of Angus reigned 2½ years.
42   Conall son of Tadc reigned 5 years.
43   Constantine son of Fergus reigned 35 years.   95
44   Angus son of Fergus reigned 12 years.
45–6   Drust son of Constantine and Talorcan son of W[r] Thoil
        however reigned together 3 years.
47   Ewen son of Angus reigned 3 years.
48   Wr Ad son of Bargoit [reigned] 3 [years.]
49   and Bred reigned 1 year.   100

The author infixed devices that guarantee the integrity of discrete parts of the narrative.

In line 45 about four men named Gart Naith and a reign of nine years there are four words after iiij and nine words before ix.

In line 46 the seventh syllable is the first of vij.

In line 49 there are two words after ij.

In lines 52–3, reckoning Roman numerals as single syllables, the first syllable of *nono decimo* is the nineteenth.

In line 54 the fourth word is iiij.

In line 66 the fifth word is v, which is followed by five syllables.

In line 67 there are seven syllables before vij.

In line 73 the eighth word of sentence 20 is *octauo*, after which there are eight words to the end of the sentence.

In line 76 there are nineteen letters before xix.

In line 77 the fourth word is iiij.

In line 78 there are five syllables after v.

In lines 80 and 84 the fourth word is iiij.

In line 86 the fifteenth letter from the end of the sentence is the first of xv.

In line 87 the fifth word is v, which is followed by five letters.

In line 89 there are two words after ij.

In line 91 there are three words before iiij.

In line 92 the fourth word is iiij, and there are five syllables after v.

In lines 94 and 95 there are five syllables after v.

In line 96 there are twelve syllables apart from xij.

In line 97 there are three words after iij.

In line 98 there are three words before iij.

The author infixed devices that guarantee the integrity of larger units of the narrative.

There are fifty words before .l., line 14.

There are thirty words from | *Circin* 4 to | xxx 16. From the space after .l., line 14, to the space after xxx., line 16, there are thirty letters and spaces between words.

There are 150 words before .c.l., line 32, between which and xl, line 35, there are forty letters.

Accounts of eight kings precede the eight-lined passage about Nechtan Morbet, 55–6, which exhibits a chiastic structure of eight parts before and after the crux.

56	A	regni
56	B	ad Britanniam
57	C	Nectonius
57	D	Deo
57	E	Sancte
57	F	Brigide
58	G1	Obtulit
58	G2	Nectonius
58	H	a lapide in Abur Feirc
58	H'	usque ad lapidem iuxta Ceir Fuill
59	G'1	oblationis
60	G'2	Nectonius
60	F'	Brigidam
60	E'	Sanctam
60	D'	Deum
60	C'	pro se [*i.e.* Nectonio]
62	B'	ad patriam tuam [*i.e.* Britanniam]
62	A'	regnum.

The 127 words from *Tertio* 56 to *possidebis* 62 inclusive divide by extreme and mean ratio at 78 and 49. There are forty-nine words from | *obtulit* 58 to *oblationis* | 59 inclusive. There are seventy-eight words from | *Pictorum* 58 to *Pictorum* | 62. From | *Sancte Brigide* 58 to the end there are seventy-eight words. Of the two other references to Brigit in this passage there are twenty-six words before | *Sancte Brigide* 57, twenty-six words from | *Brigidam Sanctam* 60 to the end, and fifty-two words from | *Sancte Brigide* 58 to | *Brigidam Sanctam* 60. There are twenty-three letters and spaces before | *Dar Lugdach* 56 and twenty-three words between *Dar Lugdach* | 56 and | *Dar Lugdach* 57. There are twenty-three words from the beginning to *Apur* | *Nethige* 57 and twenty-three words between *Apur Nethige* | 57 and | *Apur Nethige* 58. There are thirty-nine words before *Nectonius* 58, and *Nectonius* 60 is the thirty-ninth word from the end.

The author also infixed devices that guarantee the integrity of the entire narrative.

The thirty-four letters in the title, *Cronica de Origine Antiquorum Pictorum*, provide the key to the thirty-four sentences in the first part of the text.[8]

In the second part of the text the seven divisions coincide with the statement in *De Situ Albanie* that the country was divided into seven parts.[9] Three groups of fourteen names in I–II, III–IIII, V–VI are modelled upon the list of three groups of fourteen generations in the genealogy of Jesus in Matthew I 1–17.[10] Part VII contains forty-nine names (7 x 7).

The 100 lines of text from *Cruidne filius Cinge* to *Bred j anno regnauit* divide by extreme and mean ratio at 62 and 38, at the end of line 62, at the end of the passage about *Necton Morbet filius Erip*.

The 409 words of the first part relate to the 661 words of the second part by extreme and mean ratio, the golden section of 1070 falling at 661 and 409. The 1070 words of the complete text about Picts and their kings coincide with the length of Pictish dominion, *mille septuaginta annorum*, according to the author of *De Situ Albanie*.[11]

Here is clear evidence of a writer who absorbed the Late Latin traditions of Jerome's *Biblia Vulgata* and Isidore's *Etymologiae*, the Cambro-Latin tradition of the *Historia Brittonum*,[12] the Hiberno-Latin traditions of Patrick, Brigit, Darlugdach, and Columba,[13] the Anglo-Latin and Old English traditions of arranging genealogical lists in groups of fourteen, at no point merely copying, but selecting and weaving elements from which he composed a text that is in its own terms intellectually coherent, arithmetically exact, and, some may think, beautiful.

8 See above p. 4 and below pp. 85, 89, 96, 102, 115, 141, 150, 152, 155, 186–7.
9 See above p. 30.
10 For another reflex of the Matthaean pattern see Howlett, *British Books in Biblical Style*, pp. 327–31.
11 See above pp. 36–8.
12 Howlett, *Cambro-Latin Compositions*, pp. 69–83.
13 Howlett, *Liber Epistolarum Sancti Patricii Episcopi, Celtic Latin Tradition*, pp. 65–6, 138–52, 243–9, 253–8, 342–6, 353–4, '*Vita Prima Sanctae Brigitae*', pp. 1–23.

'CHRONICLE OF THE KINGS OF ALBA'

Directly after the end of *Cronica de Origine Antiquorum Pictorum* follows a 'Chronicle of the Kings of Alba' on folios 28va–29va.[1] I have arranged the text in lines, the numbers of which are mine and putatively authorial. I have suggested rhymes by italics and marked the rhythms of the cursus. The dates *Anno Domini* to the right of the text are mine and putatively authorial.

A.D.

Cinadius igitur filius Alpini primus Scottorum rexit feliciter
    istam annis sédecim *Pictáuiam*   850–865
Pictauia autem a Pictis est nominata quos ut diximus Cinádius del*éuit*
Deus enim eos pro merito sue malitie alienos ac otiosos hereditate
    dignátus est fá*cere*
qui illi non solum Domini missam ac precéptum spre*uérunt*
sed et in iure equitatis aliis equiparáre nol*uérunt* .   5
Iste uero biennio antequam ueniret Pictauiam Dalriete régnum susc*épit*   848–849
Septimo anno regni sui reliquias Sancti Columbe transportauit ad
    ecclésiam . quàm constrúx*it*   856
et inuasit sexies Saxoniam et concremauit Dunbarre atque Málros usurpát*a* .
Britanni autem concremauerunt Dulblaa*n* atque Danari uastauerunt
    Pictauiam ad Clúanan èt Duncálde*n* .
Mortuus est tandem tumore ante idus Februarii   Tuesday 6 Feb. 865
    feria tertia in palátio *Fothiúrthabaicht* .   10
Douenaldus frater eius tenuit idem regnum quátuor *ánnis*   865–868
In huius tempore iura ac leges regni Edi filii Ecdach fecerunt
    Goedeli cum rege súo i *Fothiúrthabaicht* .
Obiit in palatio Cinn Belathoir ídus Apríl*is* .   Tuesday 13 Apr. 868
Constantinus filius Cinadii regnauit ánnos sé*decim*   868–883
Primo eius anno Maelsechnaill rex Hiberniénsium *óbiit*   15
et Aed . filius Neil ténuit ré*gnum*
ac post duos annos uastauit Amlaib cum gentibus súis *Pictáuiam*   869
et habitauit eam a kalendis Ianuarii usque ad festum Sáncti Patrícii   1 Jan.–17 Mar.
Tertio iterum anno Amlaib trahens celtem . a Constantíno occísus *est*   870
Paulo post ab eo bello in decimo quarto eius anno facto in Dolair   881
    inter Danarios et Scottos occisi sunt Scotti co Athcochla*m*   20

---

1   *BCLL*, no. 1038 p. 289. Skene, *Chronicles*, pp. 8–10. Anderson, *Kings and Kingship*, pp. 249–53. Benjamin T. Hudson, 'The Scottish Chronicle', *The Scottish Historical Review* LXXVII.II (October 1998), pp. 129–61.

Normanni annum integrum degérunt in Pictáui*a* .

Edus tenuit idem uno anno cuius etiam breuitas nil historie memorabile
commendauit sed in ciuitate Inuer Úrim est occí*sus* .   883–884

Eochodius autem filius Run regis Britannorum nepos Cinadii ex filia
regnauit ánnis ún*decim* .   884–894

sed Ciricium filium alii dicunt hic regnasse eo quod alumnus ordinatorque
Eochódio fié*bat*

Cuius secundo anno Aed filius Néil móritu*r* .   25   885

ac in secundo eius anno in ipso die Ciricii eclipsis sólis fãcta *est*   Wednesday 16 June 885

Eochodius cum alumno suo expúlsus est nùnc *de régno* .   894

Douenaldus filius Constantini tenuit regnum úndecim *ánnos* .   894–904

Normanni tum uastauérunt *Pictáuiam*

In huius regno bellum autem factum Innisib Solian inter Danarios et
Scottos *Scotti habuérunt uictóriam*   30

Oppidum Fother occísum est a gé*ntibus* .

Constantinus filius Edi tenuit regnum quádraginta *ánnos*   904–943

cuius tertio anno Normanni predauerunt Duncalden omnémque Albán*iam* 906

In sequenti utique anno occisi sunt in Sraith hÉrenn Norm*ánni*   907

Ac in sexto anno Constantinus rex et Cellachus episcopus leges disciplinas-
que fidei atque iura ecclesiarum euangeliorumque pariter cum Scottis 909
in Colle Credulitatis prope regali ciuitati Scoan deuouérunt custod*íre* 35

ab hoc die collis hoc meruit nomen id est Cóllis Credùlitát*is*

Et in suo octauo anno cecidit excelsissimus rex Hiberniensium et
archiepiscopus apud Laignechos id est Cormace fílius Culénn*an*   911

Et mortui sunt in tempore huius Douenaldus rex Britannorum et
Douenaldus fílius Éd*e*

Rex eligitur . et Flann filius Maelsechnaill et Niall filius Ede qui regnauit
tríbus annis póst Fl*ann*

Et bellum Tine More factum est in decimo octauo anno   921
inter Constantinum et Regnall et *Scotti habuérunt uictóriam*   40

Et bellum Duin Brunde in tricesimo quarto eius anno ubi cecidit filius   937
Constantini et post unum annum mortu*us est* .   938

Dubucan filius Indrechtaig mormair Oengusa Adalstan . filius Aduar rig
Saxan et Eochaid . filius Alpini mortui su*nt*

Et in senectute decrepitus baculum cepit et Domino seruiuit et regnum
mandauit Mael filio Dómnaill .

MAelcolaim filius Domnaill undecim ánnis regn*áuit* .   943–953

Cum exercitu suo Maelcolaim perrexit in Moreb et occidit Cell*ach*   45

In septimo anno regni sui predauit Ánglos ad àmnem Thés*is*   949
et multitudinem rapuit hominum et multa arménta péc*orum*
quam predam uocauerunt Scotti predam albidosorum ídem náinn d*isi*
alii autem dicunt Constantinum fecísse hanc préd*am*
querens a rege id est Maelcolaim regnum dari sibi ad tempus
ebdomadis ut uísitaret Ánglo*s* .
unde tamen non Máelcolaim fècit préd*am*
sed instigauit eum Constantínus ut dí*xi* .

Mortuus est autem Constantinus in decimo eius anno sub corona
penitenti in sénectute bón*a*   952

Et occiderunt uiri na Moerne Maelcolaim in Fodresach íd est in Claídeo*m*
Idulfus tenuit regnum octo annis in huius tempore oppidum Eden
    uacuatum est ac relictum est Scottis usque in hódiernum díe*m*   953–960
Classis somarlidiorum occísi sunt in Búchain .   50
Niger filius Maelcolaim regnáuit quinque *ánnis*   960–964
Fothach *epíscopus pausáuit*
Bellum inter Nigerum et Caniculum super dorsum Crup in quo Niger
    habuit uictoriam ubi cecidit Dunchad abbas Duncalden et Dubdon
    sátrapas Áthoch*lach*
Expulsus Níger *de régno*
et tenuit Caniculus bréui témpo*re*   55
Domnal filius Cairill mortu*us est* .
Culen rig quinque ánnis *regnáuit* .   964–968
Marcan filius . Breodalaig occisus est in ecclesia Sáncti Michaéli*s* .
Leot et Sluagadach exiérunt ad Róm*am*
Maelbrigde *epíscopus pausáuit* .   60
Cellach . filius Ferdálaig *regnáuit*
Maelbrigde . filius Dúbucan *óbiit* .
Culen et frater eius Eochodius occisi súnt a Brit*ónibus* .
Cinadius filius Maélcolaim regnàuit ánn*um* .   968–969
Statim predauit Británniam ex pár*te*   65
Pedestres Cinadii occisi sunt maxima céde in Moìn Ua Córua*r* .
Scotti predauerunt Saxoniam ad Stan Moir et ad Cluiam et ad stágna Der*ánni* .
Cinadius autem uallauit rípas uadòrum Fórthin
Post annum perrexit Cinadius et predauit Saxoniam et traduxit filium
    régis Sáxo*num*
Hic est qui tribuit magnam ciuitatem Bréchne Dómin*o* .   70

---

1 Kinadius. xvi. 2 ei nadius. 3 occiosos. 4 spuerut. 6 Isti. 8 marlos. 10 .iij. fothiurtabaicht. 11 Duuenaldus. .iiij. 12 legis. fochiurthabaicth. 14 Constantius. cinadi. .xvi. 15 mael seehnaill. 16 niel. 19 centum. 20 xiiij. eius facto. scoti. 21 in regrum. 22 .i. eu. eciam breuitas .l'. istorie. nrurim. 23 cinadei. .xi. 24 alumpnus. 26 ix. cirici. 27 alumpno. 28 Doniualdus. .xi. 30 inuisib^{s}olian. 31 opidum. 32 edii. .xl. 35 .vi. ewangeliorumque. 37 excelcissimus. 38 doneualdus. britanniorum. duneualdus. 39 maelsethnaill. 40 7 c. *with superscript dot for expunctuation*. .xviij. 41 xxx.iiij. 42 aduarrig. alpni. 44 .xi. 45 excercitu maelcolam. 46 vij. arege. maelcolami. maelcolam. 47 .x. 48 namoerne malcolam. 49 .viij. opidum. 50 classi. 51 .v. 53 bellum deest. et deest. ingerum canicilium. duchad. 57 .v. 62 dubican. 64 regnauit [ ] añ. 66 cinadi. 67 stangna.

Cinaed, therefore, son of Alpin first of the Scots ruled happily that Pictland for
    sixteen years.
Pictland, however, is named from Picts, whom, as we have said, Cinaed wiped out.
For God deigned to make them because of the merit of their own malice
    alien from and having no share in the inheritance,
those who not only spurned the Mass and precept of the Lord,
but also wished not to be equal to others in the law of equity.   5
That man, in truth, in the two-year-period before he came to Pictland
    received the realm of Dalriada.
In the seventh year of his own reign he transported the relics of Saint
    Columba to the church which he constructed,

and he invaded England [lit. 'Saxony'] six times and burned Dunbar and Melrose
   [was] usurped.
The Britons, however, burned Dunblane, and the Danes laid waste Pictland as
   far as Clunie and Dunkeld.
He died finally from a tumour on the third day [*i.e.* Tuesday] before the ides of
   February in the palace of Forteviot.   10
Domnall his brother held the same realm for four years.
In his time the Gaels with their own king in Forteviot made laws and statutes
   of the realm of Aed son of Eochaid.
He died in the palace of Cinn Belathoir on the ides of April.
Constantín son of Cinaed reigned for sixteen years.
In his first year Maelsechnaill King of the Irishmen died,   15
and Aed son of Niall held the realm,
and after two years Olaf with his own [pagan] peoples laid waste Pictland
and inhabited it from the kalends of January up until the feast of Saint Patrick.
In the third year again Olaf drawing a knife was killed by Constantín.
A little while after that battle made in his fourteenth year in Dollar between
   the Danes and the Scots the Scots were killed as far as Atholl.   20
The Northmen remained an entire year in Pictland.
Aed held the same for one year, the brevity of which has commended really
   nothing memorable for history, but in the city of Inver Urin he was killed.
Eochaid, however, son of Rhun King of the Britons, grandson of Cinaed by his
   daughter, reigned for eleven years,
but some say Giric the son reigned here because he was made the foster father
   and regulator [or 'manager' or 'lawman'] for Eochaid.
In whose second year Aed son of Niall dies,   25
and in his second year on the very day of [Saint] Ciricius an eclipse of the sun
   was made.
Eochaid with his own foster father was expelled now from the realm.
Domnall son of Constantín held the realm for eleven years.
The Northmen then laid waste Pictland.
In the reign of this man, however, battle being made[2] at the islands of Solian
   between the Danes and the Scots, the Scots had the victory.   30
Dunnottar was destroyed by [pagan] peoples.
Constantín son of Aed held the realm for forty years,
in whose third year the Northmen preyed upon Dunkeld and all Albany.
In the following year particularly Northmen were killed in Strathearn.
And in the sixth year King Constantín and Bishop Cellach vowed to guard the
   statutes and disciplines of the Faith and the laws of the churches and gospels
   equally with the Scots on the Hill of Belief near the royal city of Scone. 35
From this day the hill in this way has merited the name, that is the Hill of Belief.
And in his own eighth year the highest king of the Irishmen fell and the
   archbishop at the hands of the Leinstermen, that is Cormac son of Culennan.
And there died in the time of this man Domnall King of the Britons and
   Domnall son of Aed

---

2   Construing *bellum factum* as an accusative absolute.

And Flann son of Maelsechnaill is elected king and Niall son of Aed who
    reigned for three years after Flann,
and battle was made at Tine More in the eighteenth year between Constantín
    and Ragnall, and the Scots had the victory. 40
And the Battle of Brunanburh in his thirty-fourth year, where the son of
    Constantín fell and after one year died.
Dubucan son of Indrechtach mormaer of Angus, Æthelstan son of Eadweard
    King of the Saxons, and Eochaid son of Alpin died.
And decrepit in old age he took a staff and served the Lord and commended
    the realm to Mael [Coluim] son of Domnall.
Mael Coluim son of Domnall reigned for eleven years.
With his own army Mael Coluim advanced into Moray and killed Cellach. 45
In the seventh year of his own reign he preyed upon the English as far as the
    river Tees
    and took a multitude of men and many herds of domestic beasts,
    which plunder the Scots called the plunder 'albidosorum' [i.e. 'of the whitish
    things'], the same 'nainn disi' [i.e. 'of the white multitudes'];
    some, however, say that Constantín made this plunder,
    seeking from the king, that is Mael Coluim, the reign to be given to him
       for the time of the week that he would visit the English;
    whence, nonetheless, Mael Coluim did not make the plunder,
    but Constantín goaded him, as I have said.
Constantín, however, died in his tenth year under the crown for a penitent
    in a good old age,
and the men of the Mearns killed Mael Coluim in Fetheresso, that is 'Swordland'.
Illulb held the realm for eight years, in the time of which man the town of Eden
    [i.e. Edinburgh] was vacated and it has been abandoned by the Scots until
    the present day.
A fleet of somarleds were destroyed in Buchan. 50
Dub son of Mael Coluim reigned for five years.
Fothad the bishop rested.
Battle between Dub and Cuilén on the ridge of Crup, in which Dub had the
    victory, where Donnchad abbot of Dunkeld fell and Dubdon the provincial
    governor [mormaer] of Atholl.
Dub expelled from the realm,
and Cuilén held for a short time. 55
Domnall son of Cairell died.
Cuilén the king reigned for five years.
Marcan son of Breodalach was killed in the Church of Saint Michael.
Leot and Sluagadach went out to Rome.
Maelbrigde the bishop rested. 60
Cellach son of Ferdalach reigned.
Maelbrigde son of Dubucan died.
Cuilén and his brother Eochaid were killed by the Britons.
Cinaed son of Mael Coluim reigned for a year.
Immediately he preyed upon Britain in part. 65
The foot soldiers of Cinaed were killed in a very great slaughter in Moin
    Ua Coruar.

The Scots preyed upon England [lit. 'Saxony'] as far as Stane More and as far as
Cluain and as far as the swamps of Derann.
Cinaed, however, walled the banks of the fords of the Forth.
After a year Cinaed also preyed upon England [lit. 'Saxony'] and handed
over [*i.e.* 'arrested' or 'surrendered'] the son of the king of the Saxons.
This is he who gave the great city of Brechin to the Lord. 70

The author arranged many of his words and ideas in chiastic and parallel patterns.

A1a	1	Cinadius ... filius Alpini primus Scottorum rexit ... annis sedecim
A1b	1	Pictauiam
A1b'	2	Pictauia autem a Pictis nominata est
A1a'	2	quos ut diximus Cinadius deleuit
A2	3	Deus ... eos ... alienos ... dignatus est facere
		qui illi non solum Domini missam ac preceptum spreuerunt
A2'	5	sed et in iure equitatis aliis equiparare noluerunt
A1'a	6	Iste [Cinadius] antequam ueniret
A1'b	6	Pictauiam Dalriete regnum suscepit.
B	7	reliquias Sancti Columbe transportauit ad ecclesiam
C	9	Danari uastauerunt Pictauiam ad ... Duncalden
D1	10	mortuus est ... ante idus Februarii feria tertia in palatio
D2	10	Fothiurthabaicht
D3	11	Douenaldus frater eius tenuit idem regnum
D3'	12	in huius tempore
D2'	12	Fothiurthabaicht
D1'	13	obiit in palatio ... idus Aprilis
E1	14	Constantinus filius Cinadii
E2a	15	primo eius anno
E2b	16	Aed filius Neil
E3	23	Eochodius ... nepos Cinadii
E4	24	Ciricium ... alii dicunt hic regnasse ...
E3'	24	Eochodio
E2'a	25	cuius secundo anno
E2'b	25	Aed filius Neil
F1	26	ac in nono eius anno
F2	28	Douenaldus filius Constantini
F3	30	Scotti habuerunt uictoriam
G	35	in Colle Credulitatis
G'	36	id est Collis Credulitatis |
F'1	37	et in suo octauo anno
F'2	38	Douenaldus filius Ede
F'3	40	Scotti habuerunt uictoriam
E'1a	41	filius Constantini post unum annum mortuus est
E'1a	42	Dubucan ... et Eochaid filius Alpini mortui sunt

E'1b	43	in senectute ... Domino seruiuit
E'2a	44	Maelcolaim ... predauit
E'2b	46	alii dicunt Constantinum fecisse ... predam
E'2a'	46	non Maelcolaim fecit predam
E'2b'	46	sed instigauit eum Constantinus ut dixi
E'1'a	47	mortuus est ... Constantinus in decimo ... anno
E'1'b	47	sub corona penitenti in senectute bona
D'1	48	occiderunt ... in Claideom
D'2	49	in huius tempore
D'1'	50	occisi sunt in Buchain
C'1a	51	Niger ... regnauit quinque annis
C'1b	53	Caniculum
C'2	53	Niger habuit uictoriam ubi cecidit ... abbas Duncalden
C'1'a	54	expulsus Niger de regno
C'1'b	55	Caniculus
B'1a	57	Culen rig quinque annis regnauit
B'1b	58	Marcan filius Breodalaig occisus est in ecclesia Sancti Michaelis
B'2	60	Maelbrigde episcopus pausauit
B'3	61	Cellach filius Ferdalaig regnauit
B'2'	62	Maelbrigde filius Dubucan obiit
B'1'a	63	Culen
B'1'b	63	et frater eius Eochodius occisi sunt a Britonibus
A'1	64	Cinadius filius Maelcolaim regnauit annum
A'2	65	statim predauit Britanniam
A'3	66	pedestres Cinadii occisi sunt
A'2'	67	Scotti predauerunt Saxoniam
A'1'	69	post annum perrexit Cinadius ... qui tribuit ciuitatem Brechne Domino.

Much of the diction recurs only in the chiastic pairs: *Sancti Columbe ad ecclesiam* and *in ecclesia Sancti Michaelis, Duncalden, in palatio, Fothiurthabaicht, in huius tempore, Aed filius Neil, Scotti habuerunt uictoriam, collis credulitatis, in senectute, Niger, Caniculus, Culen, Maelbrigde*. Chiastic pairing of diction suggests that the words *ut diximus* in A1a' imply no loss of text by abbreviation of an earlier source, as modern critics often suppose, but refer to the statement in A1a.

Of the author's many infixed numerical devices let us consider first those that confirm the integrity of discrete sentences.

In line 1 the sixteenth letter from the end is the first of *sedecim*. Reckoning letters as numbers the name *CINADIUS* bears a numerical value of $3+9+13+1+4+9+20+18$ or 77 and the name *PICTAVIA* a value of $15+9+3+19+1+20+9+1$ or 77.[3] From the *S* of *Cinadius* to the *P* of *Pictauia* inclusive there are seventy-seven letters and spaces between words.

3   See above pp. 5, 8, 22, 35 and below pp. 84, 89, 95, 141, 159–60, 174, 184.

In line 6 there are two words before *biennio* and six words after it.

The first word of the seventh line is *septimo*.

In line 13 the thirteenth syllable is the first of *idus Aprilis*, in which from the *i* of *idus* to the punctuation point after *Aprilis*. inclusive there are thirteen characters and spaces. The *idus Aprilis* is the thirteenth day of April.

In line 14 there are sixteen syllables before *sedecim*.

In line 15 the first word is *primo*.

In line 17 there are two words before *duos*.

In line 20 the fourteenth syllable is the last of *decimo quarto*.

Reckoning letters as numbers the name *INVER URIM* bears a numerical value of 9+13+20+5+17 and 20+17+9+12 or 122. From *Edus* to the space after *occisus* inclusive there are in line 22 122 letters and spaces between words.

In line 23 there are eleven words before *annis undecim*.

In line 25 the second word is *secundo*.

In line 26 there are two words and two syllables before *secundo*. In *in ipso die Ciricii* there are sixteen letters, the day of Saint Ciricius being 16 June.

In line 32 the fortieth letter is in *quadraginta*.

In line 33 the third syllable is the first of *tertio*.

In line 35 there are six syllables in *ac in sexto anno*. The sentence contains seventy-seven syllables. Reckoning letters as numbers the name *SCOAN* bears a numerical value of 18+3+14+1+13 or 49. From | *in Colle Credulitatis* to *Scoan* | inclusive there are forty-nine letters and spaces between words; from *Scoan* | to *id | est Collis Credulitatis* there are forty-nine letters. The word *CREDULITATIS* bears a numerical value of 3+17+5+4+20+11+9+19+1+19+9+18 or 135. From the space before | *in Colle Credulitatis* to the space after *Collis Credulitatis* | inclusive there are 134 letters and spaces.

In line 37 the eighth letter is the first of *octauo*.

In line 39 there are three words after *tribus*.

In line 40 there are eighteen syllables from | *in decimo octauo anno* to the end of the clause, and thirty-four syllables from the end of the clause to *in | tricesimo quarto eius anno*.

In line 41, reading *ëius* as trisyllabic, there are thirty-four syllables from | *in tricesimo quarto eius anno* to the end of the line.

In line 44 the eleventh syllable is the last of *undecim*.

Reckoning letters as numbers the name *MAELCOLAIM* bears a numerical value of 12+1+5+11+3+14+11+1+9+12 or 79. From the space before *Maelcolaim* to the space after *Maelcolaim* inclusive there are in line 45 seventy-nine letters and spaces between words.

Line 46 begins *in septimo anno regni sui*, the sentence containing seven clauses. From | *Maelcolaim* to *Maelcolaim* | inclusive there are eighty letters, though if one adopted the manuscript spelling of the latter *Malcolam* there would be seventy-nine. This sentence reveals our author as a philologist capable of varied play on words. The raid on the English as far as the river Tees yielded a *multitudinem hominum et multa armenta pecorum quam predam uocauerunt Scotti predam albidosorum idem nainn disi.* In one respect our author plays upon words for the colour white. For the etymon of *albidosus*, an unusual word, compare Late Latin *albedo* 'whiteness' and the adjectival suffix *-osus*, our author's form being the genitive plural of an adjective used as a neuter substantive 'of the whitish things',[4] glossed in the Gaelic language of the *Scotti* as *nainn disi* 'of the white multitudes',[5] playing also upon the preceding Latin *multitudinem.* In another respect our author plays upon names of peoples and places, *dos* 'property' in tmesis within *Albi* and *-orum* 'of the men of Alba' and *Disi* 'Tees'.[6] Consistent with this is the numerical value of *ALBI* as $1+11+2+9$ or 23, there being twenty-three words in the sentence before *Albi.* The numerical value of *DOS* is $4+14+18$ or 36, there being thirty-six syllables from | *quam predam* to *hanc* | *predam.* The numerical value of *NAINN* is $13+1+9+13+13$ or 49, there being forty-nine letters and spaces in the clause before | *idem nainn disi.* The numerical value of *DISI* is $4+9+18+9$ or 40, there being forty syllables between *Thesis* | and | *Disi.*

In line 47 there are ten syllables before | *in decimo eius anno.*

In line 49 there are eight syllables before *octo.*

In line 51 the fifth word is *quinque*, after which there are five letters to the end of the line in *annis.*

In line 55 there are five words.

In line 57 the fifth syllable is the last of *quinque*, after which there are five syllables to the end of the line.

Let us consider next infixed features that confirm the text in units more extensive than the sentence.

We have observed in considering discrete sentences above that the numerical value of the name *CINADIUS* is 77. In line 7 from *Septimo anno regni sui* [*i.e. Cinadii*] | to *Constantinus filius Cinadii* | 14 there are seventy-seven words. From *Cinadius* | 2 to *Mortuus est* [*i.e. Cinadius*] | 10 there are seventy-seven words. From | *Cinadius* 64 to | *Cinadii* 66 there are seventy-seven letters, and from | *Cinadius* 64 to *Cinadius* | 68 inclusive there are seventy-seven syllables, *Cinadius* 68 being the seventh occurrence of the name.

---

4   For play upon the *albo crine* 'white hair' of the men of Alba see above pp. 40–4.

5   According to Skene, *Chronicles*, pp. xxi–xxii, '*Na* is the genitive plural of the Irish definite article; *Fionn* is Irish for *albus* or *white*, and forms *fhinn*, the *f* when aspirated being silent; *Dese* is a *multitude* or *troup*; and *albidosorum* is thus an attempt to translate *na*[*fh*]*inndisi*.'

6   For comparable bilingual play consider the last line of the Salutation in a letter from the Irish *peregrinus* Cellanus of Peronna Scottorum in Picardy to the Irish-educated Englishman Aldhelm: *in tota et tuta Trinitate salutem*, with which compare Old Irish *toth* 'the female pudenda', *túatae* 'boorish', 'ignorant', and *tríanach* 'tripartite', which allows Cellán to say in Latin 'in the whole and safe Trinity greeting' and simultaneously to imply in Irish 'a tripartite ignorant twat', the putatively effeminate Aldhelm imagined as sexually passive in his mouth, his rectum, and his *labia*, a noun attracted by Cellán from neuter to feminine gender. For other tricks of this cunning linguist see Howlett, *Celtic Latin Tradition*, pp. 108–13.

Reckoning letters as numbers the name *DOVENALDVS* bears a numerical value of 4+14+20+5+13+1+11+4+20+18 or 110, coincident with the first occurrence of the name in line 11 as the 110th word of the text.

Lines 12–13 record the reign and death of Domnall, *In huius tempore iura ac leges regni Edi filii Ecdach fecerunt Goedeli cum rege suo i Fothiurthabaicht Obiit in palatio Cinn Belathoir idus Aprilis.* The *idus Aprilis* on which he died is 13 April, the 104th day of the leap year 868. From *In huius tempore* | to the *A* of *Aprilis* inclusive there are 104 letters.

In lines 15–19 about *Maelsechnaill rex Hiberniensium* the forty-four words divide by duple ratio 2:1 at 15 and 29, at | *duos.* The twenty-nine words divide into thirds at 10 and 19, at | *tertio.* There are seventeen lines before the clause *et habitauit eam a kalendis Ianuarii usque ad festum Sancti Patricii*, which occurs on 17 March. In this clause the seventeenth syllable is the first of *usque ad festum Sancti Patricii.* From | *Primo* to | *Patricii* there are seventy-four syllables, the number of days between the kalends of January and 17 March.

We have observed in considering discrete sentences above that the numerical value of the name *MALCOLAIM* is 79. In lines 48–51 there are from | *Maelcolaim* to *Malcolaim* | inclusive seventy-nine syllables.

Reckoning letters as numbers the numerical value of the name *NIGER* is 13+9+7+5+17 or 51. In lines 53–4 from | *Nigerum* to the former *Niger* | inclusive there are fifty-one letters and spaces between words; from | *Nigerum* to the latter *Niger* | inclusive there are fifty syllables.

Reckoning letters as numbers the name *MAELBRIGDE* bears a numerical value of 12+1+5+11+2+17+9+7+4+5 or 73. In lines 60–62 from | *Maelbrigde* to *Maelbrigde* | inclusive there are seventy-four letters and spaces between words, though if one adopted the manuscript spelling of the former *Maelbrigd'* there would be seventy-three.

Let us consider next infixed features that confirm the text of the entire composition.

In line 9 from | *Britanni* to *Duncalden* | inclusive there are ninety-seven letters and spaces between words. *Duncalden* is the ninety-seventh word of the complete text.

In line 33, in which, as we have noted above, the third syllable is the first of *tertio*, there are before *tertio* 333 words of the complete text.[7]

The line in which, as we have noted above, the word *pariter* occurs, is thirty-fifth, half-way through the seventy lines. Of the 777 words in the text the central, 389th from the beginning and the end, is *credulitatis* at the end of the crux of the chiasmus.

The internal chronology of this chronicle is fixed by the absolute date of the eclipse on Saint Ciricius's Day, Wednesday, 16 June 885, confirmed by the sixteen letters in *in ipso die Ciricii*, as noted above. Sixteen lines before this one reads of the death of *Cinadius filius Alpini* after a reign of sixteen years, which fixes a date

---

7 For other examples of play on 333 see above p. 35 and below pp. 75, 83, 102.

of A.D. 850 as the beginning of the chronicle. Sixteen lines after this inclusive
one reads of the Battle of Brunanburh, the date of which is fixed by the Anglo-
Saxon Chronicle as A.D. 937.

The event at the crux of the chiasmus is also the crux of the chronology,
A.D. 909 being fifty-nine years after the accession of *Cinadius filius Alpini* in 850
and fifty-nine years before the accession of *Cinadius filius Maelcolaim* in 968.

This chronicle records the reigns of twelve kings:

1	Cinadius filius Alpini	16 years
2	Douenaldus frater eius	4
3	Constantinus filius Cinadii	16
4	Edus	1
5	Eochodius nepos Cinadii	1
6	Douenaldus filius Constantini	11
7	Constantinus filius Edi	40
8	Maelcolaim filius Domnaill	11
9	Idulfus	8
10	Niger filius Maelcolaim	5
11	Culen rig	5
12	Cinadius filius Maelcolaim	—

If the chronicler reckoned the sixteen-year reign of *Cinadius filius Alpini* to have
begun in A.D. 850[8] and he ended his reckoning after sixteen years of reign by
Cinadius filius Maelcolaim, the number of kings would be 12 and the combined years
of their reigns would be 144, the square of 12, bringing one to A.D. 994. If he ended
his reckoning after twenty-two years of reign by *Cinadius filius Maelcolaim*,[9] the
combined years of their reigns would be 150, bringing one to A.D. 1000.

From line 8 one infers that the author reckoned Dunbar and Melrose to be in
Saxonia 'England', as from line 49 one infers the same of Edinburgh. From line 9
one infers that the Britons, presumably of Strathclyde, were still formidable enough
to invade Pictland. There are repeated indications of the ability of Norsemen to
attack various parts of *Albania* or *Pictauia* as easily as territories occupied by the
Gaels.

Composition in seventy lines and 777 words is consistent with composition in
sevens in *De Situ Albanie* and *Cronica de Origine Antiquorum Pictorum* and *Vita Sancti
Reguli*. The beginning of the reign of *Cinadius filius Alpini* in A.D. 850 is consistent
with the reckoning of both *De Situ Albanie* and the *Cronica Regum Scottorum*.[10]

---

8 Compare *De Situ Albanie* above p. 36.
9 Compare *Cronica Regum Scottorum* below p. 65.
10 Compare the seven parts of *De Situ Albanie* and of *Cronica de Origine Antiquorum
    Pictorum* above pp. 29–31, 44–7, the *Cronica Regum Scottorum* below pp. 64–70, and the
    777 words of *Vita Sancti Reguli* below pp. 76–8.

It would be idle to imagine that the present analysis does more than scratch the surface of the mnemonic and structural artifice of this remarkable little chronicle. None of the devices proves the historical correctness of any statement, and the chronology of this document is inconsistent with some dates recorded in such sources as the *Annals of Ulster* and later Scottish lists of kings. This composition is, however, internally consistent in punctilious detail. Considered together the infixed devices offer fair assurance that regardless of any antecedent transmission this text has descended to us nearly as it issued from the pen of its final redactor, whom we may regard as an author more accomplished than any modern critic has yet supposed.

'CRONICA REGUM SCOTTORUM'

Directly after the 'Chronicle of the Kings of Alba' in the Poppleton manuscript follows the *Cronica Regum Scottorum* on folios 29va–31ra.[1]

CRONICA REGUM SCOTTORUM TRECENTI QUATUÓRDECIM ANNÓRUM

1 Fergus filius Eric ipse fuit primus qui de semine Chonare suscepit regnum Alban
id est a monte Drum Alban usque ad mare Hibernie et ad Inche Gal

2 Iste regnauit [.]iij. annis.
Domangrat filius eius .v. annis.
Congel filius Domangrat .xxx.iii. [annis.]
5 Goueran frater Congel .xxij. annis.
Conal filius Congel .xiiij. annis.
Edan filius Goueran [.]xxxiiij. annis.
Eochid flauus filius Edan .xvj. annis.
Kinat sinistralis filius Conal .iij. mensibus.
10 Fercar filius eius xvj annis.
Douenald uarius filius Eochid .xiiij. [annis.]
Fergar longus .xxj. [annis.]
Eochal habens curuum nasum. filius Douegarth filii Douenal uarii .iij. [annis.]
Arinchellac. filius Ferchar longi .j. anno.
15 Ewen filius Ferchar longi .xiij. [annis.]
Murechat filius Arinchellac .iij. annis.
Ewen filius Murcerdach [.]iij. [annis.]
Ed albus filius Eochal curui nasi .xxx[. annis.]
Fergus filius Hed albi .iij. [annis.]
20 Seluach filius Eogan .xxiiij. [annis.]
Eochal uenenosus. filius Ed albi .xxx[. annis.]
Dunegal filius Seluach [.]vij. [annis.]

1 *BCLL*, no. 1039 p. 289. Skene, *Chronicles*, pp. 130–4. Anderson, *Kings and Kingship*, pp. 253–8.

Alpin. filius Eochal uenenosi .iij. [annis.]
Kinetus filius Alpini primus rex Scottorum .xvj[. annis.]
25 Dolfnal filius Alpini .iiij. [annis.]
Constantinus filius Kinet .xx. [annis.]
Hed filius Kinet .j. anno.
Grig filius Dunegal .xij. [annis.]
Duuenal filius Constantini .xj. [annis.]
30 Constantinus filius Hed [.]xxv. [annis.]
Malcolin filius Duuenald [.]ix. [annis.]
Indolf filius Constantini [.]ix. [annis.]
Duf filius Malcolin .iiij. annis. et [.]vj. mensibus.
Culen filius Indulf .iiij. annis et [.]vj[.] mensibus.
35 Kinet. filius Malcolin .xxij. annis et [.]ij. mensibus.
Custantin filius Culen .j. anno et [.]iiij. mensibus.
Chinet. filius Duf .j. anno et dimidium.
Malcolin. filius Kinet .xxx[. annis.]
  Hic magnum bellum fecit apud Carrun.
40 Ipse etiam multas oblationes tam ecclesiis quam clero ea die distribuit.
Macheth. filius Findleg .xvij. [annis.]
Lulac nepos filii Boide .iiij. mensibus et dimidium.
Malcolin filius Dunec' .xxxvij. [annis] et dimidium et [.]iiij. mensibus.
  Hic fuit uir Margarite regine filie nobilissimi.
45 Matildis et Maria sui generis celsitudinem coniugio morum
    ingenuitate scientie magnitudine rerum temporalium larga in
    pauperes et in ecclesias dispensatione decenter ornauerunt.
46 Matildis enim matrimonio iuncta fuit Henrico Anglorum regi
    strenuissimo: qui de Francorum excellenti regum prosapia
    duxit originem.
47 Quorum sublimitas predicti scilicet regis et regine ad hoc usque
    perducta est ut ipsorum soboles Romani imperii tenuerunt
    dignitatem.
48 Eorum namque filia Matildis prudentia forma diuitiis digna imperio
    imperatori nupsit Romano.
49 Maria uero lege coniugii Eustachio comiti Boloniensi tradita regina
    sorore non minor extitit probitate licet regia caruerit potestate.
50 Huius itidem filia strenuum uirum comitem Stephanum sponsum
    accepit de regali simul et consulari stirpe progenitum[.]
51 Omitto filias adhuc uiuentes[.]
52 Matres defunctas exemplo propono uiuentibus
    que cum seculi pompa quod raro inuenitur diuites sanctis extitere
      uirtutibus
    pauperes utriusque sexus cuiuscumque conditionis essent ac si
      membra coluerunt Xpisti [.]

53 Religiosos clericos monachos sincero amore uelut patronos et suos futuros iudices cum Xpisto dilexerunt[.]

54 Matildis regina kalendis Maii migrauit de hac uita. anno ab incarnatione Domini .m°.c°.xviij. sepultaque est honorifice in ecclesia Beati Petri apostolorum principis Westmonasterii iuxta Londoniam Anglorum urbem nobilissimam.

55 Maria autem comitissa .ij. kalendis .Iunii. anno ab incarnatione Domini .m°.c°.xvj. apud Bermundeseiam ex altera parte prefate urbis monasterio Sancti Saluatoris in pace quieuit ubi a domino Petreio admirande sanctitatis uiro tunc priore eiusdem loci Cluniacensis sed ad caritatem specialiter pertinentis gloriose sepulta est.

56 Tumulus uero marmoreus regum et reginarum ymagines habens impressas : genus quiescentis demonstrat.

57 In superficiem eiusdem tumuli titulus aureis literis sculptus nomen et uitam et originem breuiter ita comprehendit.

58 Nobilis hic tumulata iacet comitissa Maria.

59 Actibus hec nituit larga benigna fuit.

60 Regum sanguis erat morum probitate uigebat.

61 Compatiens inopi uiuat in arce poli.

62 Edmundus uero frater earum uir strenuissimus et in Dei seruitio dum uitam ageret presentem ualde deuotus apud Montem Acutum in quadam uidelicet cella Cluniacensi que ibi sita est requiescit humatus.

63 Dolfnal frater eius regnauit annis .iiij. et [.]vij[.] mensibus.

64 Dunchadh filius Malcolin dimidium annum.

65 Eadgarus. filius Malcolin .ix[.] annis.

66 Alexander frater eius .xvij. annis. et [.]iij. mensibus[.]

67 Dauid frater eius .xxx. [annis.]

68 Erat autem rex Dauid uir piissimus. in religione. catholicus. in pauperes munificus in recuperandis basilicis studiosus satis uigiliis et orationibus in tantum studens ut plus supplicationibus ad Deum profusis quam armis bellicis uictoriam de inimicis obtineret.

69 Rex uero piissimus Dauid multa bona fecit precipue tum edes sacras ubicumque in toto regno suo uetustate collapsas conferat. pontificibus et patribus ad quorum curam pertinebant ut restaurentur imperauit. adhibens curam per legatos ut imperata perficerentur.

70 Unde sub eius imperio multa sunt reparata immo funditus edificata monasteria.

71 Sed hec precipue monasterium puellare Sancte Marie. et monasterium puellare Sancte .N. et multa alia puellaria et cetera plurima utriusque uidelicet et sexus uirorum et mulierum. quibus ueluti quibusdam lichinis totum decoratur Scotie regnum.

72   Que omnia ipse piissimus Dauid rex magnus auri et argenti
       ponderibus gemmarumque pretiosarum exornauit muneribus.

73   Amplissimis etiam honoribus ditauit et insuper quod pretiosius est
       sanctissimis reliquiarum patrociniis insigniuit.

74   Has omnes idem rex potens et piissimus honorabiliter multis
       excolebat muneribus[.]

75   Sed Melrosensem precipue inter omnes ecclesias et fideliter
       defensabat et dulciter diligebat et suis opibus exornabat.

76   Ceterum omnia eius gesta que uulgo narrantur non sunt hic propter
       uitandum fastidium legentis pleniter explanata.

77   Malcolin filius filii Dauid .xij. annis. et [.]vj. mensibus et xiij diebus.

78   Willelmus frater eius
    Ab anno primo Willelmi regnum Scottorum .anni .ccc.xv.

80   Willelmus rex rufus
    filius Henrici

5   filii Dauid
    filii Maelcolaim.
    filii Donnchada

85   qui fuit nepos Maelcolaim
    filii Cinada

10   filii Maelcolaim
    filii Domnaill.
    filii Constantin.

90   filii Cinatha.
    filii Alpin.

15   filii Echach.
    filii Eda Find
    filii Echadach.

95   filii Echach.
    filii Domongrat.

20   filii Domnail Bric.
    filii Echach Buide.
    filii Edan.

100   filii Gabran.
    filii Dommungrat.

25   filii Fergusa.
    filii Eirc.
    filii Echach Muinremuir.

105   filii Oengusa Phir.
    filii Fedilmthe Aislingig.

30   filii Oengusa Buidnig.
    filii Fedilmthe Ruamnaich.
    filii Senchormaic.

110   filii Cruitluide.
        filii Find Fece.
35   filii Achir Cir.
        filii Achach Antoit.
        filii Fiacrach Cathmail.
115   filii Echdach Riada.
        filii Conore.
40   filii Moga Landa.
        filii Luigdig Ellatig.
        filii Corpre Crumpchinn.
120   filii Dare Dornmoir.
        filii Corbre Admoir.
45   filii Conaire Moir.
        filii Etersceuil.
        filii Eogain.
125   filii Elela.
        filii Iair.
50   filii Dedaid.
        filii Sin.
        filii Rosin.
130   filii Their.
        filii Rothir.
55   filii Roin.
        filii Arandil.
        filii Maine.
135   filii Forgo.
        filii Feradaig.
60   filii Elela Arann.
        filii Fiachra Fir Mara.
        filii Oengusa Turmig.
140   filii Fir Cethairroid.
        filii Fer Roid.
65   filii Fir Anroid.
        filii Fir Aibrig.
        filii Labchore.
145   filii Echach Altlethin.
        filii Elela Casiaclaig.
70   filii Conlaith.
        filii Erero.
        filii Moalgi.
150   filii Cobthaig Coelbreg.
        filii Ugaine Moir.
75   filii Ecdaig Buadaig.
        filii Duach Lograich.
        filii Fiachraig Tollgreich.

155   filii Muredaich Bollgreich.
        filii Semoin Bricc.
 80   filii Eun Duib.
        filii Edoin Glais.
        filii Nuadat Fail.
160   filii Elchada.
        filii Olchaim.
 85   filii Sirna.
        filii Dein.
        filii Demail.
165   filii Rodchada.
        filii Ogmaich.
 90   filii Oengussa Olmochada.
        filii Fiachrach Laibrinne.
        filii Smergnaid.
170   filii Smereta.
        filii Enmotha.
 95   filii Tigernaig.
        filii Fallaig.
        filii Etheoir.
175   filii Iair.
        filii hErmeoin.
100   filii Meled Espain.
        filii Bili.
        filii Nema.
180   filii Brige.
        filii Brigoind.
105   filii Bracha.
        filii Theacha.
        filii Erchada.
185   filii Aldoit.
        filii Noda.
110   filii Nonaill Hemir.
        filii Goildil Glais.
        filii Neuil.
190   filii Fenius Farsaid.
        filii Eogani.
115   filii Glunud.
        filii Lauind.
        filii Etheoir.
195   filii Iair.
        filii Agmemnoni.
120   filii Thri.
        filii Boi.
        filii Sem.

200 filii Mair.
     filii Esro.
125 filii Aduir.
     filii Hieridach.
     filii Aoth.
205 filii Srau.
     filii Esro.
130 filii Boid.
     filii Riafich.
     filii Gomur.
210 filii Iafech.
     filii Noe.
135 filii Lamech.
     filii Matussalem.
     filii Enoc.
215 filii Iarech.
     filii Malalechel.
140 filii Cainan.
     filii Enos.
     filii Sed.
220 filii Adam.
144 filii Dei uiui.

tit. .ccc.xiiij. 1 erie. 13 curruum. 18 edalbus. 19 hedalbi. 20 eogan *altered from* eogon. 21 fochal. edalbi. 24 kynedus. 45 marie. 47 sullimitas. ab. 48 N. 49 regina. 53 scincero. uelud. 54 may. 55 domno. ammirande. duniacensis. 56 tumilus. 57 superciem. tumili. 58 tumilata. 59 intuit. 62 uidilicet. cluniaccensi. 64 dunchahd. 66 mensi. 68 pijsimus. uigilis. optineret. 69 tamen. uectate. 70 funditur. 71 uidilicet. 72 oīe. 83 fili. 85 que. Malcolaim. 88 f' 7. 90 Ernacha. 97 Domnailbrie. 103 Eire. 106 Fedilinthe. 107 Oengusabuiding. 108 Fedilintheruamnaich. 110 Cruithinde. 114 Fiaerachcathmail. 118 Luigdig f' Ellatig. 119 Corpre Crumpchimi. 121 Eorbre f' Admoir. 122 Conarremoir. 124 Eogami. 128 Siu. 129 Rosiu. 132 Rom. 134 Manine. 137 Elela Arami. 138 Fiachra f' Firmara. 139 Oengusaturuug. 140 Fircechairroid. 145 Echachaltlechin. 147 Conlaich. 154 f' Fiach^raig Duadach f' Duachlograich. 156 Semoin f' Bricc. 157 Dinb. 158 Edom f' Glais. 160–1 Elchada Olchaim. 163 Dem. 167 Oengissa f' Olmochada. 169 Sinerguaid. 171 Enmocha. 176 Hermeom. 177 Meledespam. 217 Caman.

CHRONICLE OF THE KINGS OF THE SCOTS
THREE HUNDRED FOURTEEN YEARS

1   Fergus son of Erc was he who first from the seed of Conaire received
         the rule of Alba,
     that is from the mountain of Druimm–nAlban up to the sea of Ireland
         and to Inche Gal [*i.e.* the Hebrides].

2   That man reigned for 3 years.

Domangart his son for 5 years.

Comgall son of Domangart for 33 [years].

5   Gabran brother of Comgall for 22 years.

Conall son of Comgall for 14 years.

Aidan son of Gabran for 34 years.

Eochaid Buide son of Aidan for 16 years.

Connad Cerr son of Conall for 3 months.

10   Ferchar his son for 16 years.

Donald Brecc son of Eochaid for 14 [years].

Ferchar Fota for 21 [years].

Eochaid having a curved nose son of Domangart son of Domnall Brecc
    for 3 [years].

Ainbcellach son of Ferchar Fota for 1 year.

15   Eogan son of Ferchar Fota for 13 [years].

Muiredach son of Ainbcellach for 3 years.

Eogan son of Muiredach for 3 [years].

Aed Finn son of Eochaid of the curved nose for 30 [years].

Fergus son of Aed Finn for 3 [years].

20   Selbach son of Eogan for 24 [years].

Eochaid the poisonous son of Aed Finn for 30 [years].

Dungal son of Selbach for 7 [years].

Alpin son of Eochaid the poisonous for 3 [years].

Cinaed son of Alpin first King of the Scots for 16 [years].

25   Domnall son of Alpin for 4 [years].

Constantín son of Cinaed for 20 [years].

Aed son of Cinaed for 1 year.

Giric son of Dungal for 12 [years].

Domnall son of Constantín for 11 [years].

30   Constantín son of Aed for 25 [years].

Mael Coluim son of Domnall for 9 [years].

Illulb son of Constantín for 9 [years].

Dub son of Mael Coluim for 4 years and 6 months.

Cuilén son of Illulb for 4 years and 6 months.

35   Cinaed son of Mael Coluim for 22 years and 2 months.

Constantín son of Cuilén for 1 year and a half.

Cinaed son of Dub for 1 year and 4 months.

Mael Coluim son of Cinaed for 30 [years].

    This man made a great battle at Carham.

40   The same man distributed many offerings as much to churches as to
    the clergy on that day.

Mac Bethad son of Findlaech for 17 [years].

Lulach grandson [or 'nephew'] of the son of Boide for 4 months and a half.

Mael Coluim son of Donnchad for 37 [years] and a half and 4 months.

44   This man was the husband of Margaret the queen, daughter of a most
      noble man.

45   Mathilda and Mary fitly ornamented the heavenliness of their own race
      by marriage, by nobility of morals, by greatness of knowledge, by
      generous dispensation of temporal things to poor men and to
      churches.

46   For Mathilda was joined in matrimony to Henry, the most vigorous
      king of the English, who drew his origin from the excellent stock
      of the kings of the Franks.

47   The sublimity of them, that is of the foresaid king and queen, was
      extended to this, that their offspring held the dignity of the Roman
      empire.

48   For their daughter Mathilda, worthy of empire in prudence, in beauty,
      in riches, married the Roman emperor.

49   Mary, in truth, given by the law of marriage to Eustace, Count of
      Boulogne, stood out as not less in probity than the queen, her sister,
      though she lacked royal power.

50   The daughter of this woman, moreover, received as spouse the vigorous
      man Count Stephen, begotten from royal and consular stock alike.

51   I omit the daughters living at this time.

52   The deceased mothers I bring forward as an example to the living,
      who, what is rarely found, with secular pomp stood out as women
         rich in holy virtues
      and cultivated the poor of either sex and of whatever condition as
         if they were members of Christ.

53   They loved religious, clerics, monks, with sincere love as patrons and
      their own future judges with Christ.

54   Mathilda the queen departed from this life on the kalends of May in
      the year from the Incarnation of the Lord 1118 and is buried
      honourably in the Church of Blessed Peter prince of the apostles at
      Westminster near London the most noble city of the English.

55   Mary the countess, however, rested in peace on the second from the
      kalends of June in the year from the Incarnation of the Lord 1116 at
      Bermondsey; in the other part [*i.e.* the Surrey side] of the foresaid
      city in the monastery of the Holy Saviour, where she was buried
      gloriously by the lord Petreius, a man of admirable sanctity, then
      prior of the same Cluniac place, but specially devoted to charity.

56   A marble tomb, in truth, bearing the impressed images of kings and
      queens, indicates the race of the one resting there.

57   On the surface of this tomb an inscription carved in letters of gold
      briefly describes her name and life and origin.

58   Here lies entombed the noble countess Mary.

59   In acts she shone, was kindly, generous.

60   Was of the blood of kings, in morals throve.

61   Pitying the poor, should live in heaven's arc.

62   Edmund, in truth, their brother, a most vigorous man, and while he lived the present life especially devout in the service of God, rests buried at Montague in a certain Cluniac cell, that is, which is sited there.

63   Domnall his brother reigned for 3 years and 7 months.

64   Donnchad son of Mael Coluim half a year.

65   Eadgar son of Mael Coluim for 9 years.

66   Alexander his brother for 17 years and 3 months.

67   David his brother for 30 [years].

68   David the king was, however, a man most pious, catholic in religion, munificent to paupers, zealous in restoring basilicas, attentive in vigils and prayers to such a degree that he would obtain victory over enemies more from supplications poured out to God than from warlike arms.

69   The most pious King David, in truth, did many good things, especially, then, wherever in his whole realm he would confer sacred buildings collapsed from age to bishops and fathers to whose concern they belonged, he commanded that they be restored, directing his concern through legates that the things commanded be completed.

70   Wherefore under his command many monasteries were repaired, indeed built from the foundations.

71   But these especially — the monastery of Saint Mary for women and the monastery of Saint N. for women and many other women's houses and very many others of either sex, that is, of both men and women, with which, as if with lamps, the whole realm of Scotland is decorated.

72   All which this same most pious great King David adorned with weights of gold and silver and with gifts of precious gems.

73   He also enriched with the fullest honours and with what is still more precious he made them outstanding with the most holy patrimonies of relics.

74   All these the same powerful and most pious king honourably cultivated with many gifts.

75   But Melrose especially among all the churches he both faithfully defended and sweetly loved and adorned with his own gifts.

76   For the rest, all his deeds which are commonly related are not expounded fully here on account of avoiding the distate of the reader.

77   Malcolm son of the son of David for 12 years and 6 months and 13 days.

78   William his brother; from the first year of William the rule of the Scots 315 years.

79   King William the Ruddy, son of Henry ...
son of Adam
son of the living God.

The author has infixed many devices that help to guarantee the integrity of the text of discrete sentences.

In line 2 the third word is iij.

In line 3 there are five letters after v.

In line 5 there are twenty-two letters and spaces before xxij.

In line 6 about a reign of fourteen years there are fourteen syllables.

In line 7 about a reign of thirty-four years there are thirty-four letters and spaces between words.

In line 14 there is one word after j.

In lines 16 and 17 there are three words before iij.

In line 20 there are twenty-four letters to the end of xxiiij.

In line 21 there are thirty letters to the end of xxx.

In line 24 the sixteenth syllable is the first of xvj.

In line 25 the fourth word is iiij.

In line 27 there is one word after j.

In line 29 the eleventh syllable is the first of xj.

In line 30 of letters and spaces between words the twenty-fifth is the first of xxv.

In lines 31 and 32 there are nine syllables before ix.

In lines 33 and 34 the fourth word is iiij, and there are six words before vj.

In line 35 there are twenty-two letters and spaces before xxij and two words after that before ij, which is the second word from the end.

In line 42 there are four words before iiij.

In line 63 there are three words after iij.

In line 65 there are nine syllables before ix.

In line 77 the twelfth syllable is the first of xij.

The author has infixed other devices that help to guarantee the integrity of the entire text. The words *Willelmus frater eius … Ab anno primo Willelmi regnum Scottorum anni cccxv*, with half a line blank before *Ab anno primo Willelmi*, allow us to date the text to the reign of William the Lion, the first year of whose reign began with his accession on 9 December and his inauguration on 24 December 1165. The text as presented above contains 1175 words, suggesting, perhaps, the year of its composition.[2] The twenty-seven words of 74 divide by sesquioctave ratio at 14 and 13, at *Melrosensem | precipue inter omnes ecclesias et fideliter defensabat et dulciter diligebat*, suggesting, perhaps, composition at Melrose. Inclusion of Melrose as part of *totum Scotie regnum* 71 connects our author's usage with that of *De Situ Albanie* and the *Vita Sancti Reguli* and with the usage of Symeon of Glasgow, Adam of Dryburgh, and Jocelin of Furness and a charter of a Bishop of Aberdeen.[3]

---

2   See above pp. 8, 23, 36, 59, 61 and below pp. 83–5, 89, 96, 110, 142, 150, 160, 174, 182–4.

3   See above pp. 38–9 and below pp. 94, 123, 154, 157.

From the beginning to | *Willelmus frater eius* there are seventy-seven lines, with which one may compare the seven-part structures of *De Situ Albanie* and *Cronica de Origine Antiquorum Pictorum* and the seventy lines and 777 words of the 'Chronicle of the Kings of Alba' above and the 777 words of the *Vita Sancti Reguli* below.[4] A repeated sentence connects the beginning of this text with the first sentence of part VII of *De Situ Albanie*.[5] Description of King William as *Rufus* connects this text further with *De Situ Albanie*.[6] From | *Willelmus rex rufus* to the end there are 333 words.[7] Including the title there are 222 sentences.[8] There are 144 lines from *Willelmus frater eius* to *filii Dei uiui*.[9]

The phrase *propter uitandum fastidium legentis* is a cliché, but may be included here to connect this text with the *Vita Sancti Kentigerni*, in which the phrase is borrowed from Adomnán's *Vita Sancti Columbae*, and with the *Epistola ad Adam Scottum* by John Abbot of Kelso.[10]

---

4 See above pp. 29–31, 44–7, 52–4 and below pp. 76–8.
5 See above p. 31.
6 See above p. 30.
7 See above pp. 35, 61 and below pp. 83, 102.
8 For other examples of play on 22, 222, and 2222 see *Book of Letters*, p. 43, 'Five Experiments', pp. 7–8, 15–18, 27–9, 46, *Cambro-Latin Compositions*, pp. 126, 133, 'Insular Acrostics', p. 43, '*Vita I Sanctae Brigitae*', pp. 1–23, *Sealed from Within*, pp. 43–50, 91–3. See below pp. 90, 102.
9 For other examples of play on 144 see above p. 8 and below pp. 96, 150, 174.
10 See below p. 95, 100, 165.

'VITA SANCTI REGULI'

Directly after the *Cronica Regum Scottorum* in the Poppleton manuscript follows a *Vita Sancti Reguli* on folios 31ra–32ra by an author not yet identified.[1] Capital letters and punctuation marks in boldface represent features of the manuscript. I have arranged the text *per cola et commata*, numbered the sentences, and marked the rhythms of the cursus. For assimilated *c* of the fourteenth-century manuscript I have silently restored *t* before *e* and *i* as appropriate in a twelfth-century composition. All other departures from the manuscript are recorded after the text.

[VITA SANCTI REGULI]

**QUALITER ACCIDERIT
QUOD MEMORIA SANCTI ANDREE APOSTOLI
AMPLIUS IN REGIONE PICTORUM
QUE NUNC SCOTIA DICITUR
QUAM IN CETERIS REGIONIBUS SIT :
ET QUO MODO CONTIGERIT
QUOD TANTE ABBATIE IBI FACTE ANTIQUITUS FUERUNT
QUAS MULTI ADHUC SECULARES VIRI IURE HEREDITARIO POSSIDENT**

1   '**AN**dreas' qui 'interpretatur secundum Hebream ethimologiam decorus síue
        respóndens .
        Sermone enim Greco a uiro uirílis' intèrpretátur .   10
        germanus Beati Pétri Apóstoli .
        'coheres' autem eíus 'grátia'
        secundum Iohannem euangelistam primus apostolus a Xpisto Iesu Domino
        nóstro eléctus
        secundum uero Matheum Marcúmque secúndus
2   **H**ic sorte predicationis aquilonales nationes Cithias Pictonésque postréme   15
        Achaias ipsamque ciuitatem nomine Pátras accépit .
        in qua etiam cruci suspensus est secunda kalendárum Decémbrium .
        ibíque obcúbuit
        et ibique custodita sunt óssa illíus
        usque ad tempus Constantini Magni . filii Heléne   20

1   *BCLL*, no. 1026 p. 285. Skene, *Chronicles*, pp. 138–40. Anderson, *Kings and Kingship*,
     pp. 258–60.

atque filiorum eius id est Constantíni cum Constánte
quasi spatio ducentorum septuaginta tríum annórum .

3   In quorum regno a Constantinopolitanis miro famosoque ductu inde suscepta
atque translata sunt Cónstantinópoli .

4   Et cum magna gloria et maximo honore ibidem recondita sunt [? l. súnt recóndita]

5   Et manserunt semper usque ad tempus Theodotionis Xpistiani ímperatóris .   25
spatio scilicet centum décem annórum .

6   Tunc diuino instinctu Rex Pictorum nomine Ungus filius . Urguist cum exercitu
mágno consúrg*ens*

Britannicas nationes dexteram eius insule partem inhabitantes crudelissima
uastatione ínterfici*ens* .

postremo peruenit úsque ad cámpum Merc

7   Íllic hiemáuit .   30

8   Eo tempore omnes pene totius insule gentes unanimo impetu uenientes
círcumdedèrunt éum .

uolentes eum cum exercitu suo pénitus delé*re* .

9   Altera autem die euenit regi predicto cum septem comitibus amicíssimis àmbulá*re* .

10   Et circumfulsit éos diuína lux

11   Et proni in facies suas non ualentes eam sustinere cecidérunt in térram   35

12   Et ecce uox de célo audíta est .

13   "Ungus Ungus audi me apostolum Xpisti Andréam nómine
qui missus sum ad te defendendum atque cústodiéndum :

14   Surge uide signum crucis Xpisti quod stat in aere atque precedet contra ínimicos
túos .

15   Verum tamen decimam hereditatis tue partem et elemosinam Deo
omnipotenti et in honore Sancti Andree apóstoli eìus óffer ."   40

16   Tertia autem die diuina uoce admonitus suum exercitum in duodecim túrmas
diuísi*t*

17   Et signum crucis unamquamque pártem precedé*bat*

18   Lux autem diuina de unius cuiusque signi cápite fulgé*bat* .

19   Tunc uictores facti Deo omnipotenti atque Sancto Andree apostolo grátias
egérun*t* .

20   Patriam autem uenientes incolumes decimam sue hereditatis partem Deo et
Sancto Andree apostolo uenerabili uoléntes offèrre .   45

impléndo quod scríptum est

21   Date elemosinam et omnia múnda sunt uóbis

22   Incertum uero habebant in quo loco specialiter uectigalem Deo . principalem
ciuitatem Sancto Andree apóstolo òrdinárent .

23   Tunc unito concilio binis . ternis . quatriduanis diébus ieiu*n*ántes   50
atque Dei omnipotentis misericórdiam . pòstu*l*ántes
unus custodientium corpus Sancti Andree apostoli Cónstantinópoli
uisione diuina et reuelatione admonitus atque instrúctus est dicénte .

24   'Exi de terra tua et de cognatione tua .
et de domo patris *tui* .   55

25   Et uade in terram quam monstrauero *tibi* .'

26   Tunc uenit ángelo còmitá*n*te
atque uiam illius cústodié*n*te
prospere peruenit ad uerticem montis régis id est Ríg Mund .

27   **E**adem autem hora qua illic lassus sederet cum suis séptem comítibus   60
      lux circumfulsit diuina regem Pictorum uenientem cum suo exercitu ád
          speciàlem lócum
      qui dícitur Kar Ténan
28   Et claritatem non ferentes ceciderunt in fácies súas
29   Et sanati sunt claudi et ceci número séptem
30   Et unus a natiuitate cecus ílluminátus est .   65
31   **Et** inde *uidit locum plenum uisitatióne angelórum*
32   Et tunc uoce mágna clamàuit dícens
      "*Video locum plenum uisitatióne angelórum*"
33   **P**ostremo Dei ordinatione rex cum suo exercitu uénit ad lócum
      quem Dominus illi ceco qui illuminatus fúerat osténdit   70
34   **R**egulus uero monachus a Constantinopolitana úrbe peregrínus
      regi obuiauit cum reliquiis Sancti Andrée apóstoli
      quas secum hinc huc adduxerat ad portam que dicitur Matha íd est Mordúrus .
35   Salutauerunt se . in uicem cíues et hóspites
      atque tentoria ibi fixerunt ubi núnc est aula régis .   75
36   **Rex** uero Ungus hunc locum et hanc ciuitatem Deo omnipotenti Sanctoque
          Andree apostolo ea semper líbertate dédit
      ut sit caput et mater omnium ecclesiarum que sunt in régno Pictórum
37   **A**d istam enim ciuitatem conueniunt peregrini palmarii dé Ierúsalem .
      Romani Greci . Armenii Theutonii Alimánni Sáx*ones* .
      Dani Galliciani Galli . Ánglici Brít*ones*   80
      uíri et fémine
      díuites et paúperes
      sani córpore et égri
      claúdi et céci
      in equis et curribus debiles húc deferúntur   85
      atque per Dei misericordias ad honorem et gloriam sui summi Sancti apostoli
          Andree infestíssimi curántur
38   **V**irtutes et signa et innumerabilia prodigia per suum Sanctum apóstolum Andréam
      Dominus fecit . hic fácit et factúrus est .
      que hic nón possunt scríbi .
39   **R**egulus uero abbas atque monachus cum suis cáris comítibus   90
      habitauit in loco isto . in monáchica uíta
      seruiens Deo die ac nocte in sanctitate et iustitia cunctis diébus uite súe .
40 . **Q**uorum corpora híc requiéscent
41   **I**ste Regulus tertiam partem totius Scotie in manu sua et potestáte hábuit
      et per abbatias ordinauit átque distríbuit .   95
42   **P**atria illa 'siquidem Pictis Scottis Dacis Nórguagénsibus
      ceterisque qui ad uastandum insulam applicuerant situ locorum' amenitáteque
          'patúerat'
43   **E**t si aliquando refugii opus fuisset tutum receptaculum eis sémper prestábat
44   Et se se infra eam quasi in propria cástra recepérunt .   99

9 decoris. 12 choeres. 13 ewangelistam. 16 achaidas *with* d *subpuncted for deletion.* 17 .ij .
descimbrum. 22 .cc.lxx. 23 fauoso. 26 .c.x. . 27 excercitu. 28 insule inhabitantes. 32
excercitu. 38 sed. 39 aiere. precedat. 40 Verumptamen decimam partem hereditatis tue
partem. sancte andre eius. 41 ammonitus suum excercitum. .xij. dimisit . 45 in colimes.

hereditates. 49 i cet'm. andreo. 50 initto. 53 ammonitus. 59 Rigmud. 61 excercitu. 62 que. 66 fidit. 67 uideo plenum. 69 excercitu. 70 illo. 77 capud. 80 gallicani. 86 infestissime. 97 amenitatique pauerat.

[THE LIFE OF SAINT RULE]

HOW IT HAPPENED
THAT THE MEMORY OF SAINT ANDREW THE APOSTLE
IS GREATER IN THE REGION OF THE PICTS
WHICH IS NOW CALLED SCOTLAND
THAN IN OTHER REGIONS:
AND HOW IT BEFELL
THAT SUCH GREAT ABBEYS WERE MADE THERE IN ANTIQUITY
WHICH MANY SECULAR MEN POSSESS NOW BY HEREDITARY RIGHT

1   'Andrew, which is interpreted according to Hebrew etymology "handsome" or "responding"

in Greek speech, nonetheless, is interpreted "manly" from "man"',   10
the brother of blessed Peter the apostle,
his 'fellow heir', however, 'by grace',
according to John the evangelist the first apostle chosen by Christ
    Jesus our Lord,
according to Matthew and Mark, in truth, second.

2   This man by lot of the most remote preaching received the northern nations,
    Scythian and Pictish,   15
and the same city Achaean Patras by name,
in which he was also suspended on a cross on the second of the kalends
    of December,
and there he died,
and there his bones were guarded
until the time of Constantine the Great, son of Helena,   20
and of his sons, that is of Constantine with Constans,
as if through a space of two hundred seventy-three years.

3   In the reign of whom in a wondrous and famous journey they were taken up
    thence by Constantinopolitans and translated to Constantinople.

4   And with great glory and the greatest honour they were reburied there.

5   And they remained always until the time of Theodotion the Christian emperor, 25
through a space, that is, of one hundred ten years.

6   Then by divine urging the King of the Picts, Ungus by name, son of Urguist,
    rising with a great army,
killing with the cruellest devastation the British nations inhabiting the right-
    hand [i.e. southern] part of the island,
finally came through as far as the plain of Merc.

7   There he wintered.   30

8   At that time almost all the peoples of the entire island with a single-minded
    onrush surrounded him,
wishing to wipe him out entirely with his army.

9   On the second day it occurred to the foresaid king to walk with seven most
       loved companions.

10   And a divine light shone round them.

11   And prone on their faces, not able to sustain it, they fell to the earth.   35

12   And lo a voice was heard from heaven:

13   "Ungus, Ungus, hear me, apostle of Christ, Andrew by name,
       who have been sent for defending and guarding you.

14   Rise, see the sign of the Cross of Christ which stands in the air and will
       precede against your enemies.

15   A tenth part, nevertheless, of your inheritance and alms offer to almighty
       God and in honour of His apostle Saint Andrew."   40

16   On the third day, however, admonished by the divine voice, he divided his
       army into twelve troops.

17   And the sign of the Cross preceded each part.

18   A divine light, however, shone from the head of each and every sign.

19   Then, made victors, they gave thanks to almighty God and to Saint Andrew
       the apostle.

20   Coming unharmed, however, to the fatherland, wishing to offer a tenth part
       of his inheritance to God and to Saint Andrew the venerable apostle,
       fulfilling what has been written,

21   'Give alms and all things are clean for you'.

22   They considered it uncertain in what place they should order specially for
       God a principal city yielding revenue for Saint Andrew the apostle.

23   Then in united council, fasting on the second, third, fourth days,   50
       and seeking the mercy of God almighty,
       one of those guarding the body of Saint Andrew the apostle at Constantinople,
       admonished and instructed by a divine vision and revelation, saying,

24   'Go out from your land and from your family,
       and from the house of your father.   55

25   And go into the land which I will have shown to you.'

26   Then came an accompanying angel,
       and guarding the way of that man
       he came through prosperously to the ridge of the mountain of the king, that
       is Rig Monaid.

27   In the same hour, however, in which worn out he sat there with his seven
       companions,   60
       a divine light shone round the King of the Picts coming with his army to the
       special place,
       which is called Kar Tenan.

28   And not bearing the brightness they fell on their faces.

29   And lame men and blind men were healed there, seven in number.

30   And one man blind from birth was given light.   65

31   And thence he saw a place filled with a visitation of angels.

32   And then with a great voice he called, saying,
       "I see a place filled with a visitation of angels".

33   Finally by the ordering of God the king comes with his army to the place
       which the Lord shows to the blind man who had been given light.   70

34   Rule, in truth, a monk, a pilgrim from the Constantinopolitan city,

stood in the way of the king with the relics of Saint Andrew the apostle,
which he had brought thence hither to the gate which is called Matha, that is
    Mordurus.

35   They greeted each other in turn, citizen and guest,
and fixed tents there, where the hall of the king is now.   75

36   King Ungus, in truth, gave this place and this city to almighty God and to Saint
    Andrew the apostle with that liberty forever,
that it might be the head and mother of all the churches which are in the
    realm of the Picts.

37   For to this city come together palmer pilgrims from Jerusalem,
Romans, Greeks, Armenians, Teutons, Allemans, Saxons,
Danes, Galicians, Gauls, Englishmen, Britons,   80
men and women,
rich men and poor men,
men sound in body and sick men,
lame men and blind men,
on horses and in carts the weak are borne hither,   85
and through the mercies of God to the honour and glory of His own highest
    saint, the apostle Andrew those most ill are cured.

38   Virtues and signs and innumerable prodigies through His own saint the apostle
    Andrew
the Lord has performed here, performs, and will have performed,
which cannot be written here.

39   Rule the abbot and monk, in truth, with his own dear companions   90
dwelt in this place in monastic life,
serving God by day and by night in holiness and justice all the days of his life.

40   Of whom the bodies will rest here.

41   This Rule had the third part of the whole of Scotland in his own hand and
    power
and through abbeys ordered and distributed [it].   95

42   That fatherland, 'indeed, to Picts, Scots, Danes, Norwegians,
and to others who had approached for devastating the island lay open by the
    site' and amenity 'of its places'.

43   And if at some time there was need of a refuge it always offered to them a safe
    shelter.

44   And they received themselves within it as if in their own camps.   99

The author has arranged his words and ideas in chiastic and parallel patterns.

tit.	A1	Reguli
	A2	Scotia
	A3	abbatie
9	B1	Andreas
13	B2	Domino
19	C	ossa illius
22	D	Constantinopolitanis
27	E1	Tunc
27	E2	diuino instinctu
27	E3	rex Pictorum nomine Ungus filius Urguist

27	E4	cum exercito magno
29	E5	peruenit usque ad campum
33	F1	cum septem comitibus
34	F2	circumfulsit eos diuina lux
35	F3	in facies suas non ualentes eam sustinere ceciderunt in terram
36	F4	uox
38	G	custodiendum
39	H1	signum crucis
39	H2	precedet
40	H3	decimam partem hereditatis tue
40	H4	Deo
40	H5	et
40	H6	Sancti Andree apostoli
40	H7	offer
42	H1'	signum crucis
42	H2'	precedebat
45	H3'	decimam sue hereditatis partem
45	H4'	Deo
45	H5'	et
45	H6'	Sancto Andree apostolo
45	H7'	offerre
49	I1	Deo
49	I2	Sancto Andree apostolo
50	K	Tunc unito concilio
50	K'	| binis |
50	K"	ternis quadriduanis diebus ieiunantes
51	I'1	Dei
52	I'2	Sancti Andree apostoli
54	H'1	Exi de terra tua
55	H'2	et de cognatione tua
56	H'2'	et de domo patris tui
57	H'1'	Et uade in terram quam monstrauero tibi
58	G'	custodiente
60	F'1	cum suis septem comitibus
61	F'2	lux circumfulsit diuina
63	F'3	claritatem non ferentes ceciderunt in facies suas
67	F'4	uoce
69	E'1	Postremo
69	E'2	Dei ordinatione
69	E'3	rex
69	E'4	cum suo exercitu
69	E'5	uenit ad locum
71	D'	a Constantinopolitana urbe
72	C'	reliquiis Sancti Andree apostoli
87	B'1	Andream
88	B'2	Dominus

94	A'1	Regulus
94	A'2	Scotie
95	A'3	abbatias.

The crux of the chiasmus occurs at the central fiftieth of ninety-nine lines. The 777^2 words of the complete text divide into 'two' parts round the central word *binis*.

The author has infixed many features that guarantee the integrity of discrete sentences.

In 1 from | *Andreas* to *Xpisto Iesu Domino* |, who lived thirty-three years, there are thirty-three words.[3]

In 2 the nine words *in qua etiam cruci suspensus est secunda kalendarum Decembrium* divide by duple ratio 2:1 at | *secunda*. The six words *quasi spatio ducenti septuaginta trium annorum* divide into two parts at *ducenti* and into thirds at *trium*. The 334 letters of the complete sentence coincide with Andrew's martyrdom, commemorated on *secunda kalendarum Decembrium*, the 334th day of the year.

In 9 there are seven words before *septem*.

In 16 *Tertia autem die diuina uoce admonitus suum exercitum in duodecim turmas diuisit* there are twelve words.

In 23 the eight words *Tunc unito concilio binis ternis quatriduanis diebus ieiunantes* divide into two parts at *binis* |, into fourths at *quatriduanis* |, by sesquialter ratio 3:2 at | *binis* and *ternis* |, by sesquitertian ratio 4:3 at *ternis* | *quatriduanis*. All twenty-nine words divide by sesquioctave ratio 9:8, *epogdous* 'one above eight' at 15 and 14, at *unus* |. Note the sequence *unito, binis, ternis, quatriduanis* in line 50, in which *binis, ternis*, and *quatriduanis* are the second, third, and fourth words after *unito*.

In 29 there are seven words before *septem*.

In 37 note the coincidence of geographic origins of visitors to Saint Andrews with classes of people healed there, twelve of each: *peregrini palmarii de Ierusalem, Romani, Greci, Armenii, Theutonii, Alimanni, Saxones, Dani, Galliciani, Galli, Anglici, Britones*, and *uiri et femine, diuites et pauperes, sani corpore et egri, claudi et ceci, in equis et curribus debiles*, and *infestissimi*.

In 39, line 90, there are nine words.

In 41 the third word is *tertiam*.

In 44 there are forty-four letters.

The author has infixed other features that connect discrete sentences.

In 1–2 from | *Andreas* to *suspensus est* | *secunda kalendarum Decembrium* there are sixty words, coincident with the traditional date of Andrew's martyrdom, A.D. 60.

Playing with duple ratio 2:1 the author wrote between *primus* 1 and *secundus* 2 eleven words, but from | *secundus* 2 to *secunda* | 4 inclusive twenty-two words, an echo of the same trick with homophonous but distinct *secundum* 1, from which to *secundum* 1 inclusive there are also twenty-two words.

2   For other examples of play on 77 and 777 see above, pp. 29–31, 40–7, 52–4.

3   For other examples of play on 33 and 333 see above pp. 35, 61, 75 and below p. 102.

In 2–5 *ducentorum septuaginta trium annorum In quorum regno a Constantinopolitanis miro famosoque ductu inde suscepta atque translata sunt Constantinopoli et cum magna gloria et maximo honore ibidem recondita sunt et manserunt semper usque ad tempus Theodotionis Xpistiani imperatoris spatio scilicet centum decem annorum* there are from the beginning to the last *m* inclusive 273 letters.

In 15–21 *Verum tamen decimam partem hereditatis tue partem et elemosinam … offer.* … *decimam sue hereditatis partem … uolentes offerre implendo quod scriptum est Date elemosinam* occupy seventy-eight words, a tenth part of the entire text.

In 27–29 from | *septem* the seventy-seventh syllable is the first of *septem*.

Reckoning letters as numerals *A*=1, *B*=2, *C*=3 … *X*=21, *Y*=22, *Z*=23 the name *ANDREAS* bears a numerical value of 1+13+4+17+5+1+18 or 59. Before *Andree* 76 there are fifty-nine letters. The name *UNGUS* bears a numerical value of 20+13+7+20+18 or 78. After *Ungus* | 27 the seventy-eighth word is *Ungus* | *Ungus* 37.[4]

There are eighty-nine lines before the naming of *Regulus* 90, from which inclusive to the end of the text there are eighty-nine words, coincident with the eighty-nine days of the year from 1 January to 30 March, on which Saint Rule is commemorated. Those eighty-nine words divide by sesquialter ratio 3:2 at 53 and 36, at *Iste Regulus tertiam* | *partem totius Scotie in manu sua et potestate habuit* 94. Besides those eighty-nine days 276 days remain in the year, the number of days from the Annunciation, celebrated on 25 March, to the Nativity, celebrated on 25 December. This use of the number 276 may connect the *Vita Sancti Reguli* with the *Vita Sancti Seruani* and the *Vita Sancti Kentigerni*.[5] Compare also the usage of Adam of Dryburgh.[6]

Let us consider the time in which these events are supposed to have occurred. The martyrdom of Saint Andrew on the 334th day of the year is marked by the 334 letters of sentence 2. The year of his martyrdom, A.D. 60, is marked by the sixty words from | *Andreas* to *suspensus est* |. His bones lay in Patras for 273 years until their translation to Constantinople, where they remained for the next 110 years, the interval being marked in the text by the 273 letters from | *ducenti septuaginta trium annorum* to *spatio scilicet centum decem annorum*|. The years 60+273+110 total 443, the year in which the king of the Picts *diuino instinctu* invaded southern Britain, saw the *diuina lux*, heard the *uox de celo*, and returned home safely. That is the year, *tunc* in sentence 23, in which Rule experienced the vision and revelation in Constantinople. The year in which Rule arrived at Rig Monaid must have been 444, *peruenit* | *ad uerticem montis regis id est Rig Mund*, the upright bar following the 444th word of the composition.

There is much to be said for the learning of the twelfth-century Scot who composed this. He may have inferred from the *Liber Epistolarum Sancti Patricii*

---

4   See above pp. 5, 8, 22, 35, 58–61 and below pp. 89, 95, 141, 159–60, 174, 184.
5   See below pp. 86–97.
6   See below pp. 157–60.

Episcopi or read in the *Annals of Ulster* that in 444 *Ard Macha fundata est.*[7] He may have known that 444 is the first year of the *Annales Cambriae.*[8] He may have known that in *De Excidio Britanniae*, composed A.D. 540, Gildas cited a letter from the Britons to *Agitio ter consuli*, requesting military help against barbarian invaders, inferring from the beginning of the third consulship of Aetius in January 446[9] that a raid by Ungus must have occurred earlier in the 440s, 443 being a credible date.

There are forty-four sentences, the last of which contains forty-four letters, in a text commemorating an event that occurred in A.D. 444.[10] The title and heading together occupy nine lines; the heading contains ninety-nine syllables, key to the ninety-nine lines of the text.[11] Title, heading, and text together contain 777 words.

The quotation of Isidore of Seville's *Etymologiae* VII IX 11 in 1 links this text to a tradition of ancient and orthodox learning and to the *Cronica de Origine Antiquorum Pictorum*, which survives in the same manuscript. So does reference to Scythia and use of *dexter* to mean 'southern'.[12] The quotation of Genesis XII 1 and Acts VII 3 in 23–26 links Rule and Andrew to a tradition of divine revelation that began with Abraham. The quotation of Mark I 11, Matthew III 17, and Luke III 22 in 12 links Ungus and Andrew with a tradition of divine revelation that began with Jesus. The quotation of Geoffrey of Monmouth's *Historia Regum Britanniae* VIII 3 from *siquidem* to *patuerat* in 42 links the text to the most famous Insular Latin 'historical' work of the early twelfth century, fixing a *terminus post quem* of March 1136 for composition of this recension of the Life.[13] The 777 words link the text specifically with the 'Chronicle of the Kings of Alba' and the *Cronica Regum Scottorum*, which survive in the same manuscript.[14] Reference to *tota Scotia* links this text with *De Situ Albanie* and the *Cronica Regum Scottorum*.[15] Use of the calendrical number 276 links it with the *Vita Sancti Seruani* and the *Vita Sancti Kentigerni* and with the work of Adam of Dryburgh.[16]

7 Howlett, *Liber Epistolarum*, p. 119.
8 Howlett, *Cambro-Latin Compositions*, p. 153.
9 *Ibid.*, pp. 42–3.
10 For another example of play on the number 444 see Howlett, *English Origins*, pp. 132–5.
11 For other examples of infixed elements that incrementally guarantee the integrity of the text see above pp. 4, 51 and below pp. 89, 96, 102, 115, 141, 150, 152, 155, 186–7.
12 See above pp. 40–1.
13 For evidence of publication of Geoffrey's *Historia Regum Britanniae* between January and March of 1136 see Howlett, *The English Origins of Old French Literature*, pp. 57–9.
14 See above pp. 52–4, 74.
15 See above pp. 38–9, 74.
16 See below pp. 86–97, 159–60.

'VITA SANCTI SERVANI'

The *Vita Sancti Seruani*, heretofore anonymous, survives in Dublin, Archbishop Marsh's Library, MS Z.4.5.5, folio 1r.[1]

INCIPIT VITA SANCTI SERVANI
QUI NUTRIVIT BEATUM KENTIGERNUM.

1   **FU**it quidam rex nobilis in terra Canaan : nomine Obeth filius Éliuð .
     et nomen uxoris eius Alpia . filia régis Arábie .

2   **A**mbo uiginti annos insimul habitantes prolem núllam h*abuérunt* .

3   **I**nde sepissime Déum rog*auérunt* .

4   Et oblationes et uictimas éi o*btulérunt* .   5
     ut eis ad expellendum obprobrium eorum sobolem condígnam do*náret* .

5   **Q**ua propter rex mandauit per uniuérsam regi*ónem*
     ut ómnes hómin*es*
     a minoribus úsque ad maiór*es*
     tribus diebus ac nóctibus ièiun*árent* .   10

6   Et assidue pro rege et regina Dei misericórdiam èxor*árent* :
     ut sterilitatis ab eis ignomíniam auérte*ret* .

7   **I**n tertia uero nocte ultimo galli cantu regi parumper dormienti in sompno
        angelus Domini appáruit dí*cens* .

8   **I**te uos in ciuitatem que uocatur Éliópoli*s* .

9   Et in ea inuenietis fóntem pulchérrimu*m* .   15

10   Et in eo tér balniáte .

11   **E**t exinde quod uos hanelátis habébiti*s*
     Exeu*ntes* . et ad fontem prenominatum péruenié*ntes*
     iuxta dictum ángeli fec*érunt* .

12   **A**c herbam iuxta fontem crescentem .scílicet. mandrág*onem*   20
     regina concupiscens éum manduc*áuit* .

13   **P**ostquam ergo comedit et copula maritali facta ílico concép*it* .

14   **I**n nocte uero subsequente **a**ngelus regíne appár*uit* .
     confortans éam et dí*cens* .

---

1   *BCLL*, no. 1029 p. 286. Skene, *Chronicles*, pp. 412–20. *Pinkerton's Lives of the Scottish Saints*, rev. W.M. Metcalfe, 2 vols (Paisley: Alexander Gardner, 1889), vol. II pp. 117– 28. A. Macquarrie, 'Vita Sancti Servani: The Life of St Serf', *The Innes Review* XLIV 2 (1993), pp. 122–52, text at 136–43. Dauvit Broun, 'A third manuscript of the Life of St Serf: a probable copy of a Glasgow exemplar', *Ibid*. L (1999), pp. 80–2.

15   **N**oli regina contristári et mèsta ésse :   25
        quia ecce hábes in útero . et paries dúos fil*ios* .
        fide et ópere ópt*imos* .

16   **N**omen erit uni Generatius íd est **a**rdens gémma :
        et erit honorabilis rex super omnem terram Cánaaneóru*m* .

17   **E**st nomen alteri Malachias síue Seruánu*s* .   30
        Que nomina ei postea peracto secularis uite cursu béne conuen*érunt* .

18   **M**alachias enim interpretatur **á**ngelus Dómin*i* .
        hoc est áptum nomen *éi* .
        qui legatus sedis apostólice ext*íterit*
        nuntians uerbum per quáttuor plàgas múnd*i* .   35

19   **S**eruanus uero seruando dícitur Déo .
        eo quod operando seruiebat Domino nostro Iesu Xpisto in omni opere bono
           nócte di*éque*

20   **H**iis itaque dictis et **an**gelo discedente regina éxporrécta es*t* :
        et dicta **a**ngelica marito súo nuntiáui*t* .

21   **I**nde igitur **a**mbo exulantes : grates Deo habundánter reddid*érunt* .   40

tit. kentegernum. 1 chanaan. 5 optulerunt. 13 pari mp. 22 commedit. 29 cananeorum.
35 quatuor.

THE LIFE BEGINS OF SAINT SERF
WHO NURTURED BLESSED KENTIGERN.

1   There was a certain noble king in the land of Canaan by name Obed son of Eliud
    and the name of his wife Alpia daughter of a king of Arabia.

2   Both living together for twenty years had no progeny.

3   Thence very often they asked God.

4   And they offered offerings and victims to Him   5
    that He might give to them condign offspring for expelling their opprobrium.

5   On which account the king commanded
    that all men through the entire region,
    from lesser men up to greater men
    should fast for three days and nights.   10

6   And they should pray assiduously for the mercy of God for the king and queen,
    that He might avert the ignominy of sterility from them.

7   On the third night, in truth, at the last cockcrow [lit. 'song of the cock'] an angel
      of the Lord appeared to the king sleeping for a short while, saying,

8   'Go into the city which is called Heliopolis,

9   and in it you will find a very beautiful fountain.   15

10   And in it bathe three times.

11   And going out thence you will have what you long for.'
    And going to the forenamed fountain,
    they did according to the saying of the angel.

12   And a herb growing alongside the fountain, that is mandrake,   20
    the queen, desiring it, ate.

13   Therefore, after she ate, and with marital coupling made, she conceived from that.

14   On the following night, in truth, an angel appeared to the queen,
        comforting her and saying,
15   'Do not wish, queen, to be sad and to be mournful,   25
        because, lo, you have in the womb and will give birth to two sons,
        in faith and work the best.
16   The name for one will be Generatius, that is "ardent gem",
        and he will be an honourable king over all the land of the Canaanites.
17   The name for the other is Malachy or Servanus',   30
        which names afterwards, with the course of secular life completed, were well
            fitting for him.
18   For Malachy is interpreted 'Angel of the Lord';
        this is an apt name for him
        who has stood out as a legate of the apostolic see,
        announcing the Word through the four regions of the world.   35
19   Servanus, in truth, is said 'for serving God',
        because by working he served our Lord Jesus Christ in all good work by
            night and by day.
20   And so with these things said and the angel departing,
        the queen awakened and announced the angelic sayings to her own husband.
21   Thence, therefore, both exulting they gave back thanks to God abundantly.   40

One could hardly determine accurately at this remove whether our author inherited a hagiographic tradition about Serf or appropriated hagiographic details about other saints for his narrative about Serf[2] or invented the lot. The Prologue may be read as evidence of some philological learning applied to a coherent purpose. Our author might have derived the name of the site of his story from Isidore's *Etymologiae* XV I 33, *Heliopolis urbs Aegypti quae Latine interpretatur solis ciuitas*, and knowledge of the procreative virtue of the mandrake from the same source, XVII IX 30, *Mandragora dicta ... quod habeat radicem formam hominis similantem*. As in earlier Cambro-Latin hagiography a saint's parents often come from different kingdoms, Samson's father *Amon nomine Demetiano ex genere* and his mother *Anna nomine de Ventia*,[3] Cadog's father Gundleius from Dyfed and his mother Guladus from Brycheiniog,[4] so here Serf's parents come from *Canaan* and *Arabia*, both Biblical names. Serf's grandfather *Eliuð* bears the name of one of the ancestors of Jesus found in Matthew I 14, *Eliud* < Ελιουδ,

2   Contemporary Lives of Welsh and Breton saints exhibit frequent use of the same
        motifs, often in identical diction, as found in earlier Lives. See *Vitae Sanctorum
        Britanniae et Genealogiae*, ed. and transl. A. W. Wade-Evans, Board of Celtic Studies,
        University of Wales History and Law Series IX (Cardiff: University of Wales, 1944)
        and G.H. Doble, *Lives of the Welsh Saints*, ed. D. Simon Evans (Cardiff: University of
        Wales, 1971).
3   *La Vie Ancienne de Saint Samson de Dol*, ed. and transl. Pierre Flobert, Sources
        d'Histoire Médiévale Publiées par l'Institut de Recherche et d'Histoire des Textes
        (Paris: CNRS, 1997), p. 146.
4   Wade-Evans, *Vitae*, pp. 25–8. Howlett, *Cambro-Latin Compositions*, pp. 120–2.

explained by the seventh-century Hiberno-Latin author Aileranus Sapiens of Clonard as meaning *Deus meus*.[5] Serf's father *Obeth* bears the name of Obed < Ιωβηδ < עוֹבֵד, the son of Boaz and Ruth and grandfather of David, appropriate here as the meaning 'servant' is identical with that of the name of his son *Seruanus*. The name of Serf's mother *Alpia* suggests, with voicing of *p* as *b*, a connection with the land Serf came to serve, *Alba*. Association of *Alpia* daughter of a king of Arabia with *Alba* resembles association of *Scotta* daughter of a pharaoh, king of Egypt, with *Scotia*.[6] The meaning of *Generatius*, 'generated' after eating a mandrake, is explained in a *jeu d'esprit* as *ardens gemma*, but *angelus Domini* is a correct explanation of the meaning of *Malachias*, a name recently borne by Saint Malachy, 1094–1148, Archbishop of Armagh, pioneer of the Gregorian reform in Ireland.

The Incipit contains eight words, twenty-one syllables, and fifty-two letters. The letters offer a clear indication of calendrical composition, one for each of fifty-two weeks in a year. The syllables offer a clear indication of incremental composition, one for every sentence of the Prologue that follows.[7]

The Prologue contains forty lines and 276 words, one for every day of the year from the Annunciation, celebrated on 25 March, to the Nativity, celebrated on 25 December.[8] This calendrical feature may have seemed appropriate here because the unusual circumstances of the conception of Serf seemed comparable with the unusual circumstances of the Annunciation.[9]

The entire composition exhibits many other forms of numerical punctilio. There are twenty words before *uiginti* 3, and twenty syllables in *uiginti annos insimul habitantes prolem nullam habuerunt* 3.

The name *OBETH* bears a numerical value of 14+2+5+19+8 or 48. In line 1 *Fuit quidam rex nobilis in terra Canaan nomine Obeth* there are from the F of *Fuit* to the O of *Obeth* inclusive forty-eight letters and spaces between words.[10]

The name *ALPIA* bears a numerical value of 1+11+15+9+1 or 37. In lines 1–2 *Obeth filius Éliuð et nomen uxoris eius Alpia* there are after the O from the *b* of *Obeth* to *Alpia* | inclusive thirty-seven letters.

The name *SERVANUS* bears a numerical value of 18+5+17+20+1+13+20 +18 or 112. In lines 28–30 in *Nomen erit uni Generatius id est ardens gemma et erit honorabilis rex super omnem terram Canaaneorum Est nomen alteri Malachias siue* | *Seruanus* there are from | *Nomen* to *siue* | inclusive 112 letters. In lines 31–2 | *Que nomina ei postea peracto secularis uite cursu bene conuenerunt Malachias enim interpretatur angelus Domini* | there are from the space before *Que* to the space

5 *Ailerani Interpretatio Mystica et Moralis Progenitorum Domini Iesu Christi*, ed. and transl. Aidan Breen (Dublin: Four Courts, 1995), p. 23.
6 See above p. 40.
7 See above pp. 4, 51, 85 and below pp. 96, 102, 115, 141, 150, 152, 155, 186–7.
8 For other examples of this feature see above p. 84 and below pp. 95, 159–60.
9 The same applies to the *Vita Sancti Kentigerni* below pp. 91–7.
10 See above pp. 5, 8, 22, 35, 58–61, 84 and below pp. 95, 141, 159–60, 174, 184.

after *Domini* inclusive 112 letters and spaces between words. In lines 33–6 | *hoc est aptum nomen ei qui legatus sedis apostolice extiterit nuntians uerbum per quattuor plagas mundi Seruanus* | there are 112 letters and spaces between words. In lines 36–7 *Seruanus* | *uero seruando dicitur Deo eo quod operando seruiebat Domino nostro Iesu Xpisto in omni opere bono nocte dieque* | there are from the space before *uero* to the space after *dieque* inclusive 112 letters and spaces between words.

Let us consider the words for 'two', 'three', and 'four'. The 276 words divide by thirds at 92. After *uiginti* 3 the ninety-second word is *ter* 16, the third word for 'three', after *tribus* 10 and *tertia* 13. As those ninety-two words divide by extreme and mean ratio at 57 and 35, the division between the minor and the major part of the golden section falls exactly at | *a minoribus usque ad maiores*.[11] There are fifty-three words from *tribus* 10 to *ter* 16 inclusive, which divide by sesquialter ratio 3:2 at 32 and 20, at | *tertia* 13. After *quattuor* 35 there are forty-four words to the end of the Prologue. The 276 words divide by extreme and mean ratio at 171 and 105. From the first of the words for 'three' *tribus* 10 to *quattuor* 35 inclusive there are 171 words, which divide by duple ratio 2:1 at 114 and 57, at | *duos* 26.

The 276 words divide by one-ninth and eight-ninths at 31 and 245. Between the name of the subject *Seruanus* 30 and *Seruanus* 36 there are thirty-one words, which divide by extreme and mean ratio at 19 and 12, *nomen* | *ei* 33, *nomen* being the 222nd word of the Prologue.[12] The text divides by eight-ninths between the title and name *Domino nostro* | *Iesu Xpisto* 37.[13]

11 For other examples of play on *maior* and *minor* at the golden section see Howlett, *The English Origins of Old French Literature*, pp. 26–9, 77–8. For comparable play at the section by sesquialter ratio see Howlett, *British Books in Biblical Style*, pp. 34–7.

12 For other examples of play on 222 see above p. 75 and below p. 102.

13 For other examples of play on one-ninth and eight-months see above pp. 18, 22 and below pp. 95, 106, 160, 184.

'VITA SANCTI KENTIGERNI'

A *Vita Sancti Kentigerni*, heretofore anonymous, bears internal evidence of composition after the time of Symeon of Durham, *Symeon monachus olim Dunelmensis*, who died about 1130, and during the time of Herbert Bishop of Glasgow, *intimante uenerando Glasguensi episcopo Herberto*, A.D. 1147–64, celebrated also in William of Glasgow's *Carmen de Morte Sumerledi*.[1] I have arranged the text that follows in lines, marked the rhythms of the cursus, and suggested rhymes with italics. Capital letters and punctuation marks in boldface represent features of London, British Library, MS Cotton Titus A.XIX, folios 76r–80v. Small capital letters mark borrowings from Adomnán's *Praefatiuncula* to the *Vita Sancti Columbae*.

1   **Multas** quidem perlustráui regió*nes*
     earundem mores et cleri plebisque deuotiones diligénter perscrútan*s* .
     omnem patriam sanctos súos prouinciá*les*
     propriis et etern*is* laudum preconi*is* uenerántem inuéni .

2   **C**um autem ad regnum Scottorum démum peruénerim .   5
     illud sanctorum reliquiis uálde óptim*um* clericis prefulgid*um* . principibus
       glorió*sum* répperi .
     nihilo minus ad ceter*orum* ínstar regn*órum*
     quasi negligentie torpens ignauia in sanct*orum* su*orum* reuerentia adhuc
       pígritabátur .

3   **E**nim uero cum in spatiosis sanctorum honorificentie raritatem ánimaduérterem
     sumpto calamo ad honorem *sanctissimi confessoris atque pontíficis* **K**èntigérni   10
     qui iuxta ceteros uelut Lucifer inter ástra rútilat .
     quemadmodum **S**ymeon monachus ólim Dunelmén*sis*
     de Sancto suo Cuthberto histó*riam* contéxuit .
     ita et ego qualemcunque clericus Sáncti **K**entigérni .
     de materia in uirtutum eius codicéllo repér*ta* .   15
     et uiua uoce fidelium míhi relá*ta* .
     intimante uenerando **G**lasguensi episcopo Herberto . próut *pótui*
     deuóte comp*ósui* .

4   ***Sanct**issimi confessoris atque pontíficis* **K**èntigérni
     uitam et miracula . Xpisto iuuánte DESCRIPTÚRUS .   20

1   *BCLL*, no. 1028 p. 286. *Lives of S. Ninian and S. Kentigern*, ed. A.P. Forbes, Historians of Scotland V (Edinburgh: Edmonston and Douglas, 1874), pp. 242–52. See above pp. 24–8.

IN PRIMIS LECTUROS decénter AMMÓNEo .
UT FIDEM DÍCTIS ADHÍB*EANT* .
ET RES MAGIS QUAM VÉRBA PERPÉND*ANT* .
que etiam si FORTE illis rustice VIDEaNTUR ÉSSE compósi*ta* .
hoc recolant prouerbium Beati **I**erónimi dic*éntis*   25
Multo melius est uera rustic*e* . quam diserte falsa proferr*e* .

5   REMINIscantur insuper REGNUM DEI NON IN ELOQUENTIE ÉXUBER*ÁNTIA* .
        SED IN FIDEI CONSTARE FLÓRUL*ÉNTIA* .

6   **E**T NEC OB ALIQUA ONÓMATA INC*ÚLTA* .
        aut audientibus dícta OBSC*ÚRA* .   30
        LOCOR*Ú*MQUE VOC*ÁBULA*
        quorum barbaries UT ESTIMO EXTERE GENTIs LÍNGUAS rudífic*aNT* .
        UTILIUM ET NON SINE DIVINA OPITULATIONE GESTARUM DESPIC*IANT*
            RERUM PRONÚNTIATIÓNEM .

7   **H**OC autem omnes commúniter *sciant* .
        QUOD DE BEATE MEMORIE VIRO PLURA STUDIO BREVITATIS
            MEMORIA DIGNA ad scribéndum PRETERMíttens .   35
        QUASI PAUCA DE PLURIMIS OB EVITANDUM LECTURORUM FASTIDIUM
            stili apícibus PR*Ò*pal*ÁBO* .

8   **E**T HOC fideliter poterit QUÍSQUE ANNOTÁ*re*
        qui eius miraculis adhuc per Cambriam apparentibus diligentiam uolúerit
            àdhibé*re* .

9   **A**d horum etiam paucorum compositionem QUE NUNC BREVITER
            contéxere glísc*o* .
        sic Deo annuente . ORDíri DISPÓN*o* .,   40

4 arternis. 7 nichilominus. 10, 14, 19 Kentegerni. 19 animo *interlined for deletion.*

1   I have travelled through many regions, to be sure,
        diligently investigating the customs of the same and the devotions of clergy and
            people;
        I have found every fatherland venerating its own provincial saints
        with proper and eternal public preachings of praises.

2   When, however, I came through at last to the realm of the Scots   5
        I discovered it as the best, especially in its relics of saints, prefulgent in its clerics,
            glorious in its princes;
        nevertheless in comparison with other realms
        as if being sluggish in sloth of negligence it hung back in the reverence of its
            own saints until now.

3   For in truth when I considered [lit. 'turned the mind to'] the rarity of the doing
            of honour in extensive writings about the saints,
        with a reed pen taken up for the honour of the most holy confessor and pontiff
            Kentigern,   10
        who compared to others shines like Lucifer among the stars,
        in the same manner as Symeon, formerly a monk of Durham,
        wove together a history about his own Saint Cuthbert,
        so also I, a cleric of Saint Kentigern, such [a history]

	from matter discovered in a little codex about his virtues	15
	and related to me by the lively voice of faithful men,	
	with the venerable Bishop of Glasgow Herbert urging, as I could,	
	devoutly I composed.	18
4	With Christ helping, bound to describe the life and miracles	20
	of the most holy confessor and pontiff Kentigern,	19
	in the first place I admonish appropriately those about to read	
	that they apply faith to these sayings	
	and weigh carefully the matters rather than the words,	
	which, even if by chance they may seem to them to be composed rusticly,	
	should recall this proverb of Blessed Jerome saying,	25
	'It is much better to proffer true things rusticly than false things eloquently'.	
5	They should call to mind besides that the realm of God consists not in exubrance of eloquence	
	but in the flourishing of faith.	
6	And not on account of any uncultivated names	
	or sayings obscure to those hearing	30
	and names of places	
	the barbarities of which, as I suppose, make rude the tongues of an outlandish people,	
	should they despise the utterance of performed deeds, useful and not without divine aid.	
7	All, however, should know in common	
	that passing over in eagerness for brevity many things worthy of memory in writing about the man of blessed memory	35
	I shall mark out with the tips of the pen [or 'with high points of style'] a few things from very many for the sake of avoiding the disgust of readers.	
8	And anyone can note this faithfully	
	who may wish to apply diligence to his miracles appearing throughout Cumbria even now.	
9	For the composition of even these few things which I now glow with ardour briefly to weave together,	
	thus with God nodding in approval I arrange to begin [lit. 'lay the warp'].	40

The author has arranged his words and ideas in chiastic and parallel patterns, both in short passages

18 A	composui	24 A'	composita
22 B	dictis	25 B'	dicentis
24 C	rustice	26 C'	rustice

and in the complete Prologue

1	A	perlustraui
2	B	diligenter
5	C	ad regnum Scottorum
5	D	peruenerim

6	E1	repperi
9	E2	sumpto calamo
9	E3	sanctissimi confessoris atque pontificis Kentigerni
13	E4	historiam
14	F	ita et ego qualemcunque clericus Sancti Kentigerni
15	E'1	reperta
18	E'2	composui
19	E'3	sanctissimi confessoris atque pontificis Kentigerni
20	E'4	uitam et miracula
36	D'	propalabo
38	C'	per Cambriam
38	B'	diligentia
40	A'	ordiri dispono.

Mention of the author's arrival in Scotland implies that he was not a native Scot. The chiastic pairing of *regnum Scottorum* C and *Cambriam* C' implies that Cumbria was the focus of his interest and that he reckoned Cumbria to be part of the Kingdom of Scotland. He may have been an Angle or a Norman introduced, as Symeon had been introduced earlier to Durham,[2] during the reign of King David to bring the Church in Cumbria into conformity with Norman policy. Reference to Herbert Bishop of Glasgow fixes the period of composition to the period 1147–64.

The diction represented in small capitals derives ultimately from Sulpicius Severus's *Vita Sancti Martini*, but immediately from Adomnan's first *Praefatiuncula* to the *Vita Sancti Columbae*.[3]

Beati nostri patroni Xpisto suffragante uitam descripturus, fratrum flagitationibus obsecundare uolens, in primis eandem lecturos quosque ammonere procurabo ut fidem dictis adhibeant conpertis et res magis quam uerba perpendant, quae ut estimo inculta et uilia esse uidentur. Meminerintque regnum Dei non in eloquentiae exuberantia sed in fidei florulentia constare. Et nec ob aliqua Scotiae uilis uidelicet linguae aut humana onomata aut gentium obscura locorumque uocabula, quae ut puto inter alias exterarum gentium diuersas uilescunt linguas, utilium et non sine diuina opitulatione gestarum despiciant rerum pronuntiationem.

Sed et hoc lectorem ammonendum putauimus quod de beatae memoriae uiro plura studio breuitatis etiam memoria digna a nobis sint praetermissa, et quasi pauca de plurimis ob euitandum fastidium lecturorum sint

2 See Howlett, 'Symeon's Structural Style: Experiments in Deconstruction', in *Symeon of Durham: Historian of Durham and the North*, ed. David Rollason, Studies in North-Eastern History I (Stamford: Shaun Tyas, 1998), pp. 254–81.

3 *Adomnán's Life of Columba*, ed. and transl. A.O. and M.O. Anderson, rev. M.O. Anderson, Oxford Medieval Texts (Oxford: Clarendon Press, 1991), p. 2.

craxata. Et hoc ut arbitror quisque haec lecturus forte annotabit quod minima de maximis per populos fama de eodem beato uiro deuulgata disperserit ad horum etiam paucorum conparationem quae nunc breuiter craxare disponimus.

Hinc post hanc primam praefatiunculam de nostri uocamine praesulis in exordio secundae Deo auxiliante intimare exordiar.

Use of diction derived from Sulpicius Severus connects this Life with Late Latin tradition, as does quotation in line 26 of Jerome's *Epistula* XVIII to Pope Damasus.[4] But direct borrowing of the diction from Adomnán's *Vita Sancti Columbae* connects this Life firmly with a more domestic Insular Latin source. The phrase *ob euitandum lecturorum fastidium* is a cliché, but its inclusion here may connect this text with the *Cronica Regum Scottorum*, the *Vita Sancte Bege*, and the *Epistola ad Adam Scottum* by John Abbot of Kelso.[5]

The hagiographer states in the first lection that Kentigern's mother, the virgin Thaney, *susceperat etiam in Scotia a Beato Seruano doctore sacro fidei Xpistiane legis doctrinam*, from which one infers the existence of a legend, if not of a Life, of Saint Serf, perhaps the very *Vita Sancti Seruani* we have just considered.[6] The only other literary source adduced is that *de materia in uirtutum eius codicello reperta*, presumably an earlier Latin collection of miracles of Kentigern that has not survived independently.

There are in this Prologue to the *Vita Sancti Kentigerni*, as in the *Vita Sancti Seruani qui nutriuit Beatum Kentigernum*, exactly forty lines and 276 words.[7] The 276 words divide by one-ninth and eight-ninths at 31 and 245, at the author's reference to himself, *peruenerim* | 4 and *propalabo* | 36.[8]

The title *SANCTUS* bears a numerical value of 18+1+13+3+19+20+18 or 92 and the name *KENTIGERNUS* a value of 10+5+13+19+9+7+5+17+13 +20+18 or 136, together 228.[9] In lines 9–10 *Enim uero cum in spatiosis sanctorum honorificentie raritatem animaduerterem sumpto calamo ad honorem sanctissimi confessoris atque pontificis Kentigerni* there are 136 letters. In lines 14–19 in *Sancti Kentigerni de materia in uirtutum eius codicello reperta et uiua uoce fidelium mihi relata intimante uenerando Glasguensi episcopo Herberto prout potui deuote composui Sanctissimi confessoris atque pontificis Kentigerni* there are from the space before *Sancti Kentigerni* to the space after *pontificis Kentigerni* inclusive 228 letters and spaces between words.

Between *Kentigerni* | 10 and | *Kentigerni* 19 there are fifty-two words, one for each week of the year.[10] With synizesis of the unstressed *e* in *Symeon* there are

4 I owe thanks to Dr Carolinne White for identifying the quotation.
5 See above, p. 75, and below, pp. 100, 165.
6 See above, pp. 86–90.
7 For the calendrical significance of the number 276 see above, p. 84.
8 See above pp. 18, 22, 90 and below pp. 106, 160, 184.
9 See above pp. 5, 8, 22, 35, 58–61, 84, 89 and below pp. 141, 159–60, 174, 184.
10 Compare the play on 52 in the *Vita Sancti Seruani* above p. 89.

144 syllables between *Kentigerni* | and | *Kentigerni*.[11] Of these fifty-two words *Kentigerni* 14 is twenty-sixth. There are thirteen lines of text before *ita et ego qualemcunque clericus Sancti Kentigerni*, in which the thirteenth syllable is the first of *Sancti Kentigerni*, coincident with Saint Kentigern's Day, 13 January.[12]

The nine sentences confirm the structure of *Prologus* and eight *Lectiones*, one for each day of the octave of Saint Kentigern's Day.[13]

In the manuscript a mediaeval reader has written in the right margin against lines 12–14 *nota*, with good reason. The forty lines of the Prologue divide by sesquitertian ratio 4:3 at 23 and 17. The 276 words divide by the same ratio at 158 and 118, at the title and name of our hagiographer's patron, *Glasguensi episcopo* | *Herberto* in line 17. Sentence 3, in which this phrase occurs, contains sixty-six words, which divide by one-ninth and eight-ninths at 7 and 59, at | *Glasguensi episcopo Herberto*. The sixty-six words divide by symmetry at 33 and 33, at the reference to the text our hagiographer used as a model, *de Sancto* | *suo Cuthberto historiam* 13. Returning to the sesquitertian ratio of the whole Prologue that marks our hagiographer's patron, let us apply the same ratio to sentence 3, of which the sixty-six words divide by 4:3 at 38 and 28, at the reference to the author our hagiographer used as a model, *Symeon* | *monachus olim Dunelmensis* 12, and at the reference to himself, *ita* | *et ego qualemcunque clericus Sancti Kentigerni* 14. From this one might infer that our hagiographer bore the name *Symeon*. Reckoning letters as numbers the name *SYMEON* bears a numerical value of 18+22+12+5+14+13 or 84. In the entire Prologue there are eighty-four words to *quemadmodum* | *Symeon monachus olim Dunelmensis*. In *quemadmodum Symeon monachus olim Dunelmensis de Sancto suo Cuthberto historiam contexuit ita et ego* the *e* of *ego* is the eighty-fourth letter.

In a charter of Herbert Bishop of Glasgow to the Church of Saint Mary of Kelso the third of four named witnesses in *Sym~ Archid~ de Theudal~*.[14] In a charter of Jocelin Bishop of Glasgow to the monks of Melrose the seventh of twenty-three named witnesses, the first after the king and the bishops, is *Sim~ archid~*.[15] In a charter of Robert Auenel to the monks of Melrose the first witness is Jocelin Bishop of Glasgow and the seventh is *Symon archidiaconus*.[16] Symeon or Simon of Glasgow, an immigrant to Scotland, Archdeacon of

---

11 For other examples of play on the number 144 see above pp. 8, 75 and below pp. 150, 174.

12 For use of other calendrical numbers see above pp. 8, 23, 36, 59, 61, 74, 83–5, 89 and below pp. 110, 142, 150, 160, 174, 182–4.

13 See above pp. 4, 51, 85, 89 and below pp. 102, 115, 141, 150, 152, 155, 186–7.

14 *Liber S. Marie de Calchou, Registrum Cartarum Abbacie Tironensis de Kelso, 1113–1567*, ed. C. Innes (Edinburgh: Bannatyne Club, 1846), vol. I p. 233 no. 286 f. 112.

15 *Liber Sancte Marie de Melros. Munimenta Vetustiora Monasterii Cisterciensis de Melros* (Edinburgh: Bannatyne Club, 1837), vol. I p. 114 no. 122.

16 William Fraser, *The Scotts of Buccleuch* (Edinburgh, 1878), vol. II no. 370 p. 410, facsimile between pp. 410 and 411.

Teviotdale during the episcopates of Herbert and Jocelin, is a likely candidate for author of the *Vita Sancti Kentigerni*.[17]

The reference to *Symeon monachus olim Dunelmensis* is initially puzzling, not least because there is no extant evidence that Symeon of Durham *de Sancto suo Cuthberto historiam contexuit*. The puzzlement diminishes once one supposes that Symeon of Glasgow introduced Symeon of Durham as a cover for the modest insinuation of his own name. But he may have had another motive, associated with his official status. One reads in the *Historia Regum*[18]

> Eadulfus cognomento Rus ... sepultus est in ecclesia apud Geddewerde, sed post a Turgoto, quondam priore Dunelmensis ecclesiae et archidiacono, talis inde spurcitia projecta,

and in the *Continuatio Prima* of the *Historia Ecclesiae Dunhelmensis*[19]

> fragili fretus juvamine, suae dioceseos appenditia, scilicet Carleol et Teviettedale, revocare nequibat, quae illo [sc. Rannulfo] exulante, cum ecclesia non haberet defensorem, ad suas quidem episcoporum applicaverant.

If Symeon was the first Archdeacon of Teviotdale after its alientation from Durham and its appropriation to Glasgow there may be a hint of triumphalism in the reference to his literary model and namesake.

There may be at least two literary reflexes of this text, one in the revised *Vita Sancti Kentigerni* by Jocelin of Furness, and another in the *Miracula Sancte Margarite*.[20]

---

17 I owe thanks to Dauvit Broun for documentary references to the career of this man.
18 *Historia Regum*, ed. Thomas Arnold, *Symeonis Monachi Opera Omnia*, Rolls Series LXXV.II (London: Longman, 1885), pp. 197–8. I owe thanks to Alan Piper for this and the following reference.
19 *Historia Ecclesiae Dunhelmensis, Ibid.* LXXV.I (London: Longman, 1882), p. 139.
20 See below pp. 103–6, 116–23.

'VITA ET MIRACULA SANCTE BEGE'

The *Vita et Miracula Sancte Bege*, composed perhaps during the twelfth century, survives in a unique manuscript, London, British Library, MS Cotton Faustina B.IV, folios 124ra–140vb (*olim* 122ra–138vb).[1]

VITA SANCTE BEGE ET DE MIRACULIS EIUSDEM

INCIPIT PROLOGUS IN VITA SANCTE BEGE VIRGINIS . PRIDIE KALENDAS NOVEMBRIS .

I

1   **Si essem** scriba doctus in régno celórum .
     sciens et potens de thesauro meo proferre nóua et uétera :
     profecto eructaret cor méum uerbum bónum .
     dicens immo edicens ad honorem Regis Xpisti prima et nouissima beate
          BEGE uírginis ópera .   5
2   Sed eius uetera transierunt ex magna parte elapsa . a preséntium notítia :
     eo quod non esset cuiuspiam lingua : calamus scribe uelóciter scrìbens éa .
3   Venerabilis tamen Beda . quemdam de eius actionibus in historia súa tractàtum
          tángit :
     et multo succinctius ut pluribus uidetur quam talis tantaque materia exposcit .
          stilo currénte pertránsiit .
4   Noua uero eius opera et recentiora que in Déo sunt fácta .   10
     non obliterauit omnino obliuio : a posteriórum memória :
     quia pro patribus filii qui nati exsurrexerunt . enarrauerunt ea filiis suis .
          ut cognoscat generátio áltera .
5   Licet enim generatio adueniat . et generatio pretereat : quamdiu támen térra stat .
          BEGE uirginis beate semper in benedictione memorande memoria
     manet in generatióne sanctórum :
     crebraque miracula in presentia hominum exhibita . illam presentialiter
          cum sponso suo regnare comprobant in régno celórum .
6   Ego uero licet egenus et pauper scientia . incitante támen deuòtióne .
     ex cronicis et historiis authenticis et uirorum ueridicorum nárratiónibus :
     que fide digna docebantur . diligénter collégi :   15

---

[1] *BCLL*, no. 1030 p. 286. *The Life and Miracles of Sancta Bega*, ed. G.C. Tomlinson (Carlisle: S. Jefferson, 1842), pp. 44–60. *The Register of the Priory of St Bees*, ed. J. Wilson, Surtees Society CXXVI (Durham: Andrews and London: Bernard Quaritch, 1915), pp. 497–520.

7   Et ad edificationem filiorum ecclesie . in duos libellos uitam et miracula sancte
      uírginis **red*é*gi**
EXPLICIT PROLOGUS   17
INCIPIT VITA SANCTE BEGE VIRGINIS

8 quedam. istoria. taclatum.   14 exibita. 15 ystoriis. autenticis.

2–3 Matthew XIII 52. 13 Ecclesiasticus I 4, XLV 1. 15 Psalm LXIX 6.

THE LIFE OF SAINT BEGA AND ABOUT THE
MIRACLES OF THE SAME

THE PROLOGUE BEGINS ON THE LIFE OF SAINT BEGA THE VIRGIN
ON THE DAY BEFORE THE KALENDS OF NOVEMBER.   I

1   If I be a scribe taught in the realm of the heavens,
      knowing how and being able to bring forth from my treasure new things and
        old things,
      assuredly my heart would breathe out a good word,
      speaking, indeed, speaking out for the honour of Christ the King the prime
        and the newest works of Bega the virgin.   5
2   But her old [works] have passed away, in great part lapsed from the notice of
        present men,
      so that there may not be a particular tongue, the reed of a scribe, swiftly
        writing them.
3   The Venerable Bede, nonetheless, touches on a certain tract about her actions
        in his History,
      and passed over with a running pen much more succinctly, as it seems to many,
        than such and so great a matter demands.
4   Her new and more recent works, in truth, which have been performed in God, 10
      oblivion has not entirely obliterated from the memory of later men,
      because sons who have risen up born for their fathers have narrated them to
        their own sons so that another generation might know.
5   For though a generation should arrive and a generation should pass away, as long,
        nonetheless, as the earth stands, the memory of Bega the blessed virgin to be
        remembered always in blessing, remains in the generation of saints,
      and her famous miracles exhibited in the presence of men prove her to
        reign presently with her Spouse in the realm of the heavens.
6   I, in truth, though needy and poor in knowledge, nonetheless with devotion inciting,
        from the chronicles and authentic histories and narratives of truth-uttering
        men have collected diligently things worthy of faith which were taught.   15
7   And for the edification of sons of the Church I have redacted into two books
      the Life and the Miracles of the holy virgin.

THE PROLOGUE ENDS.   17
THE LIFE OF SAINT BEGA THE VIRGIN BEGINS.

[on folio 133ra at the end of the *Vita*]

Ego uero quia de translatione et de miraculis inibi factis non plenam notítiam
   hábe*o* :

omnia illis illa qui uiderunt . et rei interfuerunt . scribénda relínqu*o* .

Illa uero que per illam Dominus operari dignatus est apud Kirkebi Beghoc in
   Coúpelándia .

ubi prius solitaria deguit . et eius memoria cum magna ueneratióne habétur .

de quibus certioratus ésse pótero .

ad presentium et posteriorum notitiam . stilo elucidáre pertemptáb*o* .

I in truth because I do not have full notice about the translation and about the
   miracles performed therein

leave all those things to be written by those who saw them and were present at
   the affair.

Those things in truth which through that woman the Lord deigned to work at
   Kirkby Beghoc in Copeland,

where earlier she dwelt and her memory is kept with great veneration,

about which I could be made certain

I shall attempt thoroughly to elucidate with a pen for the notice of present men
   and later men.

[on folio 140vb at the end of the *Miracula*]

Multa quidem et alia signa fecit Iesu Xpisti famula uirgo Bega in nómine ips*íus* :

que non sunt scrípta in libéllo hoc .

Hec autem scripta súnt . que clar*ióra* .

et multorum testimonio célebr*ióra* .

et ideo fide dignióra cognóu*imus* :   5

cetera propter minorem certitudinem non adiacet animo relátu prósequ*i* .

et maxime ob uitandum fastidium inf*í*rm*is* lect*ó*r*í*b*us* .

Hic ergo narrand*i* f*í*nem pón*imus* :

cum tamen non sit finis miráculorum e*íus* .

Quia enim cum illo qui est finis infinítus sine f*í*n*e*   10

regnat in glória perh*é*nn*i* :

constat nimirum quod in eíus nóm*ine*

ubi . et quando et in quibus et quotiens oporteat . possit si uelit mirácula òperári

usque ad consummatiónem sécul*i* .

Sit ergo sancto sanctorum . suorumque omnium sanctificatori . glor*í*ficat*ó*r*i* .   15

uirtus . décus . et impéri*um* :

per infinita sécula sèculór*um* .   17

AMEN

EXPLICIT LIBELLUS DE VITA ET MIRACULIS SANCTE BEGE VIRGINIS.
IN PROVINCIA NORTHANHIMBRORUM
PRIME ACTU ET HABITU SANCTIMONIALIS

Many things indeed and other signs the servant of Jesus Christ,
   the virgin Bega, performed in His name
which are not written in this little book.
These things, however, are written which we have known as brighter,
and more celebrated in the testimony of many men,
and on that account worthier of faith;   5
other things on account of lesser certitude it does not lie in the
   mind to prosecute in a related narrative,
and especially for avoiding tedium in infirm readers.
Here therefore we put an end of narrating,
though it may not nonetheless be the end of her miracles.
For since with Him who is endless end without end   10
she reigns in perennial glory,
it is apparent doubtless that in His name
where and when and among whom and as many times as it
   may be fitting she can, if she will, work miracles
until the consummation of the age.
Therefore to the Holy of holies and the Sanctifier of all
   His own, the Glorifier, be   15
virtue, beauty, and empire,
through endless ages of ages.   17
Amen.

THE LITTLE BOOK ABOUT THE LIFE AND MIRACLES OF
SAINT BEGA THE VIRGIN ENDS
IN THE PROVINCE OF THE NORTHUMBRIANS
THE PRIME HOLY NUN IN DEED AND HABIT.

The author arranged the words and ideas of the Prologue in chiastic and parallel
patterns.

1	A	Incipit Prologus
1	B	uita sancte … uirginis
2	C	si essem scriba
2	D	doctus
2	E1	in regno celorum
3	E2	sciens
5	F	Regis Xpisti
5	G1	beate Bege uirginis
6	G2	presentium
10	H	Noua uero eius opera et recentiora que in Deo sunt facta

11	H'	non obliterauit omnino obliuio a posteriorum memoria
13	G'1	Bege uirginis beate
14	G'2	presentia
14	F'	Sponso suo
14	E'1	in regno celorum
15	E'2	scientia
15	D'	docebantur
15	C'	collegi
16	B'	uitam … sancte uirginis
17	A'	Explicit Prologus

The seventeen words in the Title and Incipit provide the key to the structure of this composition of seventeen lines, of which the seventeenth contains seventeen letters and space. There are comparably seventeen lines in the Epilogue and seventeen words in the Explicit.[2]

In the Prologue from | *Si essem scriba* 2 to | *beate Bege uirginis* 5 there are thirty-three words. From *Bege uirginis beate* | 13 to *Explicit Prologus* | 17 there are sixty-six words. From | *beate Bege uirginis* 5 to *Bege uirginis beate* | 13 inclusive there are ninety-nine words. From | *Vita Sancte Bege et de Miraculis Eiusdem* and *Incipit Prologus* to *Explicit Prologus* | and from | *Multa quidem et alia signa fecit to per infinita secula seculorum* | inclusive there are exactly 333 words,[3] of which the 111th is *Deo* Prologue 10 and the 222nd is *Iesu* Epilogue 1.[4] The penultimate sentence of the Prologue divides into two parts at *duos* | *libellos*.[5]

2   See above pp. 4, 51, 85, 89, 96 and below pp. 115, 141, 150, 152, 155, 186–7.
3   See above pp. 35, 61, 75, 83.
4   For other examples see above pp. 75, 90.
5   For other examples see above pp. 35, 83.

'MIRACULA SANCTE MARGARITE SCOTORUM REGINE'

The *Miracula Sancte Margarite Regine Scotorum*, completed during the second half of the thirteenth century, survive in a manuscript from Dunfermline, written 1460x1488, now Madrid, Patrimonio Nacional, Biblioteca, II.2097 (*olim* II 4 N), folios 26r–41v.[1] The same manuscript also contains texts of Turgot's *Vita Margarita Reginae* and Jocelin's *Vita Sancti Waldeui*.[2]

INCIPIT PROLOGUS
IN MIRACULIS SANCTE MARGARITE SCOTÓRUM REGÍNE

I Quam mágnus et mirábilis Déus in sànctis súis :
per quorum merita : íneffabília iugiter operándo prodígia :
nos qui adhuc temporali uita fruimur : de sua repromissionis munificentia
  certificat : insinuando uidélicet nóbis
quanta familiaritatis gratia et amoris priuilegio suos extollendo beatíficat *in cǽlis* : 5
quorum corpora multimodis signis uisitando honórat *in térris* :

II Hii sunt enim bellatores incliti : pompam mundi et omnia eius prospera uelud
  fénum calcántes .
soli Deo mente et opere fidéliter àdheréntes :
exemplar facti nobis uíte celéstis et summe beátitúdinis :
ut si fuerimus eorum imitatóres *acciónum* : 10
procul dubio erimus cohéredes mànsiónum :
De quorum glorioso contubernio lucidissima nóstra Margaríta
et secundum ewangelicum sensum pretiosa : iure celorum regno *ássimíláta* :
ubi manet eternaliter glórificáta :
Que nostris temporibus occidentales tenebras sue lúcis splendóre : 15
uelud Lucifer matutinus irradiando illustrans : quicquid tenebrarum calígine
  òbcecátum
et ignorancia ueritatis fúerat . òbdurátum
subtiliter et ártificíóse plena fíde et ràcióne :
prudens magistra agéndo que dócuit ad agnicionem ueri licet multum
  desudándo perdúxit .

III Sed quia libellus de eius uíta inscríptus : 20
qualia eius opera in presenti século fúerint .

---

1 I owe thanks to Professor Robert Bartlett, F.B.A., for collation of the manuscript.
2 See below pp. 107–15, 124–30.

quanta misericordia et pietáte clarúerint .
sufficiénter osténdit .
ego quoque licet incomposito a ueritatis tamen tramite nequaquam módo
uacillánte :
ea que post uite sue exitum diuina miseracióne coòperánte: 25
ob eíus mérita que oculis meis partim conspéxi mirácula :
partim a fidelibus didici rélatóribus
quibus Deus per ipsam : immo ipsa per Deum magnificáta est uèheménter .
litterarum memorie quod necessarium est uálde preséntibus
utile quídem pósteris   30
decreui áccomodáre .

ÉXPLICIT PRÓLOGUS
INCÍPIUNT MIRÁCULA :   33

Inc. Margarita. 16 obduratum fuerat. 17 at. 23 uacillante modo.

1 Psalm LXVII 36. 13 Matthew XIII 46.

THE PROLOGUE BEGINS
ON THE MIRACLES OF SAINT MARGARET QUEEN
OF THE SCOTS

I   How great and wonderful [is] God in His own saints,
    through whose merits continually performing ineffable prodigies
    us who at this time enjoy temporal life He makes certain by His
        munificence of promise, insinuating, that is, to us
    what great grace of familiarity and love beatifies His own with a
        privilege to be extolled in the heavens,   5
    whose bodies He honours by visiting with signs of many forms on earth.
II For these are renowned warriors trampling the pomp of the world
        and all its successes like hay,
    adhering faithfully to God alone in mind and work,
    made an exemplar for us of the celestial life and the highest beatitude,
    so that if we shall have been imitators of their actions   10
    without doubt we will be fellow heirs of the mansions,
    in whose glorious shared lodging our Margaret, most lucid,
    and, according to the evangelical meaning, 'precious', assimilated by right to
        the realm of the heavens,
    where she remains eternally glorified,
    who in our times illuminating the western shadows with the splendour of
        her own light   15
    by radiating like the morning Lucifer whatever had been obscured by the
        darkness of shadows
    and made obdurate by ignorance of the truth
    subtly and artfully, with full faith and reason,
    the prudent mistress by doing what she taught completed much, though by
        working strenuously, for acknowledgement of the truth.

III	But since the little book written about her life	20
	shows sufficiently	23
	of what sort her works were in the present age	21
	with what great mercy and piety they shone,	22
	I also, though in uncomposed manner, nonetheless by no means vacillating	
	from the track of the truth,	24
	I have decided to make available	31
	those things which after the going out of her life, with divine mercy	
	cooperating,	25
	on account of her merits miracles which partly I have beheld with my	
	own eyes,	
	partly I have learned from faithful relators,	
	by which God through her, indeed she through God, is magnified greatly,	
	to the memory of letters, which is especially necessary for present men,	
	useful, indeed, for later men.	30
	THE PROLOGUE ENDS.	32
	THE MIRACLES BEGIN.	33

The author has arranged words and ideas chiastically.

1	A1	Incipit Prologus
1	A2	in Miraculis
2	B	quam magnus et mirabilis Deus in sanctis suis
3	C	per quorum merita
4	D	uita
5	E	quanta
9	F	uite
12	G	Margarita
15	H	tenebras
15	I	sue | lucis
16	I'	lucifer
16	H'	tenebrarum
19	G'	magistra
20	F'	uita
22	E'	quanta
25	D'	uite
26	C'	ob eius merita
28	B'	Deus per ipsam immo ipsa per Deum magnificata est uehementer
32	A'1	Explicit Prologus
33	A'2	Incipiunt Miracula

There are three sentences and, including the Incipit and Explicit, thirty-three lines. The 101 words of the second sentence divide by symmetry around the allusion to Matthew XIII 46, describing Margaret as *secundum ewangelicum sensus pretiosa*. Those 101 words divide by extreme and mean ratio at 62 and 39, at

coheredes | *mansionum* and *nostris* | *temporibus*. The 227 words of the Prologue
divide by symmetry at 114, at the crux of the chiasmus, at | *lucis* 14. They divide
by duple ratio 2:1 at 76 and 151, at | *libellus de eius uita inscriptus* 19, where our
author refers in the third word of the third sentence, *libellus*, to Turgot's *Vita
Margaritae Reginae*. The 227 words divide by extreme and mean ratio at 140 and
87, where the author refers to himself and his readers, *coheredes* | *mansionum* 10,
the same point at which the 101 words of the second sentence divide by
extreme and mean ratio. The 227 words divide by one-ninth and eight-ninths at
25 and 202, where the author refers to himself, at | *didici* 26.[3]

The reference to Lucifer in line 16 may connect this text with the *Vita Sancti
Kentigerni*.[4]

3   See above pp. 18, 22, 90, 95 and below pp. 160, 184.
4   See above p. 91.

TURGOT PRIOR OF DURHAM:
'VITA MARGARITAE REGINAE: PROLOGUS'

The oldest datable Scottish Latin literary text is the *Vita Margaritae Reginae*, written by Turgot Prior of Durham, later Bishop of Saint Andrews, during the years between the marriage of Margaret's daughter Mathilda to Henry I King of England on 11 November, the eleventh day of the eleventh month of the year 1100, and the death of Margaret's son Eadgar on 8 January 1107.[1] I have arranged the text that follows in lines, marked the rhythms of the cursus, and suggested rhymes with italics. Capital letters and punctuation marks in boldface represent features of London, British Library, MS Cotton Tiberius D.III part II, folios 179v–180ra.

VITA MARGARITAE REGINAE

1   Excellenter hónorábili et honorabíliter èxcellénti reginae Anglórum Mathíld*ae*
    Turgotus seruorum Sáncti Cuthbèrti séruus .
    in praesenti pacis et salutis *bonum* :
    et in futuro bonorum ómnium *bónum* .

2   Venerandae memoriae matris uestrae placitam Deo cónuersatió*nem* .   5
    quam consona multorum laude saepius praedicari . *aúdierátis* :
    ut litteris traditam uóbis offér*rem* .
    et postulándo iuss*ístis* :
    et iubéndo p*ostulástis* .

3   Scilicet mihi praecipue in hoc credéndum *dicebátis* .   10
    quem gratia magnae apud illam famíliarit*átis* .
    magna ex parte secretorum illius conscium esse *aúdierátis* .

4   Haec iussa et haec uota ego líbens ampléc*tor* .
    amplectens múltum uéner*or* .
    uenerans uóbis congrátul*or* :   15
    quae a rege angelorum constituta regína Angl*órum* .
    uitam matris reginae quae semper ad regnum anhelábat ange*lórum* .
    nón solum aud*íre* :
    sed etiam litteris impressam desideratis iúgiter inspíc*ere* .
    ut qui faciem matris párum noue*rátis* :   20
    uirtutum eius notitiam plénius hàbe*átis* .

---

1   BCLL, no. 1009 p. 281. *Vita S. Margaretae Scotorum Reginae*, ed. J.H. Hynd in *Symeonis Dunelmensis Opera*, Surtees Society LI (Durham, 1868), pp. 234–54.

5   **Et** quidem mihi imperata perficiendi próna est uol*úntas* :
     sed fateor déest fac*últas* .

6   **M**aior est quippe huius negótii matér*ia* .
     quam mihi sit uel scribendi uel loquendi éfficác*ia* .   25

7   **D**uo namque súnt quae páti*or* .
     quibus hínc et inde tráh*or* .

8   **P**ropter magnitudinem rei oboedíre formíd*o* :
     propter iubentis auctoritatem et illius de qua dicendum est memoriam
          contradícere non aúd*eo* .

9   **S**ed quamuis sicut dignum esset tantam rem explicáre non uál*eo* :   30
     quantum tamen possum quia hoc et eius dilectio et uestra exigit iussio
          intimáre déb*eo* .

10   **G**ratia namque Sancti Spiritus quae illi dederat efficáciam uirtút*um* :
     mihi ut spero enarrandi eas subministrábit auxíl*ium* .

11   **D**ominus dabit uerbum euángeliz*ántibus* .
     et iterum . **A**peri os tuum . et ego adimplebo illud .   35

12   **N**eque enim poterit deficere uerbo : qui crédit in Vérbo .

13   **I**n principio énim erat Vérb*um* .

14   **I**n primis igitur cupio *et uos*
     et alios scire per *uos* .
     quod si omnia quae de illa noui praedicanda dícere conáb*or* .   40
     uobis propter regiae dignitatis apicem in matris laude adulári putáb*or* .

15   **S**ed procul absit a méa can*ície* .
     uirtutibus tantae feminae mendacii crímen *admíscere* .

16   **I**n quibus exponendis Deo teste ac iudice profiteor me nihil supra íd quod est
          ádd*ere* .
     sed ne incredibilia uideantur multa siléntio subprím*ere* .
     ne iuxta illud Oratoris cornicem dicar cignaeis colóribus àdorná*re* .   46

tit. INCIPIT TRANSLATIO ET VITA SCE MARGARITE REGINE SCOTIE.
2 .T.   4 *after* bonum *in a more recent hand* per Turgotum Dunelmensem.   25 michi.
33 michi. sumministrabit.   44 nichil.

34 Psalm LXVII 12.   35 Psalm LXXXVII 10.   37 John 1 1.

THE LIFE OF QUEEN MARGARET

1   For the excellently honourable and honourably excellent Queen of the English,
          Mathilda,
     Turgot, servant of the servants of Saint Cuthbert,
     in the present [wishes] the good of peace and health
     and in the future the good of all goods.

2   The conversation pleasing to God of your mother of venerable memory   5
     which you had heard to be preached quite often in the harmonious praise of
          many men
     that I should offer handed over to you in letters
     you have both in asking ordered
     and in ordering asked.

3   You kept saying, understand, that I was especially to be believed in this   10
      whom by grace of great familiarity with that woman
      you had heard to be knowledgeable about a great part of her secrets.

4   These orders and these wishes I willingly embrace; embracing I much venerate
             and venerating I congratulate you,   15
      who, by the King of the angels established as Queen of the Angles,
      the life of [your] mother the queen who always aspired to the realm of the angels
      not only to hear
      but also impressed in letters you desire continually to look on,
      so that you who knew a little the face of [your] mother   20
      might have more fully a notice of her virtues.

5   And though the will is prone to perform the things commanded of me,
      yet I confess the faculty is lacking.

6   The matter of this business is indeed greater
      than there may be power in me either of writing or of speaking.   25

7   For there are two things which I suffer,
      by which I am drawn to this side and to that side.

8   Because of the magnitude of the affair I dread to obey;
      because of the authority of the one ordering and the memory of that woman
             about whom one must speak I dare not gainsay.

9   But although I am not able to unfold so great an affair in a manner as would be
             worthy,   30
      I ought to intimate as much as I can, because both the love of her and your
             order exacts this.

10   For the grace of the Holy Spirit which had given to her the power of virtues
             will, as I hope, supply to me the aid of narrating them.

11   The Lord will give the word to those evangelizing,
      and again, 'Open your mouth and I will fill it'.   35

12   For he will not be able to lack the word who believes in the Word.

13   For 'In the beginning was the Word'.

14   In the first place therefore I want both you
      and through you others to know
      that if I shall attempt to say all the things which I have learned fit to be
             preached about her   40
      on account of the apex of royal dignity in the praise of [your] mother I
             shall be thought to flatter you.

15   But far be it from my grey-haired state
      to admix the crime of a lie with the virtues of so great a woman.

16   In expounding which, with God as witness and judge, I profess myself to add
             nothing above that which is,
      but, lest they seem incredible, to suppress many things in silence,
      lest according to that [remark] of the Orator I be said to adorn the crow
             with the colours of the swan.   46

One notes that many of Turgot's lines end with correct clausular rhythms.
   Turgot's Salutation of four lines and twenty-five words divides by symmetry
at the end of his title at the end of a central second line, *Turgotus seruorum Sancti
Cuthberti | seruus |*. The central words of the first half occur at the end of the

first line, *reginae* | *Anglorum* | *Mathildae*. The central word of the second half occurs at the end of the third line, *bonum*, which is repeated as the last word of the last line, *bonum*.

Turgot arranged his words and ideas in chiastic and parallel patterns.

5	A1	matris	
6	A2	laude	
6	B		praedicari
7	C		uobis
10	D		scilicet
10	E		credendum
21	F1		uirtutum
23	F2		deest
25	G		efficacia
29	H		iubentis
29	I		illius
29	J		dicendum
29	K		memoriam
29	J'		contradicere
31	I'		eius
31	H'		iussio
32	G'		efficaciam
32	F'1		uirtutum
36	F'2		deficere
36	E'		credit
39	D'		scire
39	C'		uos
40	B'		praedicanda
41	A'1	matris	
41	A'2	laude	

The centre of the chiasmus, in a central eighth of sixteen sentences, illustrates the purpose of the entire composition, the *memoriam* of Queen Margaret. The 320 words of the Prologue divide by extreme and mean ratio at 198 and 122, at *eius* | *notitiam*, the notice of Queen Margaret, and at *et eius dilectio et* | *uestra exigit iussio*, the love of Queen Margaret and the order of her daughter Queen Mathilda.

The forty-six lines of text represent the forty-six years of Queen Margaret's age at her death. The sixteen sentences represent 16 November, Saint Margaret's Day. The three words of the Title and the 317 words of the Prologue, together 320 words, also represent Saint Margaret's Day, the 320th of the year.[2]

---

2   See above pp. 8, 23, 36, 59, 61, 74, 83–5, 89, 96 and below pp. 142, 150, 160, 174, 182–4.

TURGOT PRIOR OF DURHAM: 'VITA MARGARITAE REGINAE: CAPITULUM XI'

In chapter XI of the Life Turgot relates a prose account of the event commemorated in the poem considered above in chapter III.[1] Capital letters and punctuation marks in boldface represent features of MS Cotton Tiberius D.III part II folio 184va–vb.

QUOD IN TESTIMONIUM SANCTAE CONVERSATIONIS EIUS QUIDDAM DOMINUS OSTENDERIT

1 **C**um ergo his et huiusmodi dedita ésset opéri*bus* **.**
et continuis laboraret ínfirmitát*ibus* **:**
ut iuxta Apostolum 'uirtus in infirmitate pérficeré*tur*'
de uirtute in uirtutem **.** de die in diem mélior rèdd*eb*á*tur* **.**

2 **T**errena omnia ménte déser*ens* **.**   5
toto desiderio ardebat caeléstia síti*ens* **.**

3 '**S**itiuit anima mea ad Deum fontem uiuum **.**

4 Quando ueniam et apparebo ante faciem Dei **?**'

5 **M**irentur alii in aliis sígna miràcul*órum* **:**

6 Ego in Margarita multo magis admiror opera mísericòrdiá*rum* **.**   10

7 **N**am signa bonis et málís sunt commún*ia* **:**

8 Opera autem uerae pietatis et caritatis bonórum própr*ia*

9 Illa sanctitatem ínterdum osténd*unt* **:**

10 ista étiam fáci*unt* **.**

11 **D**ignius inquam miremur in Margarita facta quae illam sánctam faciéba*nt* **.**   15
quam signa si aliqua fecisset **:** quae hominibus sanctam tántum osténdere*nt*

12 **D**ignius *í*lla*m* óbstupescá*mus* **.**
in qua per iustitiae pietatis **.** misericordiae et caritatis studia antiquorum
patrum facta magis quam sígn*a* consìder*á*m*us* **.**

13 **Q**uiddam támen narrá*bo* **:**
quod ad religiosae uitae illius indicium pertinere non inconuenienter
díxerim ut pút*o* **.**   20

14 **H**abuerat librum éuangelió*rum*
gemmis et aúro perornát*um* **.**
in quo quattuor euangelistarum imagines pictura auro admíxta decorá*bat* **.**
sed et capitalis quaeque littera auro tóta rutilá*bat* **.**

1 See above pp. 15–18.

15   Hunc codicem prae caeteris in quibus legendo studére consuéuerat .   25
carius semper amplexáta fúerat .

16   Quem quidem deferens dum forte per uádum transíret .
liber qui minus caute pannis fuerat obuolutus : in medias áquas cécidit .
quod ignorans portitor . iter quod inceperat secúrus perégit .

17   Cum uero postea líbrum profèrre uéllet :   30
tum primum quod perdíderat agnóuit .

18   Quaerebatur diu . nec inuéniebátur .

19   Tandem in profundo fluminis apertus iacére reperítur .
ita ut illius folia impetu aquae sine cessatione ágitaréntur .
et panniculi de serico uiolentia fluminis ábstraheréntur :   35
qui litteras aureas ne foliorum contactu obfuscaréntur . contéxerant .

20   Quis ulterius librum ualére putáret ?

21   Quis in eo uel unam litteram parére créderet ?

22   Certe integer incorruptus . illaesus . de medio flúminis extráhitur :
ita ut minime ab aqua táctus uiderétur .   40

23   Candor enim foliorum et integra in omnibus formula litterarum íta permánsit .
sicut erat antequam in flúuium cècidísset :
nisi quod in extremis foliis in parte uix aliquod humoris signum uidéri póterat .

24   Liber simul et miraculum ad regínam refértur .
quae reddita Xpisto gratiarum actione : multo carius quam antea códicem
amplèctitur .   45

25   Quare álii uídeant
quid índe séntiant .

26   Ego propter reginae uenerabilis dilectionem hoc signum a Domino
osténsum non ámbigo .

1 huiusmodo.   11 nobis.   36 offuscarentur.

3 II Corinthians XII 9. 7–8 Psalm XLII 2.

THAT FOR TESTIMONY OF HER HOLY CONVERSATION
THE LORD SHOWED SOMETHING

1   Since therefore she was given to these works and the like
and laboured in continual infirmities,
so that according to the Apostle 'Virtue was perfected in infirmity',
from virtue to virtue, from day to day, she was rendered better.

2   Abandoning all earthly things in [her] mind   5
with complete desire she burned, thirsting for heavenly things.

3   'My soul has thirsted for God, a living fountain.

4   When shall I come and appear before the face of God?'

5   Let others admire in others the signs of miracles.

6   I admire much more in Margaret the works of mercies.   10

7   For signs are common to good and evil men.

8   Works of true piety and charity, however, are proper to good men.

9   The former [works of piety] occasionally show sanctity.

10   The latter [works of charity] really make [it].

11   Let us, I say, more worthily admire in Margaret the deeds which made her holy,   15
      than the signs if she did any, which only showed her holy to men.

12   Let us more worthily be amazed at her,
          in whom through studies of justice, piety, mercy, and charity we consider the
              deeds of the holy fathers more than the signs.

13   I shall nevertheless relate something
          which I may say not inconveniently, as I think, to pertain to the showing of her
              religious life.   20

14   She had a book of the Gospels
          adorned with gems and gold,
          in which painting mixed with gold decorated images of the four evangelists,
          but also a certain capital letter gleamed complete with gold.

15   This codex beyond the others in which she was accustomed to study by reading 25
          she always embraced more dearly.

16   Which a certain man carrying, while by chance he crossed over through a ford,
          the book which had been rather incautiously wrapped in cloths fell into the
              middle of the waters,
          not knowing which the bearer continued careless on the journey which he had
              begun.

17   When in truth afterwards he wished to bring forth the book,   30
          then first he knew what he had lost.

18   He kept seeking for a long time, and it was not found.

19   Finally in the depth of the river it is found to lie open,
          so that its leaves by the onrush of the water are agitated without cessation,
          and the little cloths of silk by the violence of the river are taken away,   35
          which had covered the golden letters lest they be obscured by the contact
              of the leaves.

20   Who would think the book to have value any longer?

21   Or who would believe one letter to appear in it?

22   Certainly whole, incorrupt, undamaged, it is drawn out from the middle of
              the river,
          so that it seems not at all touched by the water.   40

23   For the whiteness of the leaves and the complete shape of the letters in all
              respects remained so,
          just as it was before it fell into the river,
          except that in the last leaves in part some sign of the liquid could barely be seen.

24   Book and miracle together is related to the queen,
          who with thanksgiving given back to Christ embraces the codex more dearly
              than before.   45

25   Wherefore let others see
          what they may feel about it.

26   I do not doubt this sign showed by the Lord on account of love of the
              venerable queen.

In the first part of the narrative, lines 1–18, Turgot states and restates words
and ideas at intervals of five words or multiples thereof. There are five words

between *infirmitatibus* | 2 and | *infirmitate* 3. After *uirtus* 3 the fifth word is *uirtute* 4. There are ten words from | *Deum* 7 to *Dei* | 8 inclusive. After *mirentur* | 9 the fifth word is *miraculorum* | 9, between which and | *admiror* 10 there are five words. Between *signa* | 9 and | *signa* 11 there are ten words, while between *signa* | 16 and | *signa* 18 there are twenty-five words. From | *opera* 10 to *opera* | 12 inclusive there are ten words. Between *misericordiarum* | 10 and | *misericordiae* 18 there are fifty words. Between *bonis* | 11 and | *bonorum* 12 there are ten words. From | *pietatis* 12 to *pietatis* | 18 inclusive there are forty words. After *caritatis* | 12 *caritatis* 18 is the fortieth word. From | *sanctitatem* 13 to *sanctam* | 15 inclusive there are fifteen words, and from | *sanctam* 15 to *sanctam* | 16 inclusive there are ten words. From | *interdum ostendunt* 13 to *tantum ostenderent* | 16 inclusive there are twenty-five words. Between *faciunt* | 14 and | *facta* 15 there are five words; from | *facta* 15 to *faciebant* | 15 inclusive there are five words; after *faciebant* | 15 the fifth word is *fecisset* | 16; after *fecisset* | 16 the twentieth word is *facta* | 18. After *dignius* | 15 the twentieth word is *dignius* | 17. From | *illam* 15 to *illam* | 17 inclusive there are fifteen words. Between *obstupescamus* | 17 and | *consideramus* 18 there are fifteen words, *consideramus* being the last word of the first part of this chapter.

In the second part of the narrative, lines 19–48, Turgot did something different, arranging his words and ideas in chiastic and parallel patterns.

19	A	quiddam tamen narrabo
25	B	codicem ... carius ... amplexata fuerat
27	C	deferens
28	D	liber
28	E	in medias aquas cecidit
33	F1	in profundo fluminis
33	F2	reperitur
34	F3	ita ut
34	F4	impetu aquae
36	F5	foliorum
38	F6	uel unam litteram parere crederet ... integer
39	G	incorruptus
39	G'	illaesus
39	F'1	de medio fluminis
39	F'2	extrahitur
40	F'3	ita ut
40	F'4	ab aqua tactus
41	F'5	foliorum
41	F'6	integra in omnibus formula litterarum ita permansit
42	E'	sicut erat antequam in fluuium cecidisset
44	D'	liber
44	C'	refertur
45	B'	multo carius quam ante codicem amplectitur
48	A'	hoc signum a Domino ostensum non ambigo.

These structural features fix exactly the order of the words. But other features fix the order and integrity of the entire chapter. The forty-eight lines divide by extreme and mean ratio at 30 and 18, exactly at the division between the first part, in which words recur at multiples of 5, and the second part, in which words recur in chiastic and parallel patterns.

The title, containing twenty-six syllables and seventy-four letters, provides the key to the structure of the chapter, in which the first of twenty-six sentences contains seventy-four syllables.[2] After *in medias* | 28 there are 150 words to the end of the text, of which the middle, seventy-fifth, is *de medio* |.

---

2   See above pp. 4, 51, 85, 89, 96, 102 and below pp. 141, 150, 152, 155, 186–7.

JOCELIN OF FURNESS:
'VITA SANCTI KENTIGERNI'

The most prolific hagiographer whose works have descended to us under his own name is Jocelin of Furness, who flourished 1185–1215. In addition to Lives of Saint Helena and Saint Patrick[1] Jocelin revised the work of Symeon of Glasgow considered above[2] to produce the *Vita Sancti Kentigerni* which follows.[3] Capital letters and punctuation marks in boldface represent features of Dublin, Archbishop Marsh's Library, MS Z.4.5.5, folios 7r–8r. Punctuation marks in square brackets represent features of London, British Library, MS Cotton Vitellius C.VIII, folio 165ra–vb, not found in the Dublin manuscript. Small capitals represent Jocelin's quotations from other texts.

**INCIPIT PROLOGUS EPISTOLARIS
IN VITAM SANCTI KENTEGERNI EPISCOPI ET CONFESSORIS .**

1　**D**omino suo **R**éuerent*íssimo*
　　et pátri kar*íssimo*
　　Iocelino Xpisto Dómini Ièsu *Xpísti*
　　Iocelinus minimus paúperum *Xpísti* :
　　cum filialis dil*ectionis* et súbiecti*ónis*　　　　　　　　　　5
　　afféctu et *efféctu*
　　utriusque hominis salutem in nóstro salutári .
2　**Q**uoniam nomen uéstrum *célebre* .
　　off*ícium* subl*íme* .
　　iud*ícium* èquil*íbre* .　　　　　　　　　　　　　　　　10
　　uita nullo sinistre FAMe fúco fuscáta .
　　RELIGIO díu probáta .
　　uos decorem domus Dei cui preestis diligere ANIMO meo satis probabíliter
　　　　pérsuad*ent* :
　　congruum duxi uobis offerre manipulorum meorum primitias que uestri et
　　　　ecclesie uestre decus et decórem rédol*ent* .
3　**C**IRCUIui enim PER PLATEAS ET VICOS CIVITATis iúxta mandàtum *uéstrum*　　15
　　QUERens uitam sancti Kentegerni descriptam . QUEM DILIGIT ÁNIMA *uéstra* :
　　cuius cathedre filiórum adòpti*óne* .

1　*BCLL*, nos 1020–1 p. 283.
2　See pp. 91–7.
3　*BCLL*, no. 1018 p. 283.

ecclesiastica électióne .
successiuo mínistério
uestram sanctitatem presidere fecit diuine DIGNATIónis grátia .   20

4   QUESIVI igitur diligenter uitam . si forte ínVENIrétur .
que maiori auctoritate et euidentiori ueritáte fulcíri .
et STILO cultiori uiderétur exarári :
quam illa quam uestra frequéntat ecclésia .
quia illam ut pluribus uidetur tincta per totum decolorat incúlta ORÁTIO .   25
obnubilat stilus íncompósitus :
quod pre hiis omnibus quilibet sane sapiens mágis abhórret :
in ipso narrationis frontispicio quiddam sane doctrine et catholice fidei
         aduersum euidénter appáret :

5   CODICulum autem alium STILO Scottico dictatum repperi per totum
         soloecísmis scaténtem : ·
diffusius tamen uitam et actus sancti pontíficis còntinéntem .   30

6   Videns igitur tam preciosi pontificis uitam signis et prodígiis glòriósam .
uirtutibus et doctrína claríssimam .
relatu peruerso et a fide auérso maculári .
aut SERMONE barbarico nímis obscurári :
condolui fateor . et moléste accépi .   35

7   Quo circa sedit ANIMO ex utroque libello materiam collectam redintegrándo
         sarcíre .
et iuxta MODULum meum et preceptum uestrum barbarice exarata Romano
SÁLE CONDÍre .

8   Absurdum arbitror thesaurum tam preciosum tam uilibus obuolui sémicínctiis .
et ideo conabor íllum coòperíre
et si non aurifrisiis aut óloséricis :   40
saltem uel líneis íntegris .

9   ADHIBui etiam OPERAM ex ueteri uase IN nouum uiuificum liquorem íta
         TRANSFÚndeRE :
ut simplicioribus sit áppetíbile .
mediocribus nón sit inútile :
sensu locupletioribus non sit cóntemptíbile [:]   45
pro uasis mediocritáte hauríre .

10   Sancti igitur présulis méritis
et precibus súffragántibus [;]
si superni inspiratoris mihi fauor applauserit : STILum síc temperábo .
ut nec nimis abiecto SERMONE in ceno repens obscuret ÓPUS suscéptum :   50
nec VERBorum FALERis secus quam decet inseruiens áltum túmeat .
ne uidear PLANTAsse NEMUS IN templo DOMINI contra eíus interdíctum .

11   Totum igitur studium húius óperis
totum fructum méi labóris
duxi uestro consecrándum nómini :   55
uestro etiam statui presentándum exámini .

12   Si quid autem illepidum procésserit . aùt insúlsum :
DISCRETIOnis uestre SALE CONDÍTUM saporétur .

13   Si quid forte minus ueritati consonum SONuerit . quod non reor
ad regulam iudicii uestri deductum limétur et cònquadrétur .   60

14   **Si** quid inuenitur a neutro dissidens uestro testimonio súbfulc*iátur* .
auctoritate uéstra robor*étur* .

15   **Et** in hiis omnibus <u>si quid</u> secus quam rem deceat CALAMO meo
mandatum in lúcem prod*íerit* .
exiguitatis mee imperítie ìmput*étur* .

16   **Et** si quid lectione dignum apparuerit élucubrátum :   65
uestre eminéncie àscribá*tur* .

17   **T**ranslationem autem sancti huius uel miracula post decessum eius descripta
nusquam reperíre pótui .
que **a**ut non sunt notata : quia forte effugerunt memóriam presént*ium* .
aut multiplicata sunt super numerum . ne infirmis lectoribus copia congesta
conférret fastíd*ium* .

18   **V**iuat et uigeat sanctitas uestra sémper in Dómino .   70

EXPLICIT PROLOGUS .

9 V sullime. 16 V diligat *corr. to* diligit. 23 V cerciori. 25 V tractata. declarat. 27 V et quod pre
iis. 29 V scotico dictarum. 30 V totam. 31 V tam. 34 V et relatu. 38 M semicintiis. *in marg.*
semicinctum i. zona ex una. parte. 40 M *in marg.* aurifriciis depictus auro. olosericis .i. totus
de serico. 44 V mediacribus. 51 V timeat *corr. to* tumeat. 57 M *in marg.* illepidus da d[um] .i.
insuauis. insipidus. 59 V reo. 60 V suffulciatur. 62 V imputetur imperieie. 64 V elugubratu.
66 M ascribatur eminencie. V scribatur eminencie. 67 V descriptionem. 69 V fortiter.

THE EPISTOLARY PROLOGUE BEGINS
ON THE LIFE OF SAINT KENTIGERN BISHOP AND CONFESSOR.

1   To his own most reverent lord
and dearest father
Jocelin the anointed of the Lord Jesus Christ
Jocelin the least of the poor of Christ   4
with affection and effect   6
of filial love and subjection   5
[wishes] salvation of either man in what brings our salvation.

2   Since your celebrated name,
sublime office,
equally balanced judgement,   10
life darkened by no dark colourant of sinister reputation,
religion commended for a long time,
persuade commendably to love sufficiently in my mind you, the adornment
of the house of God over which you are preeminent,
I have considered it fitting to offer to you the first fruits of my sheaves, which
are fragrant with the beauty and adornment of you and your Church.

3   For I went about through the squares and streets of the city according
to your command,   15
seeking a written Life of Saint Kentigern, whom your soul loves,
by the adoption of the sons of whose see,
by ecclesiastical election,

by successive service,
the grace of divine deigning has made your holiness to preside over.   20

4   I sought therefore a Life, if by chance one might be found,
which might be seen to be supported by greater authority and more evident truth
and written in more cultivated style
than that which your Church resorts to,
because it is seen by many that tainted uncultivated speech discolours
that [Life] through the whole composition;   25
ill-composed style overclouds [it];
what above all these things any soundly wise man rather abhors,
in the very frontispiece of the narration something appears evidently
contrary to sound doctrine and the catholic faith.

5   Another little codex, however, I found dictated in Scottish style, seething
with solecisms through the whole composition,
containing nonetheless rather diffusely the life and acts of the holy pontiff.   30

6   Seeing therefore the life of so precious a pontiff glorious with signs and prodigies,
very bright with virtues and doctrine,
to be spotted by a narrative perverse and averse from the faith,
to be obscured by speech too barbaric,
I grieved, I confess, and took it badly.   35

7   On which acount it has settled in the mind to mend by reintegrating the
material collected from either little book,
and according to my little measure and your precept to season with Roman
salt the things barbarously written.

8   I consider it absurd for a treasure so precious to be wrapped round with
such vile little girdles,
and consequently I shall try to cover it,
and if not with orphreys or all-silk cloths,   40
at least with intact linen cloths.

9   I have even applied effort so to pour life-giving liquor across from an old
vessel into a new one
that it may be desirable to more simple men,
that it may be not unuseful to men of middling ability,
that it may be not contemptible to men richer in sense,   45
to draw in proportion to the means of the vessel.

10   Therefore with the merits of the holy bishop
and prayers supporting,
if the favour of the supernal Inspirer should applaud me, I will temper my stylus,
that neither creeping along in slime may it obscure the received work with too
much abject speech   50
nor being servile may it swell aloft with ornaments of words otherwise than is
fitting,
lest I be seen to have planted a wood in the temple of the Lord against
His interdict.

11   Therefore the whole study of this work,
the whole fruit of my labour,
I have brought to be consecrated to your name,   55
I have even decreed to be presented for your examination.

12   If, however, anything will have proceeded ungraceful or unsalted,
        it should be made savoury, seasoned by the salt of your discretion.
13   If by chance anything will have sounded less consonant with the truth, which
            I think not [to be so],
        it should be led back filed and squared at the rule of your judgement.   60
14   If anything is found being out of alignment from either [your discretion or
            your judgement] it should be supported by your testimony,
        strengthened by your authority.
15   And in all these respects if anything commanded will have gone forth into the
            light from my reed pen otherwise than may befit the matter,
        it should be imputed to the unlearnedness of my little insignificance.
16   And if anything worthy of reading will have appeared with the midnight oil
            burned over it,   65
        it should be ascribed to your eminence.
17   The translation, however, of the saint or the miracles written down after his
            decease I have been able to find nowhere,
        which either have not been noted because by chance they have fled the
            memory of present men
        or they have been multiplied beyond number and the heaped up supply
            should not bring disgust to infirm readers.
18   May your holiness live and flourish always in the Lord.   70

THE PROLOGUE ENDS.

Jocelin arranged the words of his Salutation chiastically.

1	A	Domino
1	B1	reuerentissimo
2	B2	patri
2	B3	karissimo
3	C	Iocelino
3	D	Xpisto
3	E	Domini Iesu
3	D'	Xpisti
4	C'	Iocelinus
4	B'1	minimus pauperum
5	B'2	filialis
5	B'3	dilectionis

The twenty-nine words of the Salutation divide by symmetry 1:1 at 15 at the
end of the fourth of seven lines, *Xpisti*. The eighth word is *Xpisto* 3, from which
to *Xpisti* 4 inclusive there are eight words, between which the central fourth
word is *Xpisti* 3. The twenty-nine words divide by extreme and mean ratio at 18
and 11, at *Xpisti* | 3. Between *patri* | 2 and | *filialis* 5 there are eleven words.
Between *Iocelino* and *Iocelinus* | 3–4 and | *utriusque hominis* 7 there are eleven

words. The first word *Domino* 1 is echoed by *Domini* 3 at the crux of the chiasmus.

Jocelin arranged the words about his sources in another chiasmus.

13	A1	animo
14	A2	manipulorum meorum primitias
15	A3	mandatum uestrum
16	B	uitam
16	C	sancti Kentegerni
21	D	uitam
22	E	euidentiori
23	F	stilo
23	G	cultiori
24	H	illa
25	H'	illam
25	G'	inculta
26	F'	stilus
28	E'	euidenter
30	D'	uitam
30	C'	sancti pontificis
31	B'	uitam
36	A'1	animo
36	A'2	materiam collectam redintegrando sarcire et iuxta modulum meum
36	A'3	preceptum uestrum

The 213 words from | *quoniam nomen uestrum* 8 to *Romano sale condire* | 37 inclusive divide by symmetry at 107, *quia illam* | *ut* | *plurimis uidetur* at the end of the crux of the chiasmus.

Jocelin infixed varied devices that guarantee the integrity of the entire text precisely. The twenty-nine syllables in the title provide the key to the twenty-nine words in the Salutation. The seventy letters in the title provide the key to the seventy lines in the Prologue.

By *inclusio* the first word of the Salutation, *Domino*, is echoed not only by *Domini* at the crux of the chiasmus of the Salutation but by the last word of the Prologue, *Domino*.

Jocelin's third sentence begins with a quotation from the beginning of the third chapter of the *Canticum Canticorum*:[4]

---

4   For another example of this device see above p. 37.

in lectulo meo per noctes quaesiui quem diligit anima mea
quaesiui illum et non inueni
surgam et circuibo ciuitatem
per uicos et plateas quaeram quem diligit anima mea
quaesiui illum et non inueni.

The other words printed in small capital letters suggest that Jocelin had been reading Geoffrey of Monmouth's addresses to his prospective patrons Robert Earl of Gloucester and Waleran Count of Meulan and Alexander Bishop of Lincoln. Compare from the *Historia Regum Britanniae* the Prologue:[5]

multa ... animo reuoluens;
quendam Britannici sermonis librum uetustissimum;
perpulchris orationibus;
falerata uerba non collegerim
agresti tamen stilo propriisque calamis contentus
codicem illum in Latinum sermonem transferre curaui;
tedium legentibus ingererem;
sale minerue tue conditum;
operam adhibeas tuam;
codicemque ad oblectamentum tui editum;
calamum muse tue;
tuto modulamine resonare queam;

and the beginning of book VII:

uir religionis et prudentie;
nobilitatis tue dilectio;
in Latinum transferre;
istudque opus;
labor incumberet sensus meus ... ;
discretio subtilis ingenii tui donaret
agrestem calamum meum labellis apposui
et plebeia modulatione ignotum tibi interpretatus sum sermonem;
dignatus eras.

The principal difference is that Geoffrey of Monmouth adduced a beautiful and authoritative written source in Brittonic, *Britannici sermonis librum uetustissimum*, and Jocelin decried the only available literary sources for the Life of Kentigern. The passage in lines 15–37 has led some scholars to suppose that Jocelin referred to an early Life in Scottish Gaelic or even Brittonic. If one supposed such a text

5   Howlett, *The English Origins of Old French Literature*, pp. 36–48.

had ever existed a difficulty would remain in that Jocelin provides no evidence of ability to read either language. A conclusive argument is that *barbarismus* and *soloecismus* are vices of Latin, not vernacular, composition. Jocelin refers here to the Latin *Vita Sancti Kentigerni* considered above, written by Symeon of Glasgow who states explicitly that he was not a native Scot, and to what Symeon described as *materia in uirtutum eius codicello reperta*.[6] In *codiculum autem alium stilo Scottico dictatum* Jocelin refers to the work of another earlier Scottish Latin writer. From this one infers that Jocelin, like the authors of *De Situ Albanie* and the *Cronica Regum Scottorum* and the *Vita Sancti Reguli* and Adam of Dryburgh, used *Scotticus* in its politically extended sense appropriate to the later twelfth century.

In writing *adhibui etiam operam ex ueteri uase nouum uiuificum liquorem ita transfundere* Jocelin faintly echoes Rhygyfarch ap Sulien in *Ricemarch de Psalterio*:[7]

> Ebraeumque iuuar suffuscat nube Latina
> Nam tepefacta ferum dant tertia labra saporem
> Sed sacer Hieronimus Ebraeo fonte repletus
> Lucidius uerum nudat breuiusque ministrat
> Namque secunda creat Nam tertia uascula uitat.

> It darkens the Hebrew radiance with a Latin cloud,
> for third vats, made tepid, give an uncultivated savour.
> But holy Jerome, refilled from the Hebrew fountain,
> lays bare the truth more lucidly and serves [it] more briefly,
> for he creates second, for he avoids third vessels.

In sentence 9, writing about pouring the vivifying liquor into a new vessel, as in the Salutation in sentence 1, Jocelin uses twenty-nine words. From | *adhibui etiam operam* to *pro uasis mediocritate* | 'in proportion to the means of the vessel' there are twenty-eight words, which divide by extreme and mean ratio at 17 and 11, at *mediocribus* |. The same passage contains eighty syllables, which divide by the same ratio at 49 and 31, at the same place. The 474 words of the entire Prologue divide by extreme and mean ratio at 293 and 181, at | *mediocritate*.

In sentence 10 line 52 Jocelin, writing *ne uidear plantasse nemus in templo Domini contra eius interdictum*, alludes ultimately to Deuteronomy XVI 21, *non plantabis lucum et omnem arborem iuxta altare Domini Dei tui*. But his diction suggests that he had read the letter of A.D. 1180 from John Abbot of Kelso to Adam of Dryburgh: *memores illius precepti quo prohibetur nemus plantari in domo Domini*.[8]

---

6   See above p. 91.
7   Howlett, *Cambro-Latin Compositions*, pp. 104–7.
8   See below pp. 162, 174.

JOCELIN OF FURNESS:
'VITA SANCTI WALTHEUI'

Jocelin's *Vita Sancti Waltheui* survives in a manuscript from Dunfermline, written 1460×1488, now Madrid, Patrimonio Nacional, Biblioteca, II.2097 (*olim* II 4 N), folios 41r–68.[1] Capital letters and punctuation marks in boldface represent features of the manuscript.

ILLUSTRISSIMIS VIRIS	2	7	19
WILHELMO RÉGI SCÓTIE	3	8	18
ET ALEXANDRO FÍLIO EÍUS	4	10	20
ET CÓMITI DÁVID :	3	6	13
FRÁTER IOCELÍNUS	2	6	15
QUALISCUMQUE MÓNACHUS FURNÉSII	3	11	28
UTRIUSQUE HOMINIS SALUTE IN DÓMINO P*OTÍRI* :	6	17	36
ET UTRIUSQUE VITE FELICITÁTEM S*ORTÍRI* :	5	15	33
	28	80	182

1 **S**epius mente reuoluens de cuius uitis radice palmites prodúcti pullulá*stis* :
intueor excellentissimam ex summa ingenuitate totíus Euró*pe*
uos originariam particulam tráxisse *cárnis* :

2 **S**ancte namque Margarete mater Ágatha nómin*e* :
filia fuit Germani Henrici clarissimi imperató*ris* Roman*órum* .   5
cuius posteritas illustrat Román*um* impéri*um* :

3 **S**oror eiusdem Agathe regina éxtit*it* Ùngar*órum* :
cuius uteri fructus successiuus réges gérminan*s* :
non solum eiusdem regni póssidet prìncipá*tum*
sed etiam aliorum regnorum plurium náctus est scép*trum* :   10

4 **G**enitor nihilominus ipse Beáte Margaré*te*
dictus Edwardus nepos et heres legitimus sanctissimi confessoris Edwardi régis
    Ángli*e*
iure héreditári*o*
Anglici regni per lineas rectas et directas successiue generationis in uós deuolú*to*
uos sceptrígeros *èffecísset* .   15

---

1 *BCLL*, no. 1019 p. 283. *Latin Writers*, no. 555 p. 198. Ed. W. Cooper, *Acta Sanctorum*, Aug. I (1733), pp. 248–76. I owe thanks to Professor Robert Bartlett, F.B.A., for collation of the manuscript.

    nisi uiolenta Normannorum direptio Deo permittente usque ad tempus prefinítum
        prepedísset .

5   Nec solum in illo glorioso stemmate regum Anglicorum in diuitiis et gloria in
        regno potentíssimi prèfulsérunt .
    sed etiam in sanctitate et iustitia magna Deo placentes in uita et post mortem
        miraculis multimodis magnífice clàruérunt .

6   A sancto namque rege Adwolfo qui totam Angliam decimans decimam Deo et
        ecclésie cònsecráuit .
    nouem numerántur reges sáncti :   20
    quórum postérior
    priori persóna prestántior
    in Xpistiana religione emicuísse dignóscitur .

7   In decimo uero Sancto Edwardo cunctorum predecessorum summitas quasi
        transfúsa conflúxit .
    et sic ex illo tamquam fonte lucidissimo uite religióse ríuulus   25
    in Sanctam Margarétam pronèptem eíus :
    et ex illa in filium súum
    regem Dáuid auum uéstrum :
    et ex eo in Malcolmum regem fratrem uéstrum emanáuit .

8   Ceterum auia uestra Mathildis regina Scotie proneptis erat Wilhelmi
        strenuissimi ducis qui Ángliam dèbelláuit   30
    et comitis Waltheui sancti mátris filia
    ac mater sanctissimi abbatis de Melros pátrui uéstri :

9   Ipse etiam decus et decor prosápie uéstre :
    regni tutor tutéla pátrie :
    titulus púdicítie :   35
    gemma uíte canónice :
    speculum monástice dìsciplíne :

10   Hic inquam degens in mundo fuit cléri solátium :
    paúperum erárium :
    egenorum sústentáculum   40
    infirmórum remédium :
    uirtutum preclarum dómicílium :

11   Huius córpus sanctíssimum
    totius adhuc corruptionis expers future resurrectionis preclarum préfert indícium :
    et fidei ac spei nostre probabile ac palpabile prébet expèriméntum :   45

12   Huius itaque dilecti Deo et hominibus cuius memoria in bénedictióne est .
    utpote quem Dominus similem illi fecit in glória sanctórum
    uitam uirtútibus uernántem :
    miráculis glòriósam :
    theoriis precláris sublimátam   50
    et mortem in conspectu Dómini glòriósam :
    petente ac precipiente domino Patricio abbáte de Mélros :

13   Sed heu morte prematura prerepto tándem suscépi :
    dictatam excellentie uestre congruentius quam cuilibet alteri déstinandam dúxi :

14   Huic igitur libellum crebro coram uobis lectum et intellectum cum ágnouéritis : 55
    habebitis in eo lucidissimum specular ímitatiónis .
    admirationis et éxultatiónis :

15 Admiratio magna clarescit in miráculis exhíb*itis* :
exultationis prerogatiua uobis attribuitur in communión*e* gén*eris*
et germine natiue própag*atiónis* :   60

16 **I**mitatio proponitur uobis et ceteris in uirtutum studiis et misericordie opéribus
èxercénd*is* :

17 **C**um ergo traduce nature et tam clara et superexcellenti genealogia sitis utrímque
deriuát*i* :
ab illa uos esse degeneres dédignémin*i*
et sancte propaginis exsórtes fier*i* :

18 **A**ttendite igitur ad petram iugiter iuxta Isaie admonitionem *dé qua exc*ì*si éstis* :   65
et ad cauernam laci *dé qua pre*c*ìsi éstis* :
illisque conformari studete moribus et áctibus sánc*tis* :

19 **I**n primis Dei legibus custodiendis atténtius inténd*ite* :
uestigiis sancte progeniei de qua materiam traxistis carnis firmiter ìnherét*e* :
sanctissimi patrui uestri abbatis Waltheui frequenter commendate uos méritis et
précíb*us* :   70
diligite . uisitate ueneramini locum requiétionis *eíus* .

20 **O**rdinem monachicum et precipue Císterciéns*em*
et maxime Melrosénsem abbátia*m*
in qua deguit . cui etiam prefuit et profuit : promouéte protég*ite*
et aduersus aduersantium incursus brachium defensiónis oppón*ite* :   75

21 **E**xhortor et súpplico non sólum u*os*
sed etiam omnes opusculum illud lectúros uel aùditúr*os*
ut dictis fidem adhíbe*ant* .
nullaque in eis ueritáte oppósita
sed quod a uiris ueridicis senioribus dómus Melrosénsis   80
omni exceptione maióribus accép*i*
me scripsisse fidéliter agnósc*ant* .

22 **I**n dictando meum ita stýlum temperáu*i* :
ut nec humi repat nec túmeat in ál*tum* :
modum eligendo propter simplices planum et perlucidum ét circumspéc*tum* :   85
et uitando iuxta Tullium pompaticum suffúltum et ìnuolút*um* :

23 **V**aleat excellentia uestra sémp*er* in *Dómino* :
et post huius uite finem sine fine régn*et* cum *Dómino* .   88

21 MS summatas. Cooper sanctitas. 30 MS debellauit angliam.

46 Ecclesiasticus XLV 1.

FOR THE MOST ILLUSTRIOUS MEN,
WILLIAM KING OF SCOTLAND,
AND ALEXANDER HIS SON,
AND EARL DAVID:
BROTHER JOCELIN,
SOME SORT OF MONK OF FURNESS,
[WISHES] TO ATTAIN THE SALVATION OF EACH MAN IN THE LORD
AND TO ENJOY FELICITY OF EACH LIFE [OF THIS WORLD AND THE
NEXT].

1   Considering [lit. 'turning over'] quite often in the mind the shoots you,
        brought forth, have sent out from the root of that vine,
    I consider [lit. 'gaze upon'] that you have drawn the original particle of flesh,
    most excellent, from the highest free-born status of the whole of Europe.

2   For the mother of Saint Margaret, Agatha by name,
    was daughter of the German Henry, brightest Emperor of the Romans,   5
    whose posterity illuminates the Roman Empire.

3   A sister of the same Agatha stood out as Queen of the Hungarians,
    the successive fruit of whose womb, begetting kings,
    not only possesses the principate of the same realm,
    but also has acquired the sceptre of very many other realms.   10

4   The very begetter, nonetheless, of Blessed Margaret,
    the said Eadweard [the Exile], nephew and legitimate heir of the most holy
        Confessor Eadweard King of England,
    by hereditary right
    devolved to you through straight and direct lines of successive generation,
    would have made you sceptre-bearers of the English realm,   15
    if the violent depredation of the Normans, with God permitting, had not
        hindered at the prescribed time.

5   Not only did the most powerful men shine forth in riches and glory in the
        realm in that glorious lineage of English kings,
    but they also shone magnificently in great sanctity and justice, pleasing to
        God in life and after death in many-moded miracles.

6   For from the holy King Æthelwulf, who consecrated all England, tithing a
        tenth to God and the Church,
    nine holy kings are numbered,   20
    of whom a later,
    more outstanding than any earlier man in his person,
    is deemed to have shone out in the Christian religion.

7   In the tenth man, in truth, Saint Eadweard, the highness of all the predecessors
        flowed together as if transfused,
    and thus from that man as from a most lucid fountain a rivulet of religious life   25
    into Saint Margaret his great-niece,
    and from that woman into her own son,
    King David, your grandfather,
    and from him into King Malcolm your brother, has flowed.

8   For the rest your grandmother Mathilda Queen of Scotland was great-niece
        of William, the most vigorous duke who warred against England,   30
    and daughter of the mother of the holy Earl Waltheof,
    and mother of the most holy Abbot of Melrose, your paternal uncle [Waltheof].

9   The very man was also an ornament and glory of your family,
    protector of the realm, protection of the fatherland,
    epitome of chastity,   35
    jewel of canonical life,
    mirror of monastic discipline.

10   This man, I say, living in the world was the solace of the clergy,
    treasury of poor men,
    sustenance of needy men,   40

remedy of infirm men,
domicile of very bright virtues.

11   The most holy body of this man,
having no share at all of corruption to this day brings forth a very bright
      indication of the future resurrection,
and offers provable and palpable experience of our faith and hope.   45

12   Of this man, beloved of God and men, therefore, whose memory is as a blessing,
as if the Lord made him like Him in the glory of the saints,
a life flourishing in virtues,
glorious in miracles,
made sublime by very bright contemplations,   50
and [his] death glorious in the sight of the Lord,
with the lord Abbot Patrick of Melrose praying and teaching.

13   I have undertaken at last, but alas, from one snatched away by a premature death,
something dictated I have considered to be sent to your excellency more
      fittingly than to any other man.

14   When you will have come to know, therefore, the little book for this
      outstanding man before you, read and understood,   55
you will have in it a most lucid looking glass of imitation,
admiration, and exultation.

15   Great admiration becomes bright in exhibited miracles;
the prerogative of exultation is allotted to you in the shared quality of your
      begetting,
and in the seed of your native propagation.   60

16   Imitation is offered to you and others in the studies of virtues and in works
      of mercy to be exercised.

17   Since therefore you are descended on both sides by a transmission of
      nature in a genealogy both so bright and superexcellent,
you should disdain to be degenerate from it,
and be made to have no share of this holy progeny.

18   Turn your attention continually therefore to the rock, according to the
      admonition of Isaiah, from which you have been cut out,   65
and to the cave of the pit from which you have been cut clearly,
and study to be conformed to those customs and holy acts.

19   Turn your attention quite attentively to keeping the first laws of God;
inhere firmly to the tracks of the holy progeny from which you have
      drawn the material of your flesh;
commend yourselves frequently to the merits and prayers of your most
      holy paternal uncle the Abbot Waltheof;   70
love, visit, venerate the place of his resting.

20   The monastic order and particularly the Cistercian,
and especially the abbey of Melrose,
in which he lived, over which he was preeminent, and to which he was
      beneficial, promote, protect,
and place the arm of defence against the incursions of adversaries.   75

21   I exhort and supplicate not only you,
but also all those who will read or hear that little work,
that they give faith to its words,

among them none opposite from the truth,
but what from truth-uttering elder men of the house of Melrose, 80
with every reception from the greater men I have received,
they should know me to have written faithfully.

22 In dictating I have so tempered my style
that neither should it creep on the ground nor should it swell toward the height,
choosing on account of simple men a plain manner both pellucid and
circumspect, 85
and avoiding according to Tully [a manner] pompous, suffused, and involved.

23 May your excellence thrive always in the Lord,
and after the end of this life reign without end with the Lord. 88

Jocelin arranged his words and ideas in chiastic and parallel order.

Sal.	A	regi
Sal.	B	in Domino
1	C1	reuoluens
2	C2	excellentissimam
3	D	particulam traxisse carnis
18	E	miraculis
25	F	ex illo ... fonte lucidissimo
32	G	abbatis de Melros
32	H	patrui
42	I1	uirtutum
42	I2	preclarum
43–4	J	expers
44	K	preclarum prefert indicium
45	L	fidei
45	M	ac
45	L'	spei nostre
45	K'	probabile ac palpabile prebet
45	J'	experimentum
48	I'1	uirtutibus
50	I'2	preclaris
52	H'	Patricio
52	G'	abbate de Melros
56	F'	in eo lucidissimum specular
58	E'	miraculis
69	D'	materiam traxistis carnis
86	C'1	inuolutum
87	C'2	excellentia
87	B'	in Domino
88	A'	regnet

The first word of the chiastic pattern is the fourth word from the beginning of the passage, and after the last word there are four syllables to the end of the passage. Sentence 1 contains twenty-two words, the first of twenty-two sentences of the Prologue proper. The crux of the chiasmus occurs in the eleventh of twenty-two sentences of the Prologue proper. The word at the very crux of the chiasmus occurs in a central forty-fifth of eighty-eight lines of the Prologue, the central 296th of 591 words of the Prologue proper.

Jocelin begins in the Salutation as he means to go on in the Prologue. He places his name *Iocelinus* | at the central fourteenth of twenty-eight words and his title *monachus Furnesii* | at the golden section, seventeenth of twenty-eight words. The eleven words of the minor part of the golden section comprise the last two rhyming lines.

The eight lines and eighty syllables of the Salutation introduce eighty-eight lines in the Prologue that follows.

Jocelin fixes his colours to the mast and flies them clearly. He addresses William King of Scotland, whose descent he traces through an English line that would have made him King of England but for the *uiolenta Normannorum direptio*. Jocelin writes of the Conqueror as *Wilhelmus strenuissimus dux qui Angliam debellauit*, but of the English ancestors as *heres legitimus sanctissimi confessoris Edwardi regis Anglie, non solum ... potentissimi ... sed etiam in sanctitate et iustitia magna Deo placentes, reges sancti, prestantior in Xpistiana religione, clara et superexcellenti genealogia, sancte propaginis, sancte progeniei*. Jocelin's English sympathy and Scottish loyalty are as clear as they could be. In this he resembles, as we shall see below, Adam of Dryburgh, *Anglus natione*, but *nunc in regno Scottorum positi*,[2] and the author of the *Cronica de Mailros*, who, writing in Scotland, described English Bede as *decus et gloria **nostrae** gentis Beda uenerabilis*.[3]

2   See below p. 157.
3   See below pp. 181–4.

RALPH ABBOT OF MELROSE:
'EULOGIUM
IN IOCELINUM EPISCOPUM GLASGUENSEM'

After the death of Jocelin Bishop of Glasgow in 1199 Ralph Abbot of Melrose composed the following Eulogy, which survives in Oxford, Bodleian Library, MS Rawlinson G.38, folios 55r–56v, written in script of the early thirteenth century.[1] Capital letters and punctuation marks in boldface represent features of the manuscript. I have arranged the text *per cola et commata* and marked the rhythms of the cursus.

1   Uniuersis **S**ancte **M**atris **E**cclésie filiis [.]
       precipue autem uíris **R**elìgiósis [.]
       ad quos presentis scripti página peruénerit :
       Fráter **R**[adúlphus].
       Séruus **S**eruòrum **D**éi [.]   5
       Apud **M**elros Deo séruiéncium :
       Humilisque eiusdem **L**óci **C**onuèntus [**Á**bbas .]
       Salutem et óraciónes .   8

2   **M**undane uarietatis . **E**cliptica uicissitudo parte quicquid orbis in qualibet
         mortales ante conspectus quasi próuehit àd pe*rfèctum*
       e lapsu temporis ad memoriam satis exigui irreparabilem uelud ex inuidia
         deiécit in de*féctum* .   10

3   **S**iquidem glorie cuiuslibet terrene inquam quantumlibet inclita celsitudo
         in hac incolatus nostri breuitate propter productionem aliquam si cui forte
         diuina uideatur : in moménto deícitur .
       relictaque sui uix mencione nullo nature beneficio . nulla ingenii sagacitate in
         statum omnino pristinum réstitúitur .

4   **S**ic ipsius nature sic omne artis opificium operosa quamuis industria diligénter
         excúltum :
       ab ipsa statim sui consummacione festinat sub breuitáte consúmi .

5   **D**ecorem enim primo inditum paulatim exuens fuco quodam deformitátis
         ob*dúcitur*   15
       nec ea assiduitate ad summum sue statim essencie per increménta prouéh*itur*
       qua per detrimenta continua incessanter ad non ésse de*dúcitur* .

6   **I**n his autem omnibus imperiosa sub celo pre omnibus humane sublimitas
         excellencie lapsu deiectióre collí*ditur* .
       et quo ad eminenciorem gloriam concenderit : eo dimissius in térram detrú*ditur* .

1   *BCLL*, no. 1022 p. 284. *Lives of S. Ninian and S. Kentigern*, ed. A.P. Forbes, Historians of Scotland V (Edinburgh: Edmonston and Douglas, 1874), pp. 308–12.

7 Indidit enim homini inter subcelestia dingnitas condiciónis impérium . 20
   set induxit ex delicto condicio mortalitátis excídium .
8 Vnde et quanto potencius plurima sibi subicit ex imperio quantoque
      admiracior in prelacióne conspícitur :
   tanto miserabilior compáret in cásu .
   tantoque abiectius córruit èx deféctu .
9 A turribus in térram prostérnitur : 25
   a sericis in cilícium deuóluitur :
   a purpura in púluerem depónitur .
10 Sicque demum a superstitum conspéctu subtráctus :
   sub cespite collocatur beniuolis pro beneficiis dolórem :
   Inuidis autem relínquens detràctiónem . 30
11 Sic est humane glorie calamitósa felícitas .
12 Sic procurat perniciem comes assidua ex commisso contrácta calámitas .
13 Sic defectum inducit irreparabilem ruine semper exposita officiósa fragílitas .
14 Sic in nostra dissolucione trihumphat hostis publici consíliósa callíditas .
15 Hinc misera nostre mortalitátis oppréssio . 35
16 Hinc miserabilis oppressionis nostre désolácio
   dum in diebus hiis dierum nostrorum décus et glória
   Venerabilis Pater Iocelínus Epíscopus
   redeunte utinam in celo spiritu carnis ónus depósitum
   nobis reliquit in térra deponéndum . 40
17 Cuius quanto fuit apud homines commendabilior cónuersácio :
   tanto nobis et specialius ei subditis et coniunctiori deuocione deuinctis maior
      conquestiónis occásio :
   et ad quos deuoluta fuerit : fauorabilior debet esse cómmemorácio .
18 Ipsa enim adholescencie ipsius primordia quasi certa future in eo dingnitatis
      indícia prèsingnábant .
   et insingne quiddam innuencia : quasi ex designacione diuina Ecclesie Dei
      rectorem . ydóneum prèparábant . 45
19 Ita siquidem erat in géstu conpósitus .
   In Áctu próuidus .
   In Sermóne discrétus
   ut ipsa morum conposicio singularem ei quemdam fauorem in oculis intuéncium
      cònpararet .
20 Vnde et adhuc inpubes ad sanctam Melrossensem Ecclesiam tanquam a Domino
      míssus accéssit 50
   et in conspectu sancti patris Waldeui cui Spiritus Domini bónus . non défuit .
   specialem gratiam promeruit intra dies paucos ab eo ad conuersiónem illéctus :
   et post susceptum habitum quasi ex presagio de die in diem pro sanctorum
      sub discreto patre disciplinate conuersancium arbitrio mágis diléctus .
21 Vir quippe sanctus ut quodam quasi uaticinio consilii celestis infallibilem
      prouidenciam mangnum aliquid circa iuuenem disposuisse préosténderet
   quem in familiarem et filium specialiter ádoptáuerat 55
22 Quamlibet ei fere monasterii admini•tracionem ut in singulis excercitátum rédderet :
   suis successiue tempóribus còmmittébat .
23 Sicque factum est ut post decessum patris beningnissimi elapsis Annis aliquot
      uno interposito quasi sic uir sanctus destinasset concurrentibus uotis omnium
      secundus ípse succéderet .

24 Qui patris ac predecessoris e uestigio uias secutus in gerendis ita negociis
    circumspécte agébat
    in regendis fratribus regulariter ádeo ìncedébat :   60
    quod sicut ex religióne modéstia :
    ita mansuetudo creuisse in eo uidebatur ex prépositúra .

25 Ea tamen in omnibus discrecio seruabatur ut et delictis disciplína non párceret
    et delinquentibus corrépcio nòn deésset .

26 In corrigendis ac ulciscendis excessibus moderacione adhibita ut cum admissi
    immanitas debitam quandoque seueritátem expéteret .   65
    Agendi micius si qua reperiri pósset occásio :
    rigorem ordinis consueta beníngnitas tèmperáret .

27 Erat etiam tante apud subditos réueréncie :
    tantumque terroris eius inferébat offénsa :
    ut ipsius non solum metus set et mencio a conmittendo plerósque conpésceret   70
    qui tam ex singulari industria quam ex officiorum fere omnium ádministràcióne .
    cogitaciones eum quorumlibet congnoscere árbitrabántur .

28 Talis ac tante uir sagacitatis et prudencie tocius ordinis Cisterciénsis grátiam .
    tocius in quo manebat rengni fauorem facile sibi quasi ex debito cónciliáuerat .

29 Post modicum autem set decursis annis aliquibus dáto témpore   75
    cum defuncto pio patre Engerrámo Epíscopo
    sancta uacaret Glasguénsis Ecclésia
    ad populi peticionem . a clero Ecclesie canonice et unanímiter eléctus
    et illustrissimi Scottorum Regis Willelmi incontinenti quasi ex ipsius principis
    deuocione cum consensu grátiam adéptus :
    non prius ad ipsam accessit ecclesiam non ante susceptam ádministràciónem :   80
    quam et a sancto Cisterciensi Capitulo eius approbarétur eléctio .
    et ipsius generalis concilii suscipiendi regimen ipse precéptum accepísset .

30 Sicque sanctissimi patris cuius memoria in bénedictióne est .
    Alexandri pape tercii autoritate uices summi pontificis circa hóc exequénte .
    Venerabile Patre Escillo Dacorum Archiepiscopo qui pro Ecclesie sue
    libertate eo témpore èxulábat   85
    in sancta Clareuallensi Ecclesia tanquam manibus Apostolicis consecraciónem
    accépit .

31 Nec eum dingnitatis excellencia extollere in áliquo uìdebátur
    set eadem in omnibus grauitáte seruáta
    non géstus fráctior
    non aspéctus elácior   90
    non incéssus solúcior
    nec in aliquo uel méntis hábitus .
    uel corporis ipsius status incomposícior hàbebátur .

32 Cum tamen ei in omnibus fauere adeo fortúna uiderétur :
    ut tam principalis excellencia quam dingnitatis Ecclesiastice réueréncia .   95
    sicud et populi commúnis afféctus :
    pro maiore metueret pro patre uénerarétur .

33 Quot labores et quanta pericula pro Ecclésia súa .
    pro ipso etiam Rege Rengnoque suo frequenter susceperit et sústinúerit :
    quam liberaliter in exequendis Rengni negociis facultates súas effúderit :   100
    remote etiam prouíncie nòn ingnórant .

34   Ecclesiam suam in suscepcione sua satis exiguam quam excellenter **á**mpli*áuerit*
    quam decencia per loca in diocesi edificia constr*úxerit* :
    quantis quibusque libertatibus sicud et possessionibus rem a**ú**gment*áuerit*
    futura post multos annos témpora *nòn* tacébu*nt* .   105

35   Quanta fuerit carnis eius mundicia effantur ipsíus famìliáres .
    qui uel notam cuiusquam inquinamenti per ullam unquam coniecturam
          póterant sùspicári .

36   Assidentibus ei omnibus mensa quam dapsilis nota quam multis cópia pròtestátur .
    cum appositorum affluencia cibum ipse sibi potumque mínistr*áuerit* :
    ut non sacietatem set sustentacionem suo dumtaxat córpori pròcur*áret* .   110

37   Ordinem de quo assumptus est Cisterciensem quanta deuocióne compléxus s*it*
    quanta diligencia in se feruenter óbseru*áuerit*
    consueta uestium asperitas suo ex appetitu ciborum inuariata commúnitas reténta .
    etiam in clero circa has horas singulas regularium Idémptitas ìndicába*nt* .

38   Cuius obseruancie quam perseueranter animum óblig*áuerit* .   115
    dissimuláre non pot*érunt*
    ad quos ipse quiue ad eum eiusdem ordinis professores aut casu aut uisitandi grátia
          pèruen*érunt*.

39   Tanta erat eis cum eo familiaritas ut non prelatum aut pontificem set
          confratrem se fratribus in omni humilitáte exib*éret* .

40   Sua eis ita munifice communicabat ut acceptorum omnium singulis débitor
          uìder*étur* .

41   Si quid eis erat apud eum negocii communiter tractabat . ut suum
          éxequeb*átur* .   120

42   Qui se esse in propriis tunc démum reputába*t*
    cum data conferendi copia uel ad eum plúres confl*úerent* .
    uel ipse apud eos suis in locis aliquándo morar*étur* .

43   Precipuam autem gratiam apud religiósos assecútu*s* :
    summe apud subditos reuerencie . egregie apud omnes uéneracióni*s* .   125
    exactis in pontificatu **a**nnis circiter uiginti quattuor labores diutinos iússus
          est tèrmin*áre* .

44   Soluto itaque in capite Ieiunii quod ad diem pertinebat in prouincia
          sollémniter officio :
    Ecclesiam suam Melrossensem **q**uinta feria uisitauit ex desiderio eo
          destinátus ad réqui*em* :
    ubi suscepto habitu professus fuerat réligió*nem* .

45   Nocteque ipsa graui tactus molestia : sexta statim feria lecto decubuit et
          uelud infixa téli cúspi*de*   130
    ad conpunctionem letaliter percússus in pécto*re* :
    primos illos tredecim penitentie dies a sexta ílla féri*a*
    usque ad quartam rursum secunde quadragesimalis ebdomade feriam
          accepit ád purgació*nem* .

46   Dispositisque prudenter omnibus data assistentibus ac percepta bénedicci*óne* .
    retenta usque articulum tam memória quàm loqué*la* :   135
    celeste depositum ad superna remisit decimasexta uidelicet Kaléndas Apríli*s* .
    qua die ante **a**nnos circiter **q**uinquaginta in eodem monasterio habitum
          susceperat réligió*nis* .
    sextaque fe**r**ia decimaquarta Kalendas Aprilis qua die post emensum probácionis
          ánnum

Accepta monachali benediccione ibidem professiónem fécerat
et morum stabilitátem promíserat 140
in tumulo est uenerabíliter còllocátus .
quem ipse sibi ipsa in Ecclesia ante annos aliquot fécerat prèparári .

47 Quod si casus huiuscemodi uictu quasi diuino próueniéntes
circa ueterem aliquem diebus antiquis uelud ad nótum . concurríssent
et detractorum ora concludere et malingnandi materia omnino precídere
uìderéntur . 145
et ad perhennem memoriam scripto forte commendábili tràderétur .

48 Quoniam autem in hac peregrinacione constitutis de consuetudine ad leuam
léue est dèclináre
fraternitatem uestram cum lácrimis èxorámus
ut insufficiencie nostre suspiriis oracionum uestrarum accédant subsídia
et ad optinendam pie recordacionis patri beningnissimo perfectam summe
clemencie misericordiam supplicacionibus assíduis sùffragéntur . 150
pro nobis et nostris in conspectu Altissimi et uos oráre precámur
qui pro uobis et uestris fraterne karitatis ex debito deuóte supplicámus .

49 Valéte in Xpísto . 153

19 i.e. conscenderit. 29 beniuollis *with first* l *erased.* 35 miseria *with second* i
underdotted for erasure. 41 fu/uit. 79 W. 85 *above* tempore uel is.126 xx[ti]iiii[or].
133 x[a]lis. 136 xvi[o]. 138 vit[a]q;. xiiij[o].

83 Ecclesiasticus XLV 1.

1 To all holy mother Church's sons,
especially, however, to the religious men
to whom the page of the present script shall have come,
Brother Ralph,
servant of the servants of God 5
serving God at Melrose,
and humble [abbot] of the convent of the same place,
[sends] greeting and prayers. 8

2 The ecliptic change of worldly variety, in whatever part of the world, whatever it
brings before mortal gazes, as if to perfection,
from the lapse of little enough time, as if from envy it has cast down into defect
irreparable to the memory. 10

3 If on the one hand, I say, the renowned heavenliness of a certain earthly glory, on
account of any lengthening, should be seen to a certain degree to someone as
by chance divine, in this brevity of our indwelling, in a moment it is cast down,
and with scarcely any mention of itself left, with no benefit of nature, with no
sagacity of intellect, it is restored entirely to the pristine state.

4 So of its very nature, so all work of art, though wrought diligently by laborious
industry,
from its very consummation immediately hastens to be consumed in brevity.

5 For putting off the beauty put on a little at first, it is led away in a certain
smoke of deformity, 15
and not by assiduity is it brought forward by increments to the highest point
of its own being immediately,
by which through continuous detriments incessantly it is led away to non-being.

6   In all these things, however, the commanding sublimity of human excellence
         beyond all things under heaven is shattered by a more dejected lapse,
     and by that by which it would ascend to a more eminent glory, by that it is
         trodden down to earth to a lower level.

7   For the dignity of [his] condition put on man among creatures under the
         heavens a command,   20
     but from sin the condition of mortality led him to destruction.

8   Whence and by so much as he subjects very many things to himself by
         command and by so much as he is looked on as more admirable in prelacy,
     by that much he seems more miserable in the fall,
     and by that much he has collapsed more abjectly from the defect.

9   From towers he is laid low on to the ground;   25
     from silks he is wrapped up into goats' hair;
     from purple he is deposed into dust.

10   And so finally drawn down from the sight of those standing above
     he is placed under a sod leaving behind grief in exchange for benevolent benefits,
     detraction, however, from the envious.   30

11   So is the calamitous felicity of human glory.

12   So does calamity, an assiduous companion contracted from committed sin
         procure destruction.

13   So does exposed importunate fragility always lead on to the irreparable
         defect of ruin.

14   So does the counsel-giving craftiness of the public enemy [*i.e.* Satan]
         triumph in our dissolution.

15   From this the pitiful oppression of our mortality.   35

16   From this the pitiable desolation of our oppression,
     while in these days the ornament and glory of our days,
     the venerable father Bishop Jocelin,
     with the spirit returning, o that it would, into heaven, has left the burden
         of flesh laid down,
     to be laid down by us in the earth.   40

17   By so much as whose conversation was more commendable among men,
     by that much the greater occasion of lament to us both more specially
         subject to him
     and bound by more conjunct devotion,
     and to those to whom it will have devolved there ought to be more favourable
         commemoration.

18   For the very beginnings of the adolescence of the very man foresignaled as it
         were certain indications of future dignity in him
     and suggesting a certain outstanding sign as if from divine designation they
         were preparing a suitable rector of the Church of God.   45

19   On the one hand so composed was he in bearing,
     foresightful in act,
     discreet in speech,
     that the very composition of his morals showed a certain singular favour to
         him in the eyes of those looking on.

20   Whence even as yet before the age of puberty he approached to the holy
         Church of Melrose as if sent from the Lord   50

and in the sight of the holy father Waltheof, to whom the good Spirit of the
    Lord was not absent,

he merited special grace within a few days, enticed to conversion by him,

and after the habit undertaken, as if by presage from day to day loved more
    for the judgement of the holy men conversing with discipline under the
    discreet father.

21   Indeed the holy man, as if by a certain prophecy of heavenly counsel
        would reveal in advance that the youth had disposed an infallible
        foresight about some great thing,

[the youth] whom he had adopted specially as a familiar and a son.   55

22   Almost any administration of the monastery [Waltheof] would give to him as
        exercised by individual men

[Jocelin] completed successively in his own [*i.e.* Waltheof's] times.

23   And so it was done that with a certain number of years elapsed after the
        decease of the most benign father, with one man interposed, as if the
        holy man had so determined that the very man should succeed as
        second, with the vows of all concurring [lit. 'running together'].

24   Who, having followed the ways from the track of the father and predecessor
        used to act so circumspectly in conducting business affairs,

he used to proceed so according to rule in ruling the brothers,   60

that just as modesty from [his professed] religion,

so clemency was seen to have grown in him from [his] being placed in command.

25   Yet that discretion was preserved in all things so that he would not be
        sparing from discipline for delicts,

and correption was not absent for delinquents.

26   In correcting and avenging excesses, with moderation exhibited, so that the
        enormity of an admitted offence would demand at some time due severity, 65

if an occasion of acting more mildly could in any way be found,

his customary benignity would temper the rigour of the order.

27   He was even of such great reverence among his subordinates,

and an offence entailed so much of terror of him,

that not only the fear but even the mention of him would restrain many from
        committing an offence,   70

who as much from his singular industry as from his administration of almost all
        of the duties

judged him to understand the thoughts of each of them.

28   A man of such and so great sagacity and prudence had obtained the grace of the
        whole Cistercian order,

in which he maintained the favour of the whole realm easily as if owed to him.

29   After a little while, however, but with a few years passed, at the given time, 75
    when with the holy father Bishop Ingelram dead,
    the holy Church of Glasgow lay vacant,[2]

at the petition of the people canonically and unanimously elected by the
    clergy of the Church,[3]

and having secured grace as if with the unrestrained devotion of the most
    illustrious King of the Scots William, with the consent of the same prince, ·

2   from 2 February 1174.
3   23 May 1174.

he did not approach the same Church nor its undertaken administration
    before   80
his election would be approved also by the holy Cistercian chapter,
and he would receive the precept of the general council of the same for
    undertaking the rule.

30   And so of the most holy father whose memorial is in a blessing,
seeking concerning this the functions of the highest pontiff, by the authority
    of Pope Alexander III,
from the venerable father Eskill Archbishop of the Danes, who was in exile at
    that time for the liberty of his own Church,   85
he received consecration as from apostolic hands in the holy Church of
    Clairvaux.[4]

31   Nor was the excellence of dignity seen to carry him away in any respect,
but with the same gravity preserved in all things,
not more abrupt of gestures,
not more elated of aspect,   90
.not more disjointed of gait,
nor in any respect either of habit of mind
or of the state of his body was he considered irregular.

32   Yet since fortune was seen in all respects to favour him to so high a degree
that as much his principal excellence as reverence of his ecclesiastical dignity   95
just as also the affection of the common people
feared [him] as a greater man, venerated [him] as a father.

33   How many labours and what great perils for his own Church
for himself, even for his own king and realm, he would frequently undertake and
    sustain,
how liberally in pursuing the business affairs of the realm he would pour
    out his own faculties,   100
even remote provinces do not fail to know.

34   How excellently he amplified his own Church, little enough, by his own
    undertaking, how he constructed buildings in fitting places in the diocese,
with what great possessions and with what liberties just so he also augmented
    his concern
future times after many years will not be silent about.   105

35   How great was the cleanness of his flesh his own familiars say,
or those who could suggest a note of any impurity through any inference
    at any time.

36   To all those sitting next to him the table, how abundant, the supply, how well
    known to many, bears witness,
since he himself would serve the food and drink for himself with a large
    number of those placed round him,
so that he would procure not satiety but at most sustenance for his own body.   110

37   With what great devotion he embraced the Cistercian order by which
    he was taken up,
with what great diligence he fervently kept watch over himself

4   Whitsunday, 1 June 1175.

the customary roughness of his clothes, a common quality retained unvaried
   from his appetite for food,
also the continual sameness of observance of monastic rules with reference
   to the individual offices marked him out among the clergy.

38 To the observance of which how perseveringly he bound his spirit   115
they could not misrepresent,
he to those professors of the same order or those who came to him either by
   chance or for the sake of visiting.

39 So great was the familiarity to them with him that he would show himself
   not a prelate or a pontiff but a fellow brother to the brothers in all humility.

40 He used to share his own things with them so munificently that he seemed a
   debtor to each of all those he accepted.

41 If there was any matter of business concerning him he used to treat it in
   common with them as he pursued his own.   120

42 Who considered himself to be among his own only
when either many flowed together to him with a given opportunity of conferring
or he himself would remain with them for awhile in their own places.

43 Having achieved, however, especial grace among religious men,
of the highest reverence among subordinates, of outstanding veneration
   among all,   125
with about twenty-four years in his pontificate completed[5] he was ordered
   to end his long-lasting labours.

44 Therefore with the office which pertained to the day at the beginning of the
   [Lenten] Fast completed solemnly in the province,[6]
he visited his own Church of Melrose on the fifth day[7] out of desire, destined for
   rest in that place
where with the habit received he had professed religion.

45 And on the very night touched by a grave illness he lay down in bed
   immediately on the sixth day,[8] and as with the cusp of a spear infixed,   130
struck lethally in the breast for compunction,[9]
he received from that sixth day those first thirteen days of penitence,
until the fourth day again of the second week of the forty-day-period for
   purgation.[10]

46 With all things prudently disposed, and with a blessing given and received
   by those attending,
with memory as much as speech retained until the critical moment,   135
he sent back the heavenly deposit [i.e. the soul] to the supernal regions,
   understand, on the sixteenth of the kalends of April,[11]
on which day about fifty years before in the same monastery he had
   received the habit of religion,[12]

5 i.e. the twenty-four years from 1175 to 1199.
6 i.e. Ash Wednesday, 3 March 1199. The province is that of the Church of Glasgow.
7 i.e. Thursday, 4 March.
8 i.e. Friday, 5 March.
9 with play on 'pricking', 'stabbing'.
10 i.e. the thirteen days from Friday 5 March to Wednesday 17 March inclusive.
11 i.e. Wednesday, 17 March 1199.
12 A.D. 1147.

and on the sixth day, the fourteenth of the kalends of April, on which day,
    after a year of probation elapsed,[13]
with the benediction of a monk received in the same place that he had made
    a profession,
and had promised stability of behavioural customs,   140
he was venerably placed in a tomb,
which he himself had made to be prepared for himself in the same Church
    several years before.

47   Which if issues of this sort coming as if from a divine way of life
should concur as to a good reputation concerning a certain old man in the
    last days,
they should be seen both to stop up the mouths of detractors and to deprive
    them altogether of matter for maligning   145
and he should be handed on to perennial memory perhaps in a commendable
    script.

48   Since, however, it is a light matter for those assigned to this pilgrimage to
    decline from custom to the left,
we pray your fraternity with tears
that the supports of your prayers approach with sighs to our insufficiency
and undertake with assiduous supplications for obtaining the perfect pity of
    the highest clemency for the most benign father of holy recollection,   150
for us and ours we beseech you also to pray in the sight of the Most High,
we who supplicate devoutly for you and yours from the owed debt of fraternal
    charity.

49   Farewell in Christ.   153

The text has been carefully written and carefully corrected in a script nearly, if not exactly, contemporary with the date of composition. This affords fair certainty about details of the original orthography. The scribe wrote *s*; in lines 21, 70, 75, but *set* in full in line 88. For *-gn-* the scribe wrote *-ngn-* consistently, implying nasalization. Consistent scribal use of *c* for *t* reflects authorial pronunciation as *s*, as one infers from rhymes of *oppressio* 35 with *consolacio* 36 and of *conuersacio* 41 with *occasio* 42. Consistent with this is pronunciation of *h* in the Francophone fashion, as in *trihumphat* 34, *adholescencie* 44, and *perhennem* 146.[14]

The composition was probably delivered and received as an impressive specimen of forensic oratory, but the Salutation implies that the author hoped for a written transmission on *presentis scripti pagina*. The Salutation contains eight lines (8 x 1) and 32 words (8 x 4) centred at *Frater* | *Radulphus*, eighty-eight syllables (8 x 11) centred in the same place. From | *Uniuersis* to *frater Radulphus* | inclusive there are seventeen words, and from | *frater Radulphus* to *oraciones* | inclusive there are seventeen words, the triangular number 1+2+3+4+5+6+7+8

---

13 *i.e.* Friday, 19 March 1148.
14 According to the *Year Book of 32 Edward I* (A.D. 1304), p. 129: pas en Ersam e noun en Hersam ... ; Hengham: 'H nest pas lettre'.

+9+10+11+12+13+14+15+16+17 equalling 153, the number of lines in the composition.[15]

Reckoning letters as numbers the name *MELROS* bears a numerical value of 12+5+11+17+14+18 or 77. From the beginning of the Salutation to *eiusdem loci conuentus* inclusive there are seventy-seven syllables. The name *IOCELINUS* bears a numerical value of 9+14+3+5+11+9+13+20+18 or 102. In sentence 16 the 102nd letter is the *I* of *Iocelinus*.[16]

It is hard to know at this remove whether the author expected hearers, as distinct from readers, to recognize the beginning of a great chiastic passage after nineteen sentences and forty-nine lines and 365 words of introduction. The nineteen sentences represent the nineteen years of the cycle during which solar and lunar years come into synchrony. The forty-nine lines, like the forty-nine sentences of the entire composition, represent seven weeks of years (7 x 7), the introduction to a jubilee.

50	A1	Melrossensem Ecclesiam
52	A2	intra dies paucos
53	A3	susceptum habitum
53	A4	die
58	A5	elapsis annis aliquot
62	A6	uidebatur
67	A7	beningnitas
71	B	singulari industria
73	C1	ordinis
73	C2	Cisterciensis
74	D	rengni
76	E1	pio patre Engerramo Episcopo
77	E2	ecclesia
78	E3	ecclesie
8	E4	canonice et unanimiter electus
79	F	Scottorum Regis Willelmi ... deuocione
80	G	non prius ad ipsam accessit ecclesiam non ante susceptam administracionem
81	H	quam et a sancto Cisterciensi Capitulo eius approbaretur electio
82	G'	et ipsius generalis concilii suscipiendi regimen ipse preceptum accepisset
84	F'	Alexandri pape tercii autoritate
85	E'1	uenerabile patre Escillo Dacorum Archiepiscopo
85	E'2	ecclesie
86	E'3	ecclesia
86	E'4	consecracionem accepit
99–100	D'	rengnoque ... rengni

15   See above pp. 4, 51, 85, 89, 96, 102, 115 and below pp. 150, 152, 155, 186–7.
16   See above pp. 5, 8, 22, 35, 58–61, 84, 89, 95 and below pp. 159–60, 174, 184.

111	C'1	ordinem
111	C'2	Cisterciensem
112–114	B'	quanta diligencia ... singulas
127	A'1	Ecclesiam ... Melrossensem
127	A'2	quinta feria
128	A'3	suscepto habitu
137	A'4	die
142	A'5	ante annos aliquot
145	A'6	uiderentur
149	A'7	beningnissimo

The 153 lines of text divide by sesquioctave ratio 9:8 at 81 and 72, at the crux of the chiasmus in line 81.

Composition in calendrical numbers is apparent from the nineteen sentences and forty-nine lines and 365 words before the beginning of the chiasmus. There is another cluster of calendrical features in in lines 136–8:

> celeste depositum ad superna remisit decimasexta uidelicet Kalendas Aprilis qua die ante annos circiter quinquaginta in eodem monasterio habitum susceperat religionis sextaque feria decimaquarta Kalendas Aprilis qua die post emensum probacionis annum ...

Consistent with *decimasexta kalendas Aprilis*, 17 March, is the seventeenth syllable, *decima | sexta*. In line 136, *celeste depositum ad superna remisit decimasexta uidelicet Kalendas Aprilis.*, there are from the *c* of *celeste* to the punctuation point after *Aprilis.* inclusive seventy-six letters and punctuation point and spaces between words, 17 March being the seventy-sixth day of the year. Consistent with *sextaque feria decimaquarta kalendas Aprilis*, 19 March, is the nineteenth letter *decima | quarta*. Beginning to count at | *kalendas Aprilis*, the fiftieth letter is the last *a* of *quinquaginta*. From *qua die | ante* to *qua | die post* there are fifty syllables.

Bishop Jocelin died on the sixteenth of the kalends of April, 17 March 1199. Ralph states that *ante annos* **circiter** *quinquaginta in eodem monasterio habitum susceperat religionis*, 'about fifty' but exactly fifty-two years earlier, in A.D. 1147, a fact not unrelated to Ralph's fifty-two lines of prose before *et post susceptum habitum quasi ex presagio de die in diem pro sanctorum sub discreto patre disciplinate conuersancium arbitrio magis dilectus*, at the chiastic pair to this passage. The *sextaque feria decimaquarta Kalendas Aprilis qua die post emensum probacionis annum* of which Ralph wrote was 19 March, which in A.D. 1148 fell on a Friday. There are good reasons to trust the punctilio of such a writer.[17]

From the space before *Uniuersis* to the space after *Xpisto* inclusive there exactly 9999 letters and spaces between words in the entire composition.

---

17 See above pp. 8, 23, 36, 59, 61, 74, 83–5, 89, 96, 110 and below pp. 150, 160, 174, 182–4.

A BISHOP OF WHITHORN:
THE PROFESSION OF GILLA ALDAN
TO THURSTIN ARCHBISHOP OF YORK

London, British Library, MS Cotton Claudius B.III preserves on folio 133v a letter from Pope Honorius to Gilla Aldan, Bishop Elect of Candida Casa.[1]

[H]ONORIUS EPISCOPUS SÉRVUS SERVÒRUM DÉI .
DILECTO FILIO . ELECTO DE CÁNDIDA CÁSA .
SALUTEM ET APOSTOLICAM BÉNEDICTIÓNEM .

Cui alii a Domino preésse concéditur .
nulla suis digne subesse prelatis supérbia cònuincátur .
Ideoque per presentia scripta tíbi mandámus
ut ad karissimum fratrem nostrum Turstinum Eboracensem
   Archiepiscopum tanquam ad proprium metropolitanum tuum
   consecrándus accédas
et ab ipsius manu presente Sancti Spiritus gratia cum humilitatis
   deuotione consecratiónem accípias
Data Laterani . quinto ídus Decémbri .

HONORIUS BISHOP, SERVANT OF THE SERVANTS OF GOD,
TO A BELOVED SON, [BISHOP-]ELECT OF CANDIDA CASA,
SALUTATION AND APOSTOLIC BENEDICTION.

To him to whom it is granted by the Lord to stand out [lit. 'be before']
no pride should be demonstrated in worthily submitting to [lit. 'be
   under'] his own prelates.
And therefore through these present writings we order you
that to be consecrated you approach our dearest brother Thurstin
   Archbishop of York as your own metropolitan
and from the hand of that very man with the grace of the Holy Spirit
   present, you receive consecration with the devotion of humility.
Given at the Lateran on the fifth of the ides of December.

1   Haddan and Stubbs, *Councils*, vol. II pt I pp. 24–5. Lawrie, *Early Scottish Charters*, no. LXIII pp. 53–4.

The same manuscript preserves on folio 24r the oldest of the extant *acta* of the Bishops of Whithorn, the Profession made by Gilla Aldan to Thurstin Archbishop of York.[2]

[D]OMINO ET PATRI SUO REVERÉNDO **T**ÚRSTI*NO*
DEI GRATIA **E**BORACENSIS PROVINCIE MÉTROPOLITÁ*NO* :
GILLA **A**LDAN **H**UMILIS ELECTUS **C**ÁNDIDE **C**ÁSE
SALUTEM ET OBÉDIÉNTIAM .

Cognoui tam scriptis pátrum auctént*icis*   5
quam ueredicis antiquorum uirorum téstimón*iis* ,
quod episcopus **C**andide **C**ase ab antiquo debeat ad matrem suam
   Eboracensem metrópolim respíce*re*
et ei in hiis que ad Deum pertinent óbtemperá*re* .
Qua propter ego **G**illa **A**ldan **C**andide **C**áse eléctu*s*
sancte **E**boracénsis **E**cclés*ie*   10
et tíbi Túrst*ine*
et successoribus tuis canonice ínstituénd*is*
debitam subiectionem a sanctis pátribus ìnstitút*am*
et canonicam obédiénti*am*
me amod*o*   15
seruatúrum promítt*o* .

1 .T. . 11 Tustine.

TO HIS OWN LORD AND REVEREND FATHER THURSTIN
BY THE GRACE OF GOD METROPOLITAN OF THE PROVINCE OF YORK
GILLA ALDAN HUMBLE [BISHOP-]ELECT OF CANDIDA CASA
SALUTATION AND OBEDIENCE.

I know as well from authentic writings of the Fathers   5
as from truth–uttering testimonies of ancient men
that the Bishop of Candida Casa from ancient time ought to have a
   regard for the mother [Church] of York
and to be submissive to it in these things which pertain to God.
On which account I, Gilla Aldan [Bishop-]Elect of Candida Casa,
to the holy Church of York   10
and to you, Thurstin,
and to your successors to be instituted canonically
the owed subjection instituted by the holy Fathers
and canonical obedience
from me from now on   15
I promise to be bound to keep.

2   *BCLL*, no. 1110 p. 300. Haddan and Stubbs, *Councils*, vol. II pt I p. 25. Lawrie, *Early Scottish Charters*, no. LXIV p. 54.

In the text of the Profession proper the composer has played with the ratios 1:1 and 2:1 in that the second sentence has twice as many lines as the first, 8:4, but exactly as many words, 32:32. The sixty-four words divide by duple ratio at 43 and 21. The twenty-first word is *Eboracensem* 7, after which *Eboracensis* 10 is the twenty-first word. After *Eboracensis Ecclesie* | 10 there are twenty-one words to the end of the text.

The composer has played with sesquitertian ratio 4:3, by which the sixty-four words divide at 37 and 27. The thirty-seventh word is *Gilla Aldan* | 9. From | *Candide Case* 7 to *Candide Case* | 9 inclusive there are twenty-seven words. From | *ego Gilla Aldan* 9 to *me* | 15 inclusive there are twenty-seven words, which divide in turn by sesquitertian ratio at 15 and 12, at *tibi Turstine* | 11. The number 12 divides in turn by sesquitertian ratio at 7 and 5. From | *tibi Turstine* 11 to *et successoribus tuis* | 12 inclusive there are five words.

The composer has played with sesquioctave ratio 9:8, by which the sixty-four words divide at 34 and 30. There are thirty-four words between *debeat* | 7 and | *debitam* 13.

The sixty-four words divide by one-ninth and eight-ninths at 7 and 57. There are seven words before | *antiquorum* 6. There are seven words between *antiquorum* | 6 and | *antiquo* 8. There are seven words from | *instituendis* 12 to *institutam* | 13, after which there are seven words to the end of the text.

Including the Salutation the entire text contains eighty-four words, which divide by extreme and mean ratio at 52 and 32. The major part, consisting of the Salutation and the first sentence, contains fifty-two words, and the minor part, consisting of the second sentence, contains thirty-two words. There are fifty-two words between *Eboracensis* | 2 and | *Eboracensis* 10. After *Eboracensis* | 2 the thirty-second word is *Eboracensem* | 7. From | *metropolitano* 2 to *metropolim* | 7 inclusive there are thirty-two words. After *patrum* | 5 the fifty-second word is *patribus* | 13.

The eighty-four words divide by sesquioctave ratio at 44 and 40. There are forty-four words from | *Dei* 2 to *Deum* | 8 inclusive. There are forty-four words between *electus* | 3 and | *electus* 9. After *Gilla Aldan* | 3 the forty-fourth word is *Gilla Aldan* | 9. There are forty-four words from | *Candide Case* 3 to *Candide Case* | 9 inclusive, which divide in turn by 9:8 at 23 and 21. Between *Candide Case* | 7 and | *Candide Case* 9 there are twenty-three words.

If the manuscript represents correctly the name of the bishop as *Aldan*, it might be a reflex of Old English *Healf Dene*, Old Norse *Halfdan*, Latin *Haldanus*, that survives as the modern surname Haldane, appropriate to a part of the island subject to settlement by Scandinavians. But if the *l* misrepresents *i* the name is Gaelic *Gilla Aidan* 'Servant of Aidan', appropriate to the occupant of a see in a part of the island evangelized by Saint Aidan in the seventh century.

A BISHOP OF SAINT ANDREWS: GRANT OF ROBERT RELATING TO THE CHURCH OF COLDINGHAM

Here follows the oldest of the extant *acta* of the Bishops of Saint Andrews, a grant made from Robert to the Church of Coldingham on Saint Kenelm's Day, 17 July 1127.[1]

OMNIBUS SANCTE MATRIS ECCLÉSIE FIDÉLIBUS
CLÉRICIS ET LÁICIS
TAM PRESÉNTIBUS QUÀM FUTÚRIS .
RODBERTUS DEI GRATIA SANCTI ANDRÉE EPÍSCOPUS :
SALUTEM .   5

Notum sit uobis omnibus quod nos coram domino nóstro **R**ege **D**áuid .
et Turstino **A**rchiepiscopo **É**boracénsi .
et **R**annulfo . Dunelménsi . **E**píscopo :
Iohanne **E**píscopo **G**làscuénsi .
et **G**aufrido **A**bbate **S**áncti **A**lbáni .   10
et aliis múltis persónis
conuocauimus **A**lgarum . Priorem **S**ancti **C**uthbérti de Dunélmo
ante hostium ecclesie Sancti **I**ohannis Euuangelíste in **R**ókesburc :
ibique quantum ad episcopalem auctoritátem pértinet :
presentis carte attestatióne . et munímine .   15
clamauimus . concessimus . et cónfirmáuimus
ecclesiam de **C**oldingham liberam et quiétam in perpétuum
tam a nobis quam a successóribus nóstris
ab omni calumpnia . consuetudine et . **c**ana uel **c**uneuethe
atque ab ómni seruítio   20
quod ad nos pertinet uel ad súccessores nóstros .

Quare uolumus et episcopali auctoritáte confirmámus .
quatinus ecclésia de **C**óldingham
et omnes ecclésie uèl capélle

---

1   BCLL, no. 1057 p. 293. Raine, *North Durham*, app. no. CCCCXLVI p. 81. Lawrie, *Early Scottish Charters*, no. LXXIII pp. 59–60.

que amodo canonice ad ecclesiam Sancti Cuthberti pértinúerint :   25
libere et quiete sint ín perpétuum .
ab omni episcopali auxilio et cana et coneuethe .
ita ut liberiores et quietiores sint quam alique alie ecclesie ábbatiárum
que fuerint ín Lothoneío .

Et prohibemus ne aliquis amodo episcopus . archidiáconus .
   uèl decánus .   30
aliquam omnino ulterius consuetudinem . uel auxilium áb eis éxigat :
nisi forte gratis dáre uolúerint ;

Hec omnia fecimus prece . et consilio . dómini Règis Dáuid .
et predictorum episcoporum frátrum nostrórum
pro amore Sáncti Cuthbérti .   35
et fraternitate Dunelménsium mònachórum
.XVI. kaléndis Augústi .
in festo Sancti Kénelmi mártyris.
Anno ab incarnatione Domini $M^O.C^O.XX.VII$;

Téstibus preséntibus .   40
Rodbérto fratre méo .
Blahano presbítero de Lítun .
Aldulfo presbítero de Áldehamstoc .
Henrico presbítero de Leínhale .
Orm presbítero de Édenham .   45
et Iohanne presbitero de Lédgardesuúde .
Gódwino dapífero .
Godwino . Camerário méo .
et Balsan .
cum multis aliis . persónis relìgiósis   50
tam clericorum . quám laicórum .

Raine 17, 23 Collingham.

TO ALL FAITHFUL MEN OF HOLY MOTHER CHURCH,
CLERICS AND LAYMEN,
AS MUCH PRESENT AS FUTURE,
ROBERT BY THE GRACE OF GOD BISHOP OF SAINT ANDREWS
GREETING.   5

Be it known to you all that we, in the presence of our lord King David,
and Thurstin Archbishop of York,
and Ranulf Bishop of Durham,
John Bishop of Glasgow,

and Geoffrey Abbot of Saint Alban's,   10
and many other persons,
have called together Algar Prior of Saint Cuthbert's of Durham
before the door of the Church of Saint John the Evangelist in Roxburgh
and there, as far as pertains to episcopal authority
with the attestation and corroboration of the present charter   15
have claimed and conceded and confirmed
the Church of Coldingham free and quit in perpetuity
as much from us as from our successors
from every claim to title and custom and cain or conveth
and from every service   20
which pertains to us or to our successors.

For which reason we wish and by episcopal authority confirm
in respect of the Church of Coldingham
and all churches or chapels
which from now on may canonically pertain to the Church of
    Saint Cuthbert   25
should be free and quit in perpetuity
from every episcopal aid and cain and conveth
so that they may be freer and more quit than any other
    churches of abbeys[2]
which may be in Lothian.

And we prohibit that from now on any bishop, archdeacon, or dean 30
exact any further custom altogether or aid from them,
unless by chance they should wish to give it free.

All these things we have done at the prayer and counsel of the
    lord King David
and of the foresaid bishops our brothers
for the love of Saint Cuthbert   35
and the fraternity of the monks of Durham
on the sixteenth from the kalends of August
on the feast of Saint Kenelm the martyr
in the year from the Incarnation of the Lord 1127.

Witnesses being present: 40
Robert my brother
Blahan priest of Litton
Aldwulf priest of Aldhamstock

---

2   If this exhibits use of comparative for absolute, the sense is 'as free and as quit as any
    other churches'.

Henry priest of Leinhale
Orm priest of Ednam 45
and John priest of Ledgardswood
Godwin the steward
Godwin my chamberlain
and Balsan
with many other religious persons 50
as many clerics as laymen.

The composer arranged words and ideas in chiastic and parallel patterns.

```
 2  A    clericis et laicis
 3  B1    presentibus
 4  B2      Rodbertus
 6  C1       omnibus
 6  C2        domino
 6  C3          Rege Dauid
 8  C4           Dunelmensi
 8  D              episcopo
10  E               abbate
14  F1                episcopalem auctoritatem
16  F2                 confirmauimus
17  F3                  ecclesiam de Coldingham
17  F4                   liberam et quietam
17  F5                    in perpetuum
19  F6                    ab omni
19  F7                     cana uel cuneuethe
20  G                        atque ab omni seruitio
21  G'                        quod ad nos pertinet uel ad successores
22  F'1               episcopali auctoritate
22  F'2                 confirmamus
23  F'3                  ecclesia de Coldingham
26  F'4                   libere et quiete
26  F'5                    in perpetuum
27  F'6                    ab omni
27  F'7                     cana et coneuethe
28  E'               abbatiarum
30  D'              episcopus
33  C'1        omnia
33  C'2         domini
33  C'3          Regis Dauid
36  C'4           Dunelmensium
40  B'1    presentibus
41  B'2      Rodberto
51  A'  tam clericorum quam laicorum
```

The Salutation contains nineteen words, fifty-one syllables, and 144 letters and spaces and punctuation points. The 144 characters and spaces represent the square of 12, the twelfth number in the Fibonacci sequence 1–1–2–3–5–8–13 –21–34–55–89–144, the number of cubits in the walls of the heavenly Jerusalem, and part of the number of the elect in paradise.[3] The fifty-one syllables provide the key to the fifty-one lines of text.[4]

From | *Notum sit* to | *in festo Sancti Kenelmi* there are 196 words, Saint Kenelm's Day being 15 July, the 196th day of the year. From | *in festo Sancti Kenelmi* to the end there are fifty-two words, one for each week of the year.[5]

3   For other examples of this number see above pp. 8, 75, 96 and below p. 174.
4   See above pp. 4, 51, 85, 89, 96, 102, 115, 141 and below pp. 152, 155, 186–7.
5   See above pp. 8, 23, 36, 59, 61, 74, 83–5, 89, 96, 110, 142 and below pp. 160, 174, 182–4.

A BISHOP OF GLASGOW:
GRANT OF JOHN TO THE MONKS OF KELSO

Here follows the oldest of the extant *acta* of the Bishops of Glasgow, a grant made in A.D. 1144 from John to the monks of Kelso.[1] Capital letters and punctuation marks in boldface represent features of Edinburgh, National Library of Scotland, Advocates' MS 34.5.1, folio 74v.

OMNIBUS HAS LITTERAS VISÚRIS VEL AÙDITÚRIS /
IOHANNES DEI GRATIA **E**CCLESIE **G**LASGUENSIS MINÍSTER HÚMILIS/
SALUTEM IN DÓMINO PERPÉTUAM /

Sciatis me caritátis intúitu **,**
ad petitionem dómini méi **. DAVID R**egis **S**cottórum illústr*is* **,**   5
consilio et ammonitione uirorum timéntium **D**é*um* **,**
tam clericórum quam làicór*um* **,**
ex assensu et uoluntate totius **C**apituli méi concess*ísse* **,**
et hac carta méa confirmá*sse*
Abbati et **M**onachis **C**alchouensis **M**ónastérii **,**   10
Ecclesiam de **L**esmahagu cum tota paróchia súa **,**
prout eis libuerit inperpétuum òrdinánd*am* **.**
Monachos in eadem instituendo **, e**t ipsam cum **M**onachis íbidem
    sèruitúr*is*
ab omni exactione et subiectione **E**piscopali iure perpetuo liberam
    dimisísse et quié*tam* **.**
Hec autem acta sunt coram domino méo **R**ege **.**DÁVID**.**   15
et multis aliis tam cléricis quam láic*is* **.**
Anno ab incarnatione Domini / M^{o}.C^{o}.XL°.IIIJ^{o}**.,**   17

Innes 8 7.

---

[1]   BCLL, no. 1087 p. 297. *Liber S. Marie de Calchou, Registrum Cartarum Abbacie Tironensis de Kelso 1113–1567*, ed. C. Innes, 2 vols, Bannatyne Club (Edinburgh, 1846), no. 180 vol. I p. 149. Lawrie, *Early Scottish Charters*, no. CLXXIII pp. 136–7.

TO ALL THOSE BOUND TO SEE OR HEAR THESE LETTERS
JOHN BY THE GRACE OF GOD HUMBLE MINISTER OF THE CHURCH
   OF GLASGOW
PERPETUAL GREETING IN THE LORD.

You should know me from the consideration of charity
at the petition of my lord, David the illustrious King of the Scots,   5
by the counsel and admonition of men fearing God
as many clerics as laymen
from the assent and wish of my entire chapter to have conceded
and in this my charter to have confirmed
to the abbot and monks of the monastery of Kelso   10
the Church of Lesmahagow with its own entire parish,
to be ordered just as it may please them in perpetuity,
by instituting monks in the same and with monks bound to serve it there,
[and] to have dismissed it free and quit by perpetual right from
   every exaction and episcopal subjection.
These things, however, have been done in the presence of my lord
   King David   15
and many others, as many clerics as laymen,
in the year from the Incarnation of the Lord 1144.   17

   The seventeen words of the Salutation provide the key to the seventeen lines
of text in the entire composition. The 112 letters of the Salutation provide the
key to the 112 words in the entire composition,[2] of which the central words are
monachis Calchouensis | monasterii. From | *Omnibus* to *monachis* | inclusive there
are 394 letters and spaces, and from | *Calchouensis* to *MCXLIIIJ* | inclusive there
are 394 letters and spaces. From *Omnibus* to *monachis* | inclusive there are 150
syllables, and from *Calchouensis* to the beginning of *MCXLIIIJ* there are 150
syllables. From | *domini mei Dauid regis* to *domino meo rege Dauid* | inclusive there
are seventy-seven words.

2   See above pp. 4, 51, 85, 89, 96, 102, 115, 141, 150 and below pp. 155, 186–7.

A BISHOP OF ABERDEEN: GRANT OF MATTHEW TO WILLIAM DE TATENELL

Here follows one of the oldest of the extant *acta* of the Bishops of Aberdeen, a grant made from Matthew to William de Tatenell between 2 April 1172 and 20 August 1199.[1] Capital letters and punctuation marks in boldface represent features of Edinburgh, National Library of Scotland, Advocates' MS 16.1.10, folios 68v–69r.

UNIVERSIS **S**ANCTE MATRIS ECCLESIE FILIIS .
MATHEUS DEI GRATIA **A**BERDONENSIS ECCLESIE MINISTER HUMILIS .
SALUTEM

1   **S**ciant presentes et futuri nos dedisse concessisse et hac presenti **C**arta
     nostra confirmasse . **W**illelmo de **T**atenell homini nostro in feodo
     et hereditate .
2   illas duas carucatas terre in Kyllalchmond ,
3   quas **C**omes **D**auid . ecclesie nostre et nobis dedit .
4   **T**enendas sibi et heredibus suis de nobis et successoribus nostris
     libere et quiete ab omni seruitio et exactione .
5   **R**eddendo inde annuatim nobis et successoribus nostris . de una
     carucata terre unam libram incensi .
6   de altera uero unam marcam argenti ad festum **S**ancti **M**artini .

Testibus Henrico **A**bbate de **A**birbrothoc .
Symone **A**rchidiacono .
Rogero **D**ecano .
Willelmo .
Roberto .
Matheo .
Galfrido .
Andrea . capellanis .
Willelmo persona de **A**berdour .

1   *BCLL*, no. 1115 p. 301. *Registrum Episcopatus Aberdonensis*, ed. C. Innes, 2 vols
     Maitland Club LXIII (Edinburgh, 1845), vol. I p. 13.

Andrea persona de Brechyn .
Matheo clerico nostro .
Malmore persona de Taruas .
Iohanne filio archidiaconi .

WILLELMUS DEI GRATIA SCOTTORUM REX .
OMNIBUS PROBIS HOMINIBUS TOTIUS TERRE SUE
CLERICIS ET LAICIS
SALUTEM .

Sciant presentes et futuri me concessisse et hac presenti Carta mea confirmasse .
Willelmo de Tattenell'. donationem illam quam Matheus Episcopus
Aberdonensis fecit de duabus carucatis terre quas Comes Dauid frater meus
ecclesie Aberdonensi et Matheo eiusdem loci Episcopo et successoribus suis
dedit . Tenendas sibi et heredibus suis de predicto Episcopo et successoribus
suis in feodo et hereditate ita libere et quiete plenarie et honorifice sicut
Carta prefati Episcopi testatur . Saluo seruitio meo .

Testibus hijs . [Hugone?] Cancellario nostro .
Ade abbate de Dunfermelyne .
Comite Duncano Iustitiario .
Malicio filio Comitis Ferteth .
Willelmo Comyn .
Willelmo de Haya
Willelmo de Mofforde .
Waltero de Berclay Camerario ..~

TO ALL SONS OF HOLY MOTHER CHURCH
MATTHEW BY THE GRACE OF GOD HUMBLE MINISTER OF
THE CHURCH OF ABERDEEN
GREETING.

1　　Let present and future men know that we have given, conceded, and in
　　　this our present charter confirmed to our man William de Tatenell in
　　　fee and heredity
2　　those two carrucates of land in Kennethmont
3　　which Earl David gave to our Church and us,
4　　to be held for himself and his own heirs from us and our successors
　　　freely and quit from all service and exaction,
5　　by giving back thence annually to us and our successors from one
　　　carrucate of land one pound of incense,
6　　from the other, in truth, one mark of silver at the feast of Saint Martin.

Witnesses:
Henry Abbot of Arbroath
Simon the Archdeacon
Roger the Deacon
William, Robert, Matthew, Geoffrey, Andrew chaplains
William parson of Aberdour
Andrew parson of Brechin
Matthew our cleric
Mael Muire parson of Tarves
John son of the archdeacon.

WILLIAM BY THE GRACE OF GOD KING OF THE SCOTS
TO ALL WORTHY MEN OF HIS ENTIRE LAND,
CLERICS AND LAYMEN,
GREETING.

Let present and future men know me to have conceded and in this my
present charter confirmed to William de Tatenell that gift which Matthew
Bishop of Aberdeen made of two carrucates of land which Earl David my
brother gave to the Church of Aberdeen and to Matthew bishop of this place
and to his successors, to be held for himself and his own heirs from the
foresaid bishop and his own successors in fee and heredity as freely and quit,
fully and honourably, just as the charter of the foresaid bishop bears witness,
my service excepted.

These witnesses:
[Hugo ?] our Chancellor
Adam Abbot of Dunfermline
Duncan the Earl, Justiciar
Mael Isu son of the Earl Ferteth
William Comyn
William de Haya
William de Mofford
Walter de Barclay Chamberlain.

The thirteen words of Matthew's Salutation provide the key to the thirteen
witnesses,[2] named in thirty-three words.[3] The seventy-eight words of the charter
proper in six clauses equal 13 x 6.

If the chancellor referred to in King William's confirmation was Hugh de
Roxburgh, the transaction can be dated to the period between 1189 and 10 July
1199.

2 See above pp. 4, 51, 85, 89, 96, 102, 115, 141, 150, 152 and below pp. 186–7.
3 For another example of play with 33 see above p. 4.

ADAM OF DRYBURGH:
'EPISTOLA AD ECCLESIE PREMONSTRATENSIS CANONICOS DE TRIPARTITO TABERNACULO'

Adam 'the Scot', alias 'the Englishman', 'the Premonstratensian', 'the Carthusian', or 'of Dryburgh', was born, certainly not before 1131, perhaps in 1134, of middle-class parents in Berwickshire: *fuit itaque uir iste Magister Adam in confinio Anglie et Scocie oriundus parentum mediocrum proles illustris.*[1] As an adolescent, *pius adolescens*, and therefore before his twenty-second birthday,[2] he entered, perhaps in 1155, the monastery of Premonstratensian canons which had been founded by Hugh de Moreville at Dryburgh in 1152: *in eadem prouincia monasterium quoddam canonicorum ordinis Premonstratensis quod Driburga dicitur.*[3] Ordained priest at the age of twenty-five,[4] perhaps in 1159, he appears first among the witnesses, *Hiis testibus Magistro Adam*, in a document of Kelso Abbey.[5] Sometime after the last record of Abbot Girard in 1184 and before the first record of Abbot Richard in 1190,[6] Adam was elected unanimously as Abbot of Dryburgh: *totius conuentus unanimi assensu et consensu predictus Adam in abbatem eiusdem monasterii electus est.*[7] But with the support of Saint Hugh Bishop of Lincoln he became in 1188, a Carthusian at Witham, where he lived for twenty-four years,[8] dying during the Interdict in 1212.

1   E. Margaret Thompson, 'A Fragment of a Witham Charterhouse Chronicle and Adam of Dryburgh, Premonstratensian, and Carthusian of Witham', *Bulletin of the John Rylands Library* XVI (1932), pp. 487–506 at 496.

2   *Ibid.*, p. 497. A widespread form of reckoning ages of men was *infantia* 1–7, *pueritia* 8–14, *adolescentia* 15–21, *iuuentus* 22–42, *senectus* 43 onward, so that three periods of seven years preceded one period of twenty-one years before old age.

3   *Ibid.*, p. 497. For the date of foundation before the death of King David see *Liber S. Marie de Dryburgh*, ed. John Spottiswoode (Edinburgh: Bannatyne Club, 1847), no. 240 pp. 178–9.

4   Thompson, 'Fragment', p. 498.

5   *Liber S. Marie de Calchou*, ed. C. Innes, 2 vols (Edinburgh: Bannatyne Club, 1846), no. 216 vol. I p. 178.

6   Girard received a bull from Pope Lucius III in 1184, and Richard witnessed a document relating to Kelso in 1190, Thompson, 'Fragment', p. 485.

7   *Ibid.*, p. 498. Adam of Eynsham wrote *de uiro opinatissimo, magistro scilicet Adam, qui ex abbate Driburgensi Cartusiensis apud Witham effectus est monachus, Magna Vita Sancti Hugonis, The Life of St Hugh of Lincoln*, ed. and transl. Decima L. Douie and David Hugh Farmer, 2 vols, Oxford Medieval Texts (Oxford: Clarendon Press, 1985), Book IV chapter XI, vol. II pp. 52–4.

8   *xx^{ti} pene et iiii^{or} annis* according to the Witham chronicler, Thompson, 'Fragment', p. 504, or *per quina circiter annorum lustra* according to Adam of Eynsham, p. 53.

The titles of some of his books,[9] *De Triplici Genere Contemplationis* and *De Quadripartito Exercitio Celle*, suggest that he thought in numerical patterns. Particularly noteworthy is *De Tripartitio Tabernaculo*, written in 1180,[10] when Adam was forty-six years old, while he was still a Premonstratensian at Dryburgh and while John Abbot of Kelso was still alive, and sent to the canons of Prémontré in 1182, two years after it had been written, *ante hoc biennium*.[11] The work is tripartite because of the structure of the Tabernacle and in accordance with Adam's interpretation of Holy Scripture in three senses. To this work Adam prefixed as preliminaries three letters, the first from him to the canons of Prémontré, the second from John Abbot of Kelso to him,[12] and the third from him to John.

In paragraph III of the first letter Adam places himself in Scotland and names John:

> Cum autem apud uos presentes corporáliter *essémus*
> a quibus etiam nunc **in regno Scottórum** pósit*i*
> spiritualiter abséntes nón su*mus*
> placuit uobis ex humilitáte precár*i*
> quod ex potestate uobis lícuit ìmper*áre*
> ut librum quem de tabernaculo Moysis una cum pictura ante hóc biénni*um*
> rogatu quorundam frátrum nostrór*um*
> et maxime uiri illustris Ioannis cuiusdam abbatis qui in terra nostra est cómposú*imus*
> uobis tránsmitter*émus* .

Here follows paragraph V, in which Adam names himself and describes his book.

> I   Húnc autem lí*brum*
> cuius est titulus 'De Triplici Tabernaculo una cum Pictura'
> et librum per quattuordecim sermónes distí*nctum*
> qui inscribitur 'De Nomine et Habitu atque Professione Canonicorum Ordinis
>   Prémonstraténs*is*'
> 5   in nostri memóriam habébit*is*
> ut quia nostram iugiter apud uos presentiam habere non potéstis corporá*lem*
> aliquid habeatis ex parte nostra in quo retineatis spírituá*lem*.
> II   Vestris nos precibus inté*nte* commend*ámus*
> innitimur quoque meritis uestris fiducialiter possidéntes in uó*bis*
> 10   quod in nobis deésse uidé*mus*
> certo scientes non posse nos aporiari quamdiu uos díuites fuér*itis* .

---

9 *BCLL*, nos 1011–1016 pp. 281–2.
10 *BCLL*, no. 1014 p. 282. *Patrologia Latina* CXCVIII cols 609–792. In an account of the ages of the world Adam states in Part II chapter VI § LXXXVII, col. 692B, *Sexta uero etas a primo Xpisti aduentu usque ad secundum, ex qua quidem etate iam anni mille centum octoginta transacti sunt.*
11 Adam describes John in this letter of 1182 as *qui in terra nostra est*, though John is sometimes supposed to have died in 1180.
12 See below pp. 161–75.

III   Obnixe itaque uos flexis genibus méntis obsecrámus
        tamquam pedibus uéstris prostráti
        ut nostri memores sitis in uespertinis sacrificiis uéstris
  15   compatientes multimodis fragilitátibus nóstris
        offerentes nos sanandos piis conspectibus áduocati nóstri
        iusti mitis et mánsueti Iésu
        qui quod pro se non debuit sóluit pro nóbis
        et sacerdos pro nobis fáctus et hóstia
  20   émptor et prétium
        sacrifex et sácrificium
        ac medicus uulnerum nostrórum et mèdicína
        pepéndit in lígno
        larga pii cruoris sui effusione immúndos nos ábluens
  25   et reconcílians réos
        et nunc sedens ad dexteram Patris interpéllat pro nóbis.
IIII   Mementote itaque diligentis uós peccatòris Áde
        cum de ipsis intimis altaris aurei emisso odorifero sancta sanctorum impletis
            arómatis fúmo
        et ibi quam maxime ubi Patri Fílius ìmmolátur
  30   cuius sanguis clamat de terra mélius quam Ábel.
V   Sed et hoc petitionibus nostris súperadderémus
        nisi forte temerarie foret presumptióni imputándum
        scilicet ut nomen nostrum in albo sancte congregationis uestre una cum
            uestrorum qui iam discessere nominibus post mortem iuberétis adscríbi
        quia et nós uestri súmus.
VI   Verum tamen quod nostra petere uerecúndia nòn presúmit
  36   uestra ut speramus benígnitas dábit
        quía ni fállimur
        in ipso profundo fontis diuitiárum uestrárum plus ébullit ab ímo
        quam in superficie nos hauríre audémus.
VII   Et de his usque huc.

I   This book, however,
        of which the title is 'On the Triple Tabernacle together with a Picture',
        and a book divided into fourteen sermons,
        which is inscribed 'On the Name and Habit and Profession of the Canons
            of the Order of Prémontré',
  5   you will have as a memorial of us,
        so that though you can not have our bodily presence with you,
        you may have something in which you may retain from our part a
            spiritual [presence].
II   We commend ourselves intently to your prayers;
        we lean also upon your merits, reliably possessing in you
  10   what we see to be lacking in us,
        knowing certainly that it is not possible for us to be impoverished as long as
            you may be rich.
III   And so we beseech you resolutely with the knees of the mind bent,
        as prostrate at your feet,

that you may be mindful of us in your evening sacrifices,
15   having compassion on our many-moded frailties,
offering us to be healed by the holy onlookings of our advocate,
just, mild, and gentle Jesus,
Who what He did not owe for Himself paid for us,
made for us both priest and victim,
20   purchaser and price,
sacrificer and sacrifice,
both medic of our wounds and medicine,
He hung on the wood,
washing us unclean men by the generous effusion of His own holy blood,
25   and reconciling guilty men,
and now, sitting at the right hand of the Father, He intercedes for us.
IIII   And so be mindful of Adam, a sinner loving you,
when from the very inmost parts of the golden altar you fill the holy parts of
     holy places with the scent-bearing smoke of incense sent forth,
and there especially where to the Father the Son is sacrificed,
30   Whose blood shouts from the earth better than Abel's.
V   But we should add this also to our petitions,
lest by chance it should be imputed to temerarious presumption,
understand, that our name in the white book of your holy congregation, together
     with the names of yours who have already passed away, you should order to be
     written after death,
because we also are yours.
VI   Nevertheless what our shame noes not presume to ask,
36   your benignity, as we hope, will give,
because, unless we are deceived,
in the very depth of the fountain of your riches more boils up from the bottom
than we dare to draw on the surface.
40   And concerning these things, as far as this place.

The forty lines and 276 words of this passage remind one of the same phenomena in the *Vita Sancti Reguli* and in Symeon of Glasgow's *Vita Sancti Seruani* and *Vita Sancti Kentigerni*.[13] Here Adam has infixed several other devices that confirm the integrity of the composition to the last letter. There are fourteen words in the sentence before | *per quattuordecim sermones* 3 and fourteen letters and spaces in the line before | *quattuordecim*. There are ten syllables in line 10 *quod in nobis deesse uidemus*, and ten lines of text before the ten words *certo scientes non posse nos aporiari quamdiu uos diuites fueritis* 11. In 27 *Mementote itaque diligentis uos peccatoris Ade* there are forty-six letters and spaces between words, coincident certainly with the numerical value of the name AΔAM in Greek alphabetical notation, $1+4+1+40$ or 46, and possibly with Adam's age at the time of writing. From the space before *Iesu* to the end of *Et de his usque huc* inclusive there are exactly 888 letters and spaces between words, coincident with the

13 See above pp. 86–97.

numerical value of the name IHCOYC in Greek alphabetical notation, 10+8+200+70+400+200 or 888.[14] From the space before *Hunc* to the space before *Mementote* inclusive there are exactly 1180 letters and spaces between words, representing the year in which Adam wrote the book, A.D. 1180.[15]

Let us note how often Adam refers to himself at places determined by the ratios of musical and cosmic theory. His 276 words divide by duple ratio 2:1 at 184 and 92 at *pedibus uestris prostrati* | *ut nostri memores sitis* 13. They divide by extreme and mean ratio at 171 and 105, at | *nos* 16 and *mementote itaque diligentis uos* | *peccatoris Ade* 27. The 276 words divide by sesquialter ratio 3:2 at 166 and 110, at | *nostri* 16 and | *nobis* 25. They divide by one-ninth and eight-ninths at 31 and 245, at *nostri* | 5.[16]

14 See above pp. 5–9, 22, 35, 58–61, 84, 89, 95, 141 and below pp. 174, 184 and 'Five Experiments', p. 30, *British Books in Biblical Style*, pp. 119–21, 539–40, *Cambro-Latin Compositions*, p. 82, *Sealed from Within*, pp. 89–91.

15 See above pp. 8, 23, 36, 59, 61, 74, 83–5, 89, 96, 110, 142, 150 and below pp. 174, 182–4.

16 See above pp. 18, 22, 90, 95, 106 and below p. 184.

JOHN ABBOT OF KELSO:
'EPISTOLA AD ADAM SCOTTUM DE TRIPARTITO TABERNACULO'

Directly after the letter from Adam of Dryburgh to the canons of Prémontré follows a letter, presented as from John Abbot of Kelso, exhorting Adam to write *De Tripartito Tabernaculo*.[1]

I

    DILECTISSIMO ET IN XPISTI MEMBRIS HONORANDO FILIO
       ÁDE CANÓNICO
    IOHANNES ABBAS ETERNAM IN DOMINO ÓPTAT SALÚTEM.   I

I   Considerans fili carissime quamplures circa scientiam qua diuinarum notitie
       continentur Scripturarum summo stúdio òccupári
    uehementer admiror íntentiónem
    simulque ápprobo uòluntátem
    qua eam conantur omni diligéntia cónsequí   5
    decorum utileque sibi fóre iudicántes
    si in ea quantum ualent pérfici studúerint.

II   Hanc itaque pre ceteris que ad inanem philosóphiam pértinent
    considerantes mente súpra se èxtollúntur
    meditando quam sit delectabile éam adipísci   10
    aliud intelligentes dum eam in ueritatis conspíciunt lúce
    aliud dum eam sua in uoluntáte concupíscunt.

III   Contemplantur namque perspicacius attendentes in lúce ueritátis
    quam bonum sit tripliciter omnes Scripturas íntellígere
    uniuersasque sine difficultate ad euidentiorem intelligentiam manifesto
       sénsu explanáre.   15

IIII   Hec quippe multum cóncupíscitur
    que ita in animo quasi in spéculo *uidétur*
    atque accendit studia discentium quatenus circa éam uerséntur
    eique inhient in omni studio quod tali consequende facultáti impéndunt
    ut per eam promere possint quod meditatione prenóscere *uidéntur*.   20

V   Cum igitur huiusmodi nimia cupiditate estuantes quadam ui natúre impellúntur
    ut discant uniuersarum mysteria Scripturarum se uelle scire euidentíssime
       demónstrant.

VI   Hec enim circa éos agúntur

---

1   *BCLL*, no. 1017 p. 282. *Patrologia Latina* CXCVIII cols 623C–628A.

dum operibus sanctorum qui Grecas et Hebraicas scripturas ad notitiam
  transtulerunt summam diligéntiam ádhib*ent*
admirantes constantiam e*orum contra áduersários*   25
tolerantiamque labórum propter é*os*
qui in catholica fide ab eis tunc temporis ínstruebá*ntur*.

II

VII   Dum autem eis hora necessitátis incúm*bit*
ut multa contra hereticos secus quam catholica fides habeat dogmatizá*ntes*
  scríb*erent*
eis diuinarum auctoritate Scripturarum muniti óbuiam pròcedé*ntes*   30
plerumque quía pauci é*rant*
disputando contra eos diutius láboraué*runt*.

VIII   Tandem super arenam multiplicati sanctorum scriptis sacrament*orum contra*
  áduersários
et in catholica fide uniuersalem ecclesiam preliati édocué*runt*.

VIIII   Horum igitur doctrinam nonnulli modernorum pro pósse imitá*ntes*   35
quasdam profánas nou*itátes*
que primo per Arianorum sectam in domo Dómini succréu*erant*
frequentius eis in faciem resistendo in desuetúdinem àbegé*runt*
memores illíus precép*ti*
quo prohibetur nemus plantari ín domo Dóm*ini*.   40

X   Tandem per operatiónem diuín*am*
sanctam ecclesiam illius macule incontaminatam excellentíssimam rèddidé*runt*
edificantes itaque sanctam ecclesiam per huiusmodi óccasió*nes*
prauorum sectas irremediabiliter impedire nón potu*íssent*
nisi constanter contra eos proferendo diuina eloquia íllis restit*íssent*   45
scientes quod quanquam diuina Scriptura in legendo sit éis apér*ta*
in mysterio clausa sit omníno et occúl*ta*.

XI   Postquam autem sancti doctores in altitúdinem Scrìpturár*um*
quasi in excelsum per contemplationis uigórem ascendé*ntes*
usque ad ipsam Trinitatis maiestatem spirituáliter pèruené*runt*   50
qualiter Sancta Scriptura mystice intelligi debeat in utroque Testamento
  sátis lúci*de*
quanquam non omnibus tamen sensu perfectis eorum expositiónibus
  dèmonstrá*tur*.

III

XII   Verumtamen quedam plerisque in locis summe eruditionis uiri quodammodo
  superficietenus tacta prétereú*ntes*
modernorum exercitio hec ad explanánda reseruá*runt*
et quasi ex industria in campo Scripturarum quasdam spicas post uestigia
  mínus plenas stá*ntes*   55
collígere òmisé*runt*
quatenus eas posteri in tempore triplici uírga excút*erent*
atque indigéntibus mìnistrá*rent*
ne circa sterilem philosophiam inéptius òccupá*ti*
absque fructu laboris in discussione bonorum operum coram Patrefamilias
  omnino uácui àpparé*rent*.   60

XIII   Unde quoddam quo nonnulli mouentur exempli grátia prófe*ro*

cur in Exodo tabernaculum Moysis pretergredientes excépto Iosépho
et uenerabili Béda presbýtero
cum omnes interpretari et explanare Scripturas próposúerint
in hunc locum párum scripsérunt.   65

XIIII   Cum autem circa sanctam ecclesiam et ea que ad illam pertinere uidentur
       summa illorum inténtio ésset
mirum est quare hunc locum ita prétergréssi sint
cum idem tabernaculum in nonnullis sanctam ecclesiam elegantissime
       préfiguráuerit.

XV   Attamen uenerabilis Beda doctor Anglorum pauca super hoc tabernaculo
       sue diligentie indícia pándens
cum in omnibus scriptis suis ita libens explanátor exísteret   70
ut more puerorum magistri syllabicando quéque expóneret
fastidiosis lectoribus de hoc scribens nón satisfécit.   72

IIII

XVI   Quapropter fili carissime hoc opus quod ab eis uelut omnibus eque patens
       intactum fére omíttitur
ad explanandum tue iniungo mánsuetúdini
eoquod concupiscas salutáre Dómini   75
et lex eius meditatio sít cordis túi.

XVII   Amplectens ergo confidenter preceptum que Dominus super hoc per
       Spiritum suum tibi ministráre dignábitur
in explanatione huius tabernaculi calamo famulánte manifésta.

XVIII   Tempus uacántius nón queras
dum quid futurum sit pénitus ígnoras.   80

XVIIII   Librum igitur qui historiale tabernáculum còmplectátur
qualiter in re dispositum fuit per Moysen legéntibus demónstra
quem compones ex ueracissimis orthodoxorum patrum díctis colléctum
eumque in tres partes capitibus prenotátis diuídes
unicuique parti sua proportióne assignáta.   85

XX   In hoc ergo nullius sententiam contra Éxodum ínserens
ne per errorem in diuersis multorum opinionibus aliquanto diutius
       immorári uideáris
textum istius Exodi plerúmque innécte
quatenus sic discurrente manifesta ratione liber béne formétur
contraque emulos Scripturarum congregentur téstimónia   90
quod nondum 'obstructum sit os loquéntium iníqua'.

XXI   Prima igitur pars huius libri quis artifex fuerit édificii
quibusue materiis illud uetus tabernaculum constabat querentibus uel
       scire uolentibus apérte índicet
totumque edificium cum uniuersis ad illud pertinentibus intrinsecus siue
       forinsecus euidentíssime descríbat
singulisque proprio loco positis páriétibus   95
per capita uéctium coniúnctis
edificium extensio cortinarum ceterorumque tegumentorum nouissime
       cóopériat.

V

XXII   Sed quoniam de medietáte sexti sági

qua duplicatio ad protegenda posteriora tabernáculi fiébat
a nonnullis questio oriri solet [? l. sólet oríri]   100
de ipsa latius disputatio in hac eadem parte líbri protendátur
precipueque de craticula altaris de qua tam apud Grecos quam apud Latinos
    maxima ambiguitas ésse uidétur.

XXIII   Quid autem super his diuersi expositores senserint contra multórum inuèctiónes
quasi in testimonium congerere non sit tíbi onerósum
ut eorum dentes contriti et quasi quid oblatrent non habentes in seípsis
    retundántur   105
sententiisque multorum contra illos prolatis Sancte Scripture diutius insultare
    omníno confundántur.

XXIIII   Hec igitur in prima libri huius parte propter eorum calúmnias ponénda sunt
quatenus a primo limine expulsi secretiora domus Domini secundum
    preceptum legis íngredi nòn ualéntes
procul a sanctuario uel ob malam conscientiam recedant temeritatis proprie
    discrimina sécum feréntes.

VI

XXV   In textu autem secunde partis uisibile tabernaculum in plano depingens
    oculis ínuténtium   110
quantum potest per pictam similitudinem ostendi illius formam edificii
    éxpríme
intra Sancta Sanctorum uel simpliciter Sancta ea cum omni diligentia
    ponens que Exodus inibi fuísse descríbit
eoquod illi indubitánter credéndum sit
licet non ab omnibus expresse intélligi póssit
quemadmodum sensus uerborum áccipiéndus sit.   115

XXVI   Atrii uero tentorium intra castra et edificium super columnas extendens in
    gyrum spátia et lóca
in quibus filii Israel in circuitu tabernaculi castrametabantur in pictura
    diligénter desígna
quatenus indicium illius edificii per pictam similitúdinem hábeant
qui qualiter id longis retro temporibus factum fuerat scíre desíderant.

VII

XXVII   Depictis igitur omnibus in ipsa eadem parte libri mox ípsam pictúram   120
eoquod Sacra Scriptura infirmis sensu secundum historiam humilis uidetur
    esse [? l. ésse uidétur]
in uerbis per allegoricos sénsus expóne
ut lectoris studium atque intelléctus augeátur
et intuentis animus et intelligentis per uisibilem similitudinem a malo
    declináre doceátur
et per allegoricam significationem se ad modum Scripture adaptáre
    uideátur.   125

XXVIII   Consequens enim est ut qui per bonum exemplum a uítiis se ábstinet
in bonis operibus se exercendo uirtutibus státim corúscet.

XXVIIII   In tertia uero parte que superius dicta sunt ad moralitátem retórquens
quid edificationis intuentibus pictura conferat mystica interpretatione ad
    mores corrigendos inclinare diligénter sátage.

XXX   Quilibet namque dum uerba historie simplíciter nárrat   130

quasi inchoando fundamentum edificii iáctat
et dum per allegorie exercitium mysteria história pándit
in arcem fidei fabricam méntis extóllit.

VIII

XXXI   Nouissime uero qui ex utroque mysticum intellectum per
              contemplatiónem inuéstigat
         erectum edificium diuersis uirtutibus per moralitatis gratiam quasi
              distinctis colóribus órnat.   135
XXXII   Cum autem omnia secundum administrationem diuini muneris
              uigilánter compléueris
         hanc epistolam in fronte libri excusationis grátia prescríbe
         quatenus diligens lector agnoscat non presumptionis causa te hoc ópus
              inchoásse
         Sed constrictum ui obedientie precepto pátris paruísse.
XXXIII   Sed quoniam oratio ne prolixior sermo lectori fastídium géneret   140
         iam terminanda est hec dícta sufficiant
         orantem pro nobis sanctam fraternitatem tuam gratia superni Protéctoris
              cònseruáre
         atque in bonis actionibus semper corroborare dignetur
              [? l. dignetur córroboráre].
         Amen.   144

91 Psalm LXII 12.

I

TO THE SON MOST BELOVED AND TO BE HONOURED AMONG
    THE MEMBERS OF CHRIST, CANON ADAM,
ABBOT JOHN WISHES ETERNAL SALVATION IN THE LORD.   1
I   Considering, dearest son, how many men are occupied with the highest study
              about the knowledge in which the notices of the divine Scriptures are
              contained,
         I admire greatly the intention
         and at the same time I approve the will
         with which they try to follow it with all diligence,   5
         judging it to be decorous and useful for them
         if they study as much as they are able to be perfected in that [knowledge].
II   Considering therefore this [knowledge] above all other things that pertain to
              empty philosophy
         they are lifted up above themselves in mind
         by meditating about how delectable it may be to grasp that [knowledge],   10
         understanding something while they gaze on it in the light of truth,
         something while they desire it in their own will.
III   For they contemplate more perspicaciously attending in the light of truth to
         how good it may be to understand all Scriptures in a threefold way,
         and to explain them all without difficulty for more evident understanding
              in a manifest sense.   15
IIII   This [knowledge] indeed is much desired,
         which is so seen in the spirit as in a looking glass,

and it ignites the studies of those learning so that they may be turned toward it,
and that they may sigh for it in every study that they devote to following
   such a faculty,
so that they may be able to bring forth through it what they are seen to
   know beforehand by meditation.   20

V   Since, therefore, burning with very great desire of this type they are
   impelled by a certain force of nature
that they learn that they show themselves to wish to know most evidently
   the mysteries of all the Scriptures.

VI   For these things are done concerning these men
while through the works of holy men who brought the Greek and Hebrew
   Scriptures to notice they exhibit the highest diligence,
admiring their constancy against adversaries,   25
and the bearing of labours on account of those men,
who were instructed in the Catholic Faith by them at that time.

II

VII   While, however, in the hour of need it falls to them
that they should write many things against heretics dogmatically teaching
   other than what the Catholic Faith holds,
proceeding against them fortified by the authority of the divine Scriptures,   30
and especially, though they were few,
they laboured disputing for a long time against them.

VIII   Finally multiplied beyond [the number of grains of] sand with the writings
   of the holy sacraments against their adversaries,
and having engaged in battle they taught the universal Church in the
   Catholic Faith.

VIIII   Therefore not a few of these moderns imitating the teaching according
   to their ability,   35
by resisting them quite frequently in the open they drove away into disuse   38
certain profane novelties,   36
which at first through the sect of the Arians had grown from beneath in the
   house of the Lord,   37
mindful of that precept   39
by which a wood is forbidden to be planted in the house of the Lord.   40

X   Finally, through a divine operation
they rendered the holy Church most excellent, uncontaminated by that
   blemish,
and so building the holy Church through occasions of this sort,
they would not be able to impede irremediably the sects of evil men,
unless they should stand against those men by proffering constantly against
   them divine utterances,   45
knowing that although divine Scripture might be open to them in reading,
it might be altogether closed and secret in a mystery.

XI   After, however, holy teachers into the lofty height of the Scriptures,
as if ascending into the highest region through the vigour of contemplation,
came through spiritually as far as the very majesty of the Trinity,   50
how holy Scripture ought to be mystically understood in either Testament
   lucidly enough

is shown in the perfected expositions of these men, though not, nevertheless,
in one sense to all men.

III

XII   Nevertheless men of the highest erudition in many places passing over
certain places touched superficially, so to speak,
have reserved these to be explained by the skill of modern men,
and as if after hard work in the field of the Scriptures certain ears of
corn standing less full after their traces   55
they have neglected to collect,
so that men later in time should cut them out with a triple rod,
and they should minister to the needy,
lest occupied rather ineptly with sterile philosophy
they should appear altogether empty-handed before the Father of the
family without the fruit of labour in the discussion[2] of good works.   60

XIII   Whence I bring forth something for the sake of example by which not
a few are moved,
marching past the tabernacle of Moses in Exodus, except Josephus
and the venerable priest Bede,
though all may have proposed to interpret and explain the Scriptures,
they have written little about this place [in the text].   65

XIIII   Since, however, the highest intention of those men should be about the
holy Church and the things which are seen to pertain to it,
it is wondrous why they should so have marched past this place,
since the same tabernacle most elegantly prefigured in not a few respects
the holy Church.

XV   Nevertheless the venerable Bede, teacher of the English, spreading out in
revelation a few indications of his own diligence about the tabernacle,
since in all his own writings he remained so willing an explainer   70
that in the custom of a master of boys he would expound things
articulating by the syllable,
writing about this did not satisfy fastidious readers.   72

IIII

XVI   On which account, dearest son, this work, which as by all of them equally
is omitted lying almost untouched,
I enjoin to your gentleness to be explained,
because you should desire the salvation of the Lord,   75
and His law should be the meditation of your heart.

XVII   Therefore embracing faithfully the precept, show the things which the
Lord will deign to minister to you concerning this through His own Spirit
in explanation of this tabernacle, with a reed pen serving.

XVIII   May you not seek time more leisurely
while you do not know fully what the future may be.   80

XVIIII   The book, therefore, which includes in its scope the historical tabernacle,
demonstrate to readers how it was in fact disposed by Moses,
which [book] you will compose collected from the truest sayings of the
orthodox fathers,

2   with play on 'threshing'.

and you divide it into three parts with headings noted in advance,
with its own proportion assigned to each part.   85
XX   In this, therefore, inserting the sentence of no man against Exodus,
lest you be seen to delay for somewhat too long among the diverse
   opinions of many men,
bind together especially the text of that Exodus,
so that running through with manifest reason the book may be well formed,
and against emulous men the testimonies of the Scriptures may be gathered,   90
because not yet 'may the mouth of those speaking unjust things be obstructed'.
XXI   Therefore the first part of this book who was the maker of the edifice by art,
or of what materials that old tabernacle consisted should indicate openly to
   those seeking or wishing to know,
and the whole edifice with all things pertaining to it inside or outside it
   should most evidently describe,
and on individual walls positioned in the proper place   95
conjoined through the heads of wooden bars
a stretching out of curtains and other coverings would finally cover the
   edifice.
XXII   But since from the middle of the sixth cloth,
from which a doubling was made for protecting the rear parts of the
   tabernacle,
a question customarily arises from not a few men   100
concerning the very question let a disputation be extended broadly in
   the same part of the book,
and especially about the gridiron of the altar, about which as much among
   the Greeks as among the Latins there is seen to be the greatest ambiguity.
XXIII   What, however, concerning these things diverse expositors may have
   perceived against the invectives of many men,
as if to gather together as testimony may it not be burdensome to you,
so that having gnashed their teeth and as if not having anything that they
   may bark at they may be beaten flat by themselves,   105
and with the sentences of many passages of Holy Scripture brought forth
   against them they may be confounded from mocking for quite a long time.
XXIIII   These things, therefore, should be placed in the first part of this book on
   account of their calumnies,
so that those expelled from the first threshold, not being able to enter the more
   secret parts of the house of the Lord according to the precept of the law,
should recede far from the sanctuary, bearing with them the hazards of their
   own temerity or on account of a bad conscience.
XXV   In the text of the second part, however, depicting the visible tabernacle in
   open view to the eyes of those looking on   110
express as well as can be shown through a painted representation the form
   of that edifice,
placing with all diligence within the Holy Places of Holy Things, or simply the
   Holy Places, those things which Exodus describes to have been therein,
because it should be believed undoubtingly,
although it cannot be understood expressly by all men,
nonetheless the sense of the words should be accepted.   115

XXVI   In truth the tent of the atrium within the camp and the edifice above the
        columns enlarging in a circle the spaces and places
      in which the sons of Israel pitched the camp of the tabernacle in a circuit
        show diligently in a picture,
      so that they may have an indication of that edifice through a painted
        representation,
      they who desire to know how it was made in times long ago.

XXVII   Therefore with all things painted, in the very same part of the book,   120
      because Sacred Scripture is seen to those infirm in sense to be humble
        according to history [i.e. the literal sense],
      expound the very picture in words according to the allegorical senses,
      so that the study and the understanding of the reader may be increased,
      and the spirit of one looking on and understanding may be taught by the
        visible representation to decline from evil,
      and through the allegorical significance he may be seen to adapt to a
        mode of Scripture.   125

XXVIII   For it is consequent that he who through a good example makes himself
        abstain from vices
      may immediately coruscate by exercising himself in good works.

XXVIIII   In the third part, in truth, the things which have been said above, reverting
        to morality,
      busy yourself diligently with what of edification the picture may by mystic
        interpretation confer to those looking on to incline to correct their morals.

XXX   For whoever while he narrates simply the words of history
        [i.e. the literal sense],   130
      as if by beginning lays down the foundation of the edifice,
      and while through the exercise of allegory he lays bare the mysteries of history,
      he lifts up the fabric of the mind to the ark of faith.

XXXI   Finally, in truth, he who from either mode investigates the mystic
        understanding through contemplation
      adorns the erected edifice with divine virtues through the grace of
        morality as if with distinct colours.   135

XXXII   When, however, you will have completed all things vigilantly according
        to the administration of the divine gift,
      write this letter in the front of the book for the sake of explanation,
      so that a diligent reader may know you to have begun the work not
        because of presumption,
      but constrained by the force of obedience to have obeyed the precept of a
        father.

XXXIII   But since the prayer, lest speech too prolix generate tedium to the reader,   140
      should now be ended, let these words suffice,
      praying to keep your brotherhood holy for us by the grace of the supernal
        Protector,
      and may He deign to strengthen you always in good actions.
      Amen.   144

    The author has arranged words and ideas in a remarkable series of chiastic
and parallel patterns. Let us begin with lines 1–24.

2	A1	scientiam
2	A2	notitie
2	B	scripturarum
2	C1	studio
5	C2	consequi
10	C3	meditando
11	D	intelligentes
11	E	ueritatis
11	F	luce
12	G	dum eam sua in uoluntate concupiscunt
13	G'	contemplantur namque perspicacius attendentes
13	F'	luce
13	E'	ueritatis
14–15	D'	intelligere … intelligentiam
18–19	C'1	studia … studio
19	C'2	consequende
20	C'3	meditatione
22	B'	scripturarum
22	A'1	scire
24	A'2	notitiam.

A second pattern is interlocked with this in lines 22–51.

22	A	demonstrant
24	B	Grecas et Hebraicas
24	C	scripturas
30	D	diuinarum … scripturarum
33	E1	tandem
34	E2	uniuersalem ecclesiam
34	E3	edocuerunt
37	E4	Arianorum
37	E5	sectam
37	F	in domo Domini
37	G	succreuerant
38	H	frequentius eis in faciem resistendo
		in desuetudinem abegerunt
40	G'	plantari
40	F'	in domo Domini
41	E'1	tandem
42	E'2	sanctam ecclesiam
42	E'3	reddiderunt
44	E'4	prauorum
44	E'5	sectas
46	D'	diuina scriptura

51	C'	scriptura
51	B'	in utroque Testamento
52	A'	demonstratur.

A third pattern occupies lines 53–76.

54	A	ad explananda
56	B	omiserunt
62	C	tabernaculum
62	D1	pretergredientes
63	D2	uenerabili Beda
65	E	hunc locum
66	F	circa sanctam ecclesiam
66	F'	et ea que ad illam pertinent
67	E'	hunc locum
67	D'1	pretergressi sint
69	D'2	uenerabilis Beda
69	C'	tabernaculo
73	B'	omittitur
74	A'	ad explanandum.

A fourth pattern occupies lines 77–109.

77	A	preceptum
92	B	prima igitur pars huius libri
101	C	in hac eadem parte libri
107	B'	hec igitur in prima libri huius parte
108	A'	preceptum.

The thirty-five words of sentence XVIIII divide into three parts by duple ratio 2:1 at 23 and 12, at | *eumque in tres partes capitibus prenotatis diuides* 84. The entire passage contains 284 words, which divide into three parts by duple ratio 2:1 at 189 and 95, at *manifesta ratione* | *liber bene formetur* 89. The 284 words divide by sesquialter ratio 3:2 at 170 and 114, at *prima igitur pars huius* | *libri* 92. There are from | *prima igitur pars huius libri* 92 to *in prima libri huius parte* | 107 inclusive 142 words, of which a central seventy-first word precedes | *in hac eadem parte libri* 101. The 142 words divide by sesquialter ratio 3:2 at 85 and 57, at *duplicatio* |.

A fifth pattern occupies lines 107–129.

109	A	ferentes
110	B	in textu autem secunde partis
110	C	uisibile
110	D1	depingens

110	D2	intuentium
111	E	per pictam similitudinem
111	F	illius formam edificii
112	G	exprime
112	H	intra sancta sanctorum
113	I	eoquod illi indubitanter credendum sit
114	J	licet non ab omnibus expresse intelligi possit
115	I'	quemadmodum sensus uerborum accipiendus sit
116	H'	intra castra
117	G'	designa
118	F'	indicium illius edificii
118	E'	per pictam similitudinem
120	D'1	depictis
124	D'2	intuentis
124	C'	uisibilis
128	B'	in tertia uero parte que superius dicta sunt
129	A'	conferat.

The 144 lines of the entire composition divide into two equal halves at line 72. Let us consider a chiastic pattern that links the first half.

3	A1	occupari
5	A2	omni diligentia
8	B	inanem philosophiam
14	C1	scripturas
18	C2	quatenus
35	D	modernorum
47	E	mysterio
49	F	quasi in excelsum per contemplationis uigorem ascendentes
50	F'	usque ad ipsam Trinitatis maiestatem spiritualiter peruenerunt
51	E'	mystice
54	D'	modernorum
55	C'1	scripturarum
57	C'2	quatenus
59	B'	sterilem philosophiam
59	A'1	occupati
69–70	A'2	diligentie … omnibus.

Let us consider next a chiastic pattern that links the second half.

73	A	hoc opus
75	B	eoquod
78	C	tabernaculi
86	D	Exodum
88	E	textum
90	F	contraque emulos scripturarum
90	G	congregentur
90	H	testimonia
93	I	tabernaculum
94	J	edificium
94	K	intrinsecus
94	L	et
94	K'	forinsecus
97	J'	edificium
99	I'	tabernaculi
104	H'	testimonium
104	G'	congerere
106	F'	contra illos prolatis sancte scripture
110	E'	textu
112	D'	Exodus
117	C'	tabernaculi
121	B'	eoquod
138	A'	hoc opus.

Let us consider next a chiastic pattern that links both halves.

1	A	filio
5	B	diligentia
9	C1	mente ... extolluntur
13	C2	contemplantur
4–15	D	tripliciter omnes scripturas intelligere ... intelligentiam
15	E	sensu
24	F	diligentiam
32	G	disputando
46	H	aperta
53	I	tacta
60	J	operum
61	K1	nonnulli
64	K2	explanare
65	K3	scripserunt
68	K'1	nonnullis
70	K'2	explanator
72	K'3	scribens
73	J'	opus

73	I'	intactum
93	H'	aperte
101	G'	disputatio
112,117	F'	diligentia … diligenter
121	E'	sensu
122–124	D'	per allegoricos sensus … intellectus … intelligentis
133	C'1	mentis extollit
134	C'2	contemplationem
138	B'	diligens
139	A'	patris.

Let us consider finally a parallelism that binds the entire composition.

2	A	fili carissime	73	A'	fili carissime
16	B	concupiscitur	75	B'	concupiscas
20	C	meditatione	76	C'	meditatio
54	D	ad explananda	78	D'	in explanatione
60	E	uacui	79	E'	uacantius
62	F	tabernaculum	81	F'	tabernaculum
62	G	Moysis	82	G'	Moysen
64	H	scripturas	121	H'	scriptura
72	I	fastidiosis lectoribus	140	I'	lectori fastidium.

One notes that in many instances these chiastic and parallel examples account for all the occurrences of unusual words in the entire composition.

In the Salutation the phrase *Dilectissimo et in Xpisti membris honorando filio Ade* contains forty-six letters, coincident with the numerical value of the name ΑΔΑΜ in Greek alphabetical notation, $1+4+1+40$ or 46.[3] From the space before *Dilectissimo* to the space after *salutem* inclusive there are 111 letters and spaces. There are thirty-three sentences and 144 lines. There are 1180 words, coincident with the year of publication, A.D. 1180.[4] In conformity with the widespread tradition of reference to an author's addressee and work the 1180 words divide by sesquioctave ratio 9:8 at 625 and 555, at *quapropter fili carissime hoc | opus* 73.

There is a reflex of this text in the *Vita Sancti Kentigerni* by Jocelin of Furness.[5]

The English orientation of John of Kelso appears in a memorandum of agreement with the monks of Saint Cuthbert in Durham Cathedral Library MS B.IV.24, folio 5v:[6]

3   See above pp. 5, 8, 22, 35, 58–61, 84, 89, 95, 141, 159–60 and below p. 184.
4   See above pp. 8, 23, 36, 59, 61, 74, 83–5, 89, 96, 110, 142, 150, 160 and below 182–4.
5   See above pp. 117, 123.
6   I owe thanks to Mr Roger Norris of Durham Cathedral Library for supply of a facsimile of this folio.

In obitu **D**omni **J**ohannis **A**bbátis de **K**élcho*u* :
fiet pro eo unum seruitium plenárie ìn conuént*u* .
Sicut pro fratre extra ęcclesiam decedente fieri sóle*t* .
Triginta misse a sacerdotibus pró eo pèrsoluént*ur* .
5   et in proximo tricenario quod post obitum eíus dic*étur* :
fiet pro eo sicut pro uno ex fratribus nostris totum seruítium commún*iter* .
Unusquisque inferioris ordinis .**L**. [*i.e.* quinquaginta] psalmos pró eo dècantábi*t* .
reliqui qui psálmos nésciun*t* :
quinquagies **P**ater nos*ter* .
uel **M**iserere mei **D**eus ..
11   et nomen eius in **M**artirologio taliter nomina frátrum pon*étur* .

On the death of the master John Abbot of Kelso
there will be made for him one service fully in the convent,
just as is accustomed to be made for a brother dying outside the church.
Thirty masses will be offered up for him by the priests,
5   and in the next trental that will be said after his death
there will be made for him just as for one of our brothers the whole service
         communally.
Each member of a lower order will sing fifty psalms for him;
the rest who do not know the psalms [will sing]
'Our Father' fifty times
or 'Have mercy on me, God'.
11   And his name will be placed like the names of brothers in the Martyrology.

In line 2 the eight words divide by the ratio 1:1 at *unum* |. In line 6 the twelve words divide by the ratio 1:1 at *uno* |. The eleventh word of the complete text is *unum*. Between *triginta misse* | and | *et in proximo tricenario* there are thirty letters. There are thirty-three words before *tricenario*. The fifty-fifth word of the complete text is *quinquaginta*. From the space after *quinquaginta* exclusive to the space before *quinquagies* inclusive there are fifty-five letters and spaces between words.

That a letter about discursive exegesis and a notarial instrument relating to, if not actually composed by, the same man exhibit similar structural techniques tells us much about the intellectual milieu among literate men in northern Britain.

ADAM OF DRYBURGH:
'DE TRIPARTITO TABERNACULO'
PARS I CAPUT I

After the tripartite introduction Adam begins *De Tripartito Tabernaculo* with a tripartite chapter of thirty-three lines (3 x 11) exhibiting six rhymes (3 x 2), parts I, II, III containing respectively three, four, and five sentences,[1] together twelve (3 x 4), and 414 words, CCCCXIIII (3 x 138).

I

I   Quia uestre pater uenerande placet éxcelléntie   a
ut qualiter uetus illud tabernaculum Moysi in re factum fuerit et
dispositum nos quoque osténdere conémur   b
oportet nimirum deuotis uos precibus summum illum ac uerum Artíficem
èxoráre   a
quatenus uestrum etiam Beseleel quo uel aliquantulam tante rei
ostensionem effundere possit Spiritu Sancto replére dignétur .   b

II   Scit enim euidenter paternitas uestra nullum omnino hominum hoc in
témpore ésse   5 a
qui predictum edificium corporali uiderit aspectu ac per hoc mírum
non ésse   a
si in corporali eius factura et dispositione nos quóque caligémus .   c

III   Quod si dixerit quis ex libri Exodi dictis predicti tabernaculi facturam et
dispositionem materialem plene nos conícere pósse   a
sciat mirum non esse si prefati libri uerba nequaquam nos plene iuxta
litteram íntelligámus   c
cum nonnulli doctores eximii longe a nobis tam sanctitate uite quam
sublimitate scientie remoti diuersa super eorumdem uerborum
intellectu litterali sensisse ínueniántur .   10 b

II

IIII   Ut enim de multis paúca proferámus   c
pater et aduocatus noster doctorque ecclesie incomparabilis Aurelius
Augustinus multis in locis ut asserunt qui legerunt altare thymiamatis
intra uelum dícit fuísse   a
cum Iosephus et omnes fere Sancte Scripture expositores illud inter
candelabrum et mensam propositionis extra uelum contra arcam
testamenti positum fuisse affírment .   d

---

1   For composition on the series 3–4–5 see above pp. 11, 14.

V   Dicit preterea idem reuerendissimus doctor quod singulis tabulis que in
                tribus tabernaculi parietibus erant non bine bases *súpponebántur*   b

sed quod una basis tabule *súpponebátur*   15 b

alia súper*ponebátur*   b

ut basis superior quasi cápitellum és*set*   d

cum euidenter dicat Scriptura duas singulis tabulis per duos angulos bases
    suppósitas *fuísse*   a

dicente Domino ad Moysen 'Bine bases singulis tabulis per duos angulos
    súbic*iántur*'   b

et item 'Duabus basibus per unam tábulam sùpput*átis*' .   20 c

VI   Venerabilem etiam Bedam presbyterum doctorem Anglorum non solum
          diligentem uerbi Dei scrutatorem sed et ueracem fuisse expositórem
          quis nésci*at* .   d

VII   Ab eodem tamen doctore in extensione cortinarum et sagorum ad
          operiendum tabernaculi tectum et sexti sagi in fronte tecti
          duplicatione magister Andreas múltum dissénti*t* .   d

III

VIII   Hec uobis pater carissime ídeo díxerim

ut cogitetis non esse mirum si égo succúm*bo*   e

dum tam graue infirmis meis ceruicibus ónus impóni*tis*   25 c

et si in illius solis radiis ego talpa caligem in quibus tales tanteque aquile
    caligare *ínueniúntir* .   b

VIIII   Igitur quia de materiali factura et dispositione tabernaculi meam prodere
          insipiéntiam impéllo*r*   b

primum quidem quantum capere potero osténdere studé*bo*   e

qualiter tres tabernaculi parietes ex tábulis constába*nt*   d

qualiterque eedem tabule ad inuicem érant coniúnct*e* .   30 a

X   Secundo uero quomodo etiam tabule connexe et firmate et parietes cum
          introitu érant erécti .   f

XI   Tertio qualiter predicti parietes cortinis et sagis pellibusque rubricatis
          et hyacinthinis fuére coopérti .   f

XII   Cumque hoc modo fuerit tabernaculum perfectum de his que intra
          illud et exterius erant circa illud prout conicere potero tractáre tentá*bo* . 33 e

19 Exodus XXVI 16. 20 Exodus XXVI 25.

I

I   Because, venerable father, it is pleasing to your excellency
        that even we should try to show how that old tabernacle of Moses
          was in actuality made and arranged,
        it is fitting doubtless that you beseech that highest and true Artificer in prayers
        that He may deign to fill your Beseleel also with the Holy Spirit, by
          Whom he can if you like fashion some sort of showing of so great an
          actuality.

II   For your fatherliness knows evidently that no man at all exists in this time   5
        who will have seen the foresaid edifice with corporal sight, and because of
          this it is not wondrous
        if even we have a cloudy vision of its corporal making and arrangement.

III   Because if anyone should say that it is possible for us to conjecture fully from
          the sayings of the book of Exodus the making and arrangement of the
          foresaid tabernacle,
       he would know that it is not wondrous if we should in no way understand
          the words of the foresaid book fully according to the letter,
       since not a few excellent teachers far removed from us as much in sanctity
          of life as in sublimity of knowing may be found to have sensed diverse
          things about the literal understanding of the same words.   10

II

IIII   For so that we may proffer a few things from among many,
       the father and our advocate and incomparable teacher of the Church Aurelius
          Augustine in many places, as they assert who have read, says that the altar of
          incense was within the veil,
       though Josephus and almost all expositors of Holy Scripture affirm that to
          have been placed between the candelabrum and the table of offering
          outside the veil against the ark of the covenant.

V   The same most reverend teacher says besides that not two bases were placed
          beneath single frames which were on the three walls of the tabernacle,
       but that one base of a frame was placed beneath;   15
       the other was placed above,
       so that the superior base would be like a capital,
       though Scripture evidently says that two bases were placed beneath single
          frames on two corners,
       with the Lord saying to Moses, 'Two bases should be set beneath single
          frames on two corners',
       and similarly, 'You reckon two bases for one frame'.   20

VI   Who does not know also that the Venerable Bede, priest, teacher of the
          English, was not only a diligent examiner of the word of God but also
          a true expositor?

VII   From this same teacher, however, master Andrew [of Saint Victor] dissents
          much about the extending of the curtains and cloths for covering the
          roof of the tabernacle and about the doubling of the sixth cloth on the
          front of the roof.

III

VIII   These things, then, most beloved father, I would say to you,
       so that you might think it is not wondrous if I succumb
       when you place a heavy burden on my infirm neck,   25
       and if in the rays of that sun in which such and so great eagles are found to
          have cloudy vision I see dimly as a mole.

VIIII   Therefore, because I am impelled to bring forth my foolishness about the
          material making and arrangement of the tabernacle,
       I will study to show as much as I shall be able to undertake first
       how the three walls of the tabernacle stood from three frames,
       and how the same frames were joined to each other.   30

X   In the second place, in truth, how the same frames were joined together
          and made firm and the walls were erected with an entrance.

XI   In the third place how the foresaid walls were covered with curtains
          and cloths and skins reddened and hyacinthine.

XII   And when in this manner the tabernacle was perfected I shall attempt
             to treat as I can conjecture about these things which were within it and
             outside about it.   33

Even the most cursory reader must notice the stated and restated diction that
Adam used to link sentences in Part I. First within sentence I *re* and *rei* and
within sentence III *libri* and *libri* and *intelligamus* and *intellectu*. Then between
sentence I *uestre pater, uetus illud tabernaculum, nos quoque*, and sentence II *paternitas
uestra, predictum edificium, nos quoque*. Then between sentence II *scit, mirum non esse
si*, and sentence III *sciat, mirum non esse si*. Then among all three sentences *factum
et dispositum, factura et dispositione, facturam et dispositionem*, and *nos, nos, nos*.

Similarly in Part II within sentence IIII *intra uelum fuisse* and *extra uelum fuisse*,
and between adjacent sentences *Scripture* IIII and *Scriptura* V, and among all four
sentences *doctorque* IIII, *doctor* V, *doctorem* VI, *doctore* VIII.

Similarly in Part III in adjacent sentences *parietes* VIIII, X, and XI.

He linked Part I *Moysi* with Part II *Moysen*.

He linked Part I *pater, tabernaculum, mirum non esse si, in corporali eius factura et
dispositione, caligemus, tabernaculi*, and *inueniantur* with Part III *pater, tabernaculum,
non esse mirum si, de materiali factura et dispositione, caligem* and *caligare, tabernaculi*,
and *inueniuntur*.

The mathematical patterning is equally notable. Part I contains 137 words,
which divide by extreme and mean ratio at 85 and 52, so that minor and major
parts of the golden section fall at references to Adam's patron John Abbot of
Kelso, | *quia uestre pater* 1 and | *paternitas uestra* 5. The first fifty-two words divide
by extreme and mean ratio at 32 and 20 at Adam's reference to himself, *nos
quoque* | 2. There is another golden section at references to Adam's subject, in
the eighty-five words from | *uetus illud tabernaculum* 2 to *predicti tabernaculi* | 8
inclusive. Those eighty-five words divide by extreme and mean ratio at 53 and
32, at *predictum edificium* | [*i.e. tabernaculum*] 6. Adam refers to himself eight-
ninths of the way through the paragraph at *nobis* | 9.

Part II has been elaborately wrought. The eighteen words of line 14 divide by
sesquialter ratio 3:2 at 11 and 7, at *tribus* |. The seven words divide by the ratio
3:2 at | *bine*. The six words of line 15 divide by symmetry 1:1 at *una* |. The
thirteen words of line 18 divide by the ratio 3:2 at 8 and 5, in the five words
from | *duas* to *duos* | inclusive. The twelve words of line 19 divide by duple ratio
2:1 at 8 and 4, at | *bine*. The last eight words divide by the same ratio at 5 and 3,
at | *duos*. The eight words of line 20 divide by the same ratio at *duabus* |. Part II
contains 158 words, which divide by duple ratio 2:1 at 105 and 53, so that the
paragraph divides into thirds in the fifty-three words from | *tribus* 14 to *unam* |
20. Those fifty-three words divide by the same ratio at 35 and 18. There are
thirty-five words from | *bine* 14 to *bine* | 19 inclusive. There are thirty-five
words from | *una* 15 to *duos* | 19 inclusive. There are eighteen words between
duos | 18 and | *duabus* 20, of which a central ninth word is *bine* | 19.

Part III contains 119 words, which divide by symmetry at *tres tabernaculi parietes* 29. The 119 words divide by extreme and mean ratio at 74 and 45, at | *tabernaculi* 27. From | *tres tabernaculi parietes* 29 to *tabernaculum* | 33 inclusive there are forty-five words. The 119 words divide by sesquitertian ratio 4:3 at 68 and 51, at the fifty-first word, *primum* | 28. The next fifty-one words divide by the same ratio at 29 and 22, at the twenty-second word, *secundo uero* | 31. The next twenty-two words divide by the same ratio at 13 and 9, at the thirteenth word, *tertio* | 32. Adam refers to himself one-ninth of the way through the paragraph at *ego* | 24.

Parts I, II, and III together contain 414 words, which divide by symmetry 1:1 at 207 and 207, at | *una* 15. The 414 words divide by duple ratio at 276 and 138, the 138th word being the first of the central part II. The 414 words divide by extreme and mean ratio at 256 and 158, the central part II containing 158 words. The 414 words divide by sesquialter ratio 3:2 at 248 and 166, at *duabus basibus* | 20. The 414 words divide by sesquitertian ratio 4:3 at 237 and 177, at *bine* | *bases* 19.

'CRONICA DE MAILROS'

The most important and extensive Scottish historical text of the twelfth century is the *Cronica de Mailros*, compiled from about 1185, extant in London, British Library, MS Cotton Faustina B.IX.[1] I have represented capital letters and punctuation marks of the manuscript with boldface, suggested rhymes with italics, and marked the rhythms of the cursus.

CRONICA DE MAILROS

1	**P**ostquam ueridicus hystoriographus et dóctor exím*ius* .		a
	decus et gloria nostrae gentis Beda uenerabilis scríbere cessáu*it* :		b
	non inuenti sunt aliqui quantum perpendere potuimus certi uel contínui rèlatór*es* .		a
	qui in annorum et temporum euéntibus rècitánd*is* .		a
	et ad instruendam posteritatis nostrae ignoránti*am* .	5	c
	et dubietates aetatis huius omníno tollén*das* :		a
	qualem deceret óperam impénderen*t* .		b
2	**Q**uod ánimaduertént*es* .		a
	quantum pigritia nóstra permítt*it* .		b
	aliquantulam dédimus óper*am* .	10	c
	rei ueritatem quantum sufficere potuimus diligénter indagáre .		d
3	**A**b eo igitur tempore id est ab his tribus annis quibus praedictus et uenerabilis **G**yruensis siue **W**eremuthensis monasterii presbyter et monachus Beda finem fécit recitáre :		d
	seriem et statum temporum breuissime tamen decúrrere aggrédimur .		e
	et ab ipsius Bedae uerbis exórdium súmim*us* .		a
	quorum hanc esse formam certíssime cónsta*t* .	15	b

1   *BCLL*, no. 1041 p. 290. *Chronica de Mailros e Codice Unico in Bibliotheca Cottoniana Servato, Nunc Iterum in Lucem Edita. Notulis Indiceque Aucta*, ed J. Stevenson (Edinburgh: Bannatyne Club, 1835), p. 1. *The Chronicle of Melrose from the Cottonian Manuscript, Faustina B.IX in the British Museum*, (facsimile) with an Introduction by A.O. Anderson, M.O. Anderson, W.C. Dickinson (London: Percy Lund Humphries, 1936).

1 After the truth-uttering writer of history and exceptional teacher,
   the honour and glory of our people, the venerable Bede, ceased to write,
   there have not been found, as far as we have been able to assess, any sure or
    continuous relaters,
   who in events of years and times to be recited
   for both instructing the ignorance of our posterity   5
   and taking away altogether the dubieties of this age
   might weigh out such effort as would be fitting.

2 Turning our minds to which,
   as far as our laziness permits,
   we have given a certain little effort,   10
   as far as we have been able to suffice, diligently to ascertain the truth of the
    matter.

3 Therefore from that time, that is from the three 'years' in which the foresaid
    and venerable priest and monk Bede of the monastery of Jarrow or
    Wearmouth recited the end,
   we are advancing to run through the series and condition of the times,
    though most briefly,
   and we are taking up the beginning from the words of the same Bede,
   of which this happens most surely to be the form.   15

This copy is good, but not the original text, as one infers from the thirteenth-century script, the spelling *pigricia*, as distinct from *pigritia*, the use of *e caudata ę* for the Classical diphthong *ae*, and use of abbreviations that obscure the letter count. The only apparent oddity in this Prologue is the reference to the *tribus annis quibus … Beda finem fecit recitare.* Bede is widely known to have brought the *Historia Ecclesiastica Gentis Anglorum* to an end in a single year, A.D. 731. Our author alludes to Bede's use in the account of that year of the word *annus* three times.

> *Anno* DCCXXXI Berctuald archiepiscopus obiit. *Anno eodem* Tatuini consecratus archiepiscopus nonus Doruuernensis ecclesiae, Aedilbaldo rege Merciorum XV agente *annum* imperii.

Bede's sentence of twenty words divides into thirds at the second usage, *anno eodem* |. In the *Cronica de Mailros* the Prologue contains three sentences and 730 letters, or including a single punctuation point after *constat*, 731 characters. This suggests that our author understood the structure of Bede's Preface from *Historia Ecclesiastica Gentis Anglorum Praefatio* to *Explicit Praefatio* inclusive as arranged in one hundred lines with exactly 731 words.[2]

 Our author has ordered his words and ideas in chiastic and parallel patterns.

---

2 Howlett, 'Insular Latin Writers' Rhythms', pp. 110–16.

2	A1	Beda
3	A2	certi
4	B	temporum
4	C	recitandis
5	D1	posteritatis nostrae ignorantiam
7	D2	operam
8	E	quod animaduertentes
9	D'1	pigritia nostra
10	D'2	operam
12	C'	recitare
13	B'	temporum
14	A'1	ipsius Bedae
15	A'2	certissime.

The author begins and ends the chiasmus with references to his model Bede, and he refers to himself at the crux of the chiasmus, where he 'turns the mind', *animaduertentes*.

The author has further disposed words at intervals determined by arithmetic ratios. In this passage of 111 words there are eleven words before | *Beda* 2 and eleven words from | *ipsius Bedae* to the end.[3]

As the 111 words divide by duple ratio 2:1 at 74 and 37, the Prologue divides into thirds at *tribus* | *annis* 12. The Prologue exhibits duple ratio again in that the twentieth word is *quantum* 3, and there are ten words from *quantum* 9 to *quantum* 11 inclusive, between which a central fifth word is *aliquantulam* 10.

The 111 words divide by extreme and mean ratio at 69 and 42, at *aetatis* | *huius* 6 and *ab eo igitur* | *tempore* 12. There are forty-two words from *potuimus* 3 to *potuimus* 11 inclusive.

The 111 words divide by sesquialter ratio 3:2 at 67 and 44. There are twelve words before *uenerabilis* 2 and thirty-two words after *uenerabilis* 12, together forty-four. As 67 divides by the same ratio at 40 and 27, one notes that there are twenty-seven words from | *uenerabilis* 2 to *posteritatis nostrae ignorantiam* | 5 inclusive and twenty-seven words from | *pigritia nostra* 9 to *uenerabilis* | 12 inclusive. As 44 divides by the same ratio at 26 and 18, one notes the twenty-sixth word *relatores* 3, between which and *tollendas* 6 there are eighteen words. After *nostrae* | 2 the forty-fourth word is *nostra* 9, there being eighteen words from | *posteritatis nostrae* 5 to *pigritia nostra* | 9 inclusive.

The 111 words divide by sesquitertian ratio 4:3 at 63 and 48. There are forty-eight words before *impenderent* 8. The number 48 divides by the same ratio at 27 and 21. Between *perpendere* 3 and *impenderent* 8 there are twenty-seven words.

---

3   For other examples of composition on the numbers 11, 111, 1111, see above pp. 14, 17, 102, 174 and below pp. 186–7.

The 111 words divide by one-ninth and eight-ninths at 12 and 99, at *Beda* |
2, the twelfth word from the beginning, and | *ab ipsius Bedae uerbis* 14, the
twelfth word from the end. Between *Beda* | 12 and | *ab ipsius Bedae uerbis* 14
there are twelve words.[4] Reckoning letters as numerals *BEDA* bears a numerical
value of 2+5+4+1 or 12.[5]

By representing the 731 words of Bede's Preface with the 731 characters of
this Prologue our author placed himself in the Anglo-Latin tradition. From the
title of Bede's work, *Historia Ecclesiastica Gentis Anglorum*, and the description of
Bede as the *decus et gloria **nostrae** gentis* one infers that our author considered
himself an Angle. Few will doubt that he also placed himself in *regno Scottorum*.

4   For reference to authors and patrons at one-ninth and eight-ninths of compositions
     see above pp. 18, 22, 90, 95, 106, 160.
5   See above pp. 5, 8, 22, 35, 58–61, 84, 89, 95, 141, 159–60, 174.

'DE SUBIECTIONE ECCLESIE CANDIDE CASE'

Another tract of the twelfth century considers the subordination of the Bishop of Whithorn to the Archbishop of York.[1] Composed about A.D. 1200, the text survives in London, British Library, MS Additional 25014, folio 118va. I have arranged the text in sentences, represented capital letters and punctuation marks in the manuscript with boldface, and marked the rhythms of the cursus.

DE EO QUOD EPISCOPI CANDIDE CASE ESSE DEBEANT SUBIECTI ARCHIEPISCOPO EBORACENSI .

1 **IN** hystoria et ueteribus **A**nglorum uoluminibus de ecclesie Candide Cáse epíscopis **:** que alio uocabulo ab incolis Hꝑítern nuncupátur **:** quoddam conscríptum repperímus **.** quod preséntium notície **:** et posteriorum memorie Latino sermone sicut inuenimus trádere curáuimus **.**

2 **AN**no septingentesimo sexagesimo secundo Friðuꝑald Hꝑiternensis episcopus óbiit nònis Maíi **.**

3 **H**ic uero sui presulatus consecrationem in Cestra quondam uilla religióne famósa **:** inter Dunelmiam et Tine fluuium suscepit decimo octauo kalendis Decembris sexto anno regni Céolꝑulfi régis **.**

4 **H**ic autem Friðuꝑald uiginti nóuem annis uíxit **:**

5 Eo uero defuncto **.** consecratus est **P**ehtꝑine in uilla que dicitur Eluete inter fluuium Tese et Tine decimo sexto kaléndis Augústi **.** et restitutus est ín loco eíus **:** in Hꝑiternénsi ecclésia **.**

6 **A**nno septingentesimo nonagesimo primo Badꝑulfus ab Eanbaldo Eboracensi árchiepíscopo **.** et Eꝑelberchto episcopo consecrationem episcopálem suscépit **:** et in ecclesia Hꝑiternensi episcopus ést constitútus **.**

7 **An**no septingentesimo septuagesimo octauo imperantibus Cineꝑulfus **.** et Offa Anglórum régibus **.** Eꝑelberchtus consecratus est episcopus in Eboraco decimo sexto kaléndis Iúlii **:** ab Eboracensi árchiepíscopo **.**

8 Et ecclesie Hꝑiternensis presulátum suscépit **.**

9 **An**no septingentesimo nonagesimo sexto passa est lúna eclípsin **.** inter galli cantum et auroram quinto kaléndis Aprílis **:**

10 Et Eardꝑulfus regnum Northanhimbrorum suscepit secúndo idus Maíi **.**

---

1 *BCLL*, no. 1044 p. 290. R.J. Brentano, 'Whithorn and York', *The Scottish Historical Review* XXXII (1953), pp. 143–6.

11   Postea uero septimo kalendis Iunii ab Eanbaldo Eboracensi árchiepíscopo . et
      Eþelberchto . et Higbaldo Líndisfarnénsi . et Badþulfo Hþiternensi episcopis eius
      súffragáneis : in Eboraco est sullimatus et in régem consecrátus .

      I have silently reduced *e̜* to *e* throughout. 1 hpltaérne. 2 .dcc°.lx°.ij°. friðupald. hpitaernensis.
      .N'. 3 .xviii. kl'. .vi°. ceolpulfi. 4 friðepald .xxix. 5 þehtpine. .xvi. kl'. piternensi. 6
      .dcc°.xx°.i°. badpúlf. enbaldo. uuiternénsi. 7 .dcc°.lxx°.viii°. sinepul. ethilbe[r]cht. .xvi. kl'. 8
      piternensis. 9 .dcc°.xc°.vi°. v kl'. 10 eardulfus. .ii. 11 .vii. Kl'. ethilberchto. [h]igbaldo. badulfo
      hpiternensi.

ABOUT THAT [FACT] THAT BISHOPS OF CANDIDA CASA
OUGHT TO BE SUBJECT TO THE ARCHBISHOP OF YORK

1   In history and the old volumes [or 'rolls'] of the English we have discovered a certain
      document about bishops of the Church of Candida Casa, which by another name is
      named Whithorn by the inhabitants, that we have taken care to hand on to the notice of
      present men and to the memory of later men in Latin speech just as we have found [it].
2   In the 762nd year Frithuwald Bishop of Whithorn died on the nones of May [*recte* 7
      May 763].
3   This man in truth received the consecration of his episcopate in Chester[-le-Street],
      formerly a town famous in religion, between Durham and the river Tyne on the
      eighteenth of the kalends of December in the sixth year of the reign of Ceolwulf the
      king [*i.e.* 14 November 735].
4   This Frithuwald, however, lived twenty-nine years.
5   With that man dead in truth Pectwine was consecrated in the town that is called Elvet
      between the river Tees and the Tyne on the sixteenth of the kalends of August [*i.e.* 17 July
      763], and he was restored in his [*i.e.* Frithuwald's] place in the Church of Whithorn.
6   In the 791st year Beaduwulf received episcopal consecration from Eanbald Archbishop
      of York [780–96] and Æthelberct Bishop [of Hexham 789–97], and he [Æthelberct] was
      constituted bishop in the Church of Whithorn [777–89].
7   In the 778th year, with Cynewulf [757–86] and Offa [757–96] kings of the English
      ruling, Æthelberct was consecrated bishop in York on the sixteenth of the kalends of
      July [*i.e.* 16 June 777] by the Archbishop of York.
8   And he received the episcopate of the Church of Whithorn.
9   In the 796th year the moon suffered eclipse between cockcrow [lit. 'the song of the
      cock'] and dawn on the fifth of the kalends of April [*i.e.* 28 March 796].
10   And Eardwulf received the kingdom of the Northumbrians on the second of the ides
      of May [*i.e.* 14 May 796].
11   Afterwards in truth on the seventh of the kalends of June [*i.e.* 26 May 796] by Eanbald
      Archbishop of York and by his suffragan bishops Æthelberct and Higbald of Lindisfarne
      and Beaduwulf of Whithorn he was elevated and consecrated as king in York.

      The author has infixed devices that guarantee incrementally the integrity of
his composition. In the title there are eleven words that introduce a text of
eleven sentences. In the title, with diaeresis in *subïecti*, there are thirty-three

syllables that introduce the first sentence of thirty-three words. The first sentence contains 223 letters, beginning a text that contains 223 words.[2]

In 3 the eighteenth word from the beginning of the sentence is the first of *decimo octauo*, of which the last syllable is eighteenth from the end of the sentence.

In 4 there are nine syllables before *nouem*. The last letter of *uiginti nouem* is the twenty-ninth of the sentence.

In 5 there are sixteen words before *decimo sexto*.

In 7 there are sixteen words before *decimo sexto*.

In 9 the ninth syllable is the first of *nonagesimo*.

In 10 there are two words after *secundo*.

For present purposes minor discrepancies of dating between this and other texts that refer to the same events matter less than the devices infixed to guarantee the integrity of this composition. In this respect, the fact of ownership of land and the fact of Duncan's kingship in the charter considered above, the topography in *De Situ Albanie*, the chronology in the 'Chronicle of the Kings of Alba', like the absolute chronology of events mentioned in this text, are less valuable to us than the picture they present of various authors' opinions about their significance.

2   For other examples of this technique see above pp. 4, 51, 85, 89, 96, 102, 115, 141, 150, 152, 155, and Howlett, 'Five Experiments', pp. 15–18, 28–30, '*Synodus Prima*', pp. 252–3, '*Liber Angeli*', p. 268, 'Insular Acrostics, Celtic Latin Colophons', pp. 27–44.

X

EPILOGUE

Twenty-three years ago, Gordon Murray, one of my colleagues as Assistant Editor of the *Supplement* to the *Oxford English Dictionary*, drafted entries for scientific words with the same care that he devoted to a private interest, trying to understand the 'grammatical' structure of pictorial elements of Pictish symbol stones and the 'syntactical' order in which one should read them.[1] Knowing my interest in the structures of Anglo-Latin and Old English texts, he asked me to analyse the *Historia Brittonum* and some early Scottish Latin historical and hagiographical texts. In Mommsen's edition for the *Monumenta Germaniae Historica* the *Historia Brittonum* seemed rebarbative, and the Scottish texts seemed even more repellent, farragos of pseudo-historical nonsense and hagiographic lies.[2] Gordon's asking in a soft but insistent voice, silenced long ago, still works in the mind, now like the voices of authors he once invited me to understand. Long delay in satisfying his request has allowed me the advantage of a journey backward in time, from works of Anglo-Latin writers to works of their Hiberno-Latin teachers, and from the Cambro-Latin writers, who taught the Irish, to their Romano-British forbears. The cumulative continuities of the Romano-British, Cambro-Latin, Hiberno-Latin, and Anglo-Latin traditions bring into sharp focus the radical discontinuities of Scottish intellectual life as recorded in Latin literature.

We may suppose that peoples who lived in what is now Scotland experienced spoken and perhaps written Latin in the course of commercial and military contacts between and around the Roman walls from the first century A.D. onward.[3] Unless we dismiss as mere rhetoric Tertullian's reference to *Britannorum inaccessa Romanis loca Xpisto uero subdita* they must have received Latin Christianity by the beginning of the third century.[4] They received Latin Christianity from

---

1   †G. Murray, 'The declining Pictish symbol — a reappraisal', *Proceedings of the Society of Antiquaries of Scotland* CXVI (1986), pp. 223–53.

2   For a fairer estimate of the *Historia Brittonum* see Howlett, *Cambro-Latin Compositions*, pp. 69–83. The change of my opinion about the Scottish texts should be apparent on every page of this book.

3   D.V. Clarke, D.J. Breeze, G. Mackay, *The Romans in Scotland, An introduction to the collections of the National Museum of Antiquities of Scotland* (Edinburgh: National Museum of Antiquities of Scotland, 1980).

4   W.H.C. Frend, 'The Christianization of Roman Britain' in M.W. Barley and R.P.C. Hanson edd. *Christianity in Roman Britain, 300–700* (Leicester University Press, 1968), p. 38. Haddan and Stubbs, *Councils*, vol. I p. 3.

the mission of Ninia around Whithorn late in the fourth century and early in the fifth, and again from another mission around Whithorn and the Rhins of Galloway late in the fifth century and early in the sixth. In a letter written during the fifth century from Ireland to the soldiers of a British tyrant named Coroticus Saint Patrick lamented the betrayal of his converts by a *traditor Xpistianorum in manus Scottorum atque Pictorum* and condemned the *socii Scottorum atque Pictorum apostatarumque*, implying that if Scots and Picts had converted to Christianity he considered them to have lapsed from it.[5] For analyses of both the artefacts associated with these missionaries and the intellectual world inhabited by them one may profitably consult the works of Professor Charles Thomas.[6] About the middle of the sixth century, from 563, the peoples of what is now Scotland received Latin Christianity from the mission of Columba on Iona.[7] The *Annales Cambriae* record *s.a.* CLXVIII, A.D. 612, *Conthigirni obitus,* 'the death of Kentigern'. In *Historia Ecclesiastica Gentis Anglorum* V XXI, published in 731, Bede records a letter, written perhaps by himself, but sent as from Abbot Ceolfrid to Nechtan King of the Picts. The letter, dealing with complexities of calculating the date of Easter, about which Bede says that the king was already well informed, *ipse in his non parua ex parte esset imbutus,* implies the presence at Nechtan's court of men who could cope with detailed arguments in written Latin.

> Sed et architectos sibi mitti petiit, qui iuxta morem Romanorum ecclesiam de lapide in gente ipsius facerent, promittens hanc in honorem beati apostolorum principis dedicandam; se quoque ipsum cum suis omnibus morem sanctae Romanae et apostolicae ecclesiae semper imitaturum, in quantum dumtaxat tam longe a Romanorum loquella et natione segregati hunc ediscere potuissent.

> 'He also asked for builders to be sent to build a church of stone in their country after the Roman fashion, promising that it should be dedicated in honour of the blessed chief of the apostles. He also said that he and all his people would always follow the customs of the holy Roman and apostolic Church, so far as they could learn them, remote though they were from the Roman people and from their language.'

5   Howlett, *Liber Epistolarum Sancti Patricii Episcopi,* pp. 26, 32.
6   C. Thomas, *Britain and Ireland in Early Christian Times, A.D. 400–800* (London: Thames and Hudson, 1971), *The Early Christian Archaeology of North Britain* (London: Oxford University Press for the University of Glasgow, 1971), *Christianity in Roman Britain to A.D. 500* (Berkeley and Los Angeles: University of California Press, 1981), *Whithorn's Christian Beginnings,* First Whithorn Lecture (Whithorn: Friends of the Whithorn Trust, 1992), 'The Early Christian Inscriptions of Southern Scotland', *Glasgow Archaeological Journal* XVII (1994 for 1991–2), pp. 1–10, 'The Conversions of Scotland', The John Jamieson Lecture, *Records of the Scottish Church History Society* XXVII (1997), pp. 1–41.
7   Anderson and Anderson, *Vita Sancti Columbae.*

This implies a desire to understand and participate in the intellectual and spiritual life of Latin Christian civilization and to live with permanent artefacts of that civilization.

So does that most spectacular monument, the Ruthwell Cross, erected probably during the episcopate of Pecthelm, who in 731 had become the first English Bishop of Whithorn *nuper* and who died in 735. The cross bears the longest extant Anglo-Latin and Old English runic inscriptions and an Old Northumbrian form of the finest Old English Christian poem.[8]

These, with ogam inscriptions and Pictish symbol stones, the restrained beauty of which must be apparent to the most casual observer, imply the existence of sophisticated literate cultures.[9] But with the possible exception of the first text considered in this book, the Liturgy from the Book of Deer, any Latin literature that may have been composed before the end of the eleventh century in Scotland has disappeared without trace. If it existed it may have been destroyed by Vikings who behaved more ruthlessly in Scotland than elsewhere in the British Isles during campaigns, based in the Shetlands, the Orkneys, the Hebrides, and Dalriada, to enrich and empower themselves to conquer Ireland, as suggested by Professor Donnchadh Ó Corráin in a brilliant O'Donnell Lecture for 1996.[10]

What we can read today emerged in a burst of creative literary activity from the end of the eleventh century to the end of the twelfth. In this literature we encounter two recurrent phenomena: plain statements that little, if any, Scottish Latin literature existed already, and recourse, both implicit and explicit, to models in earlier Cambro-Latin, Hiberno-Latin, and Anglo-Latin literatures.

Assuming that, like *entia, auctores non multiplicandi sunt preter necessitatem*, let us imagine the smallest number of writers possible, reckoning Turgot as efficient cause, if not the onlie begetter, of the diplomatic instruments of Malcolm III and Duncan II and Eadgar and Thor Longus, and composer of the verses in Saint Margaret's Gospel Book, and author of the prose *Vita Margaritae Reginae*.

Even if we suppose early forms of *Cronica de Origine Antiquorum Pictorum* and the 'Chronicle of the Kings of Alba' to have existed, the texts as preserved in the Poppleton manuscript exhibit signs of coherent editing to make them fit into a comprehensive twelfth-century collection. So carefully have they been edited that one cannot without earlier texts work backward to any antecedent form from the present form, which we should deal with as the work of a single

---

8 D. Howlett, 'Inscriptions and Design of the Ruthwell Cross', *The Ruthwell Cross*, ed. B. Cassidy, Index of Christian Art Occasional Papers I (Princeton University Press, 1992), pp. 71–93. B. Cassidy and D. Howlett, 'Some Eighteenth-Century Drawings of the Ruthwell Cross', *The Antiquaries Journal* LXXII (1992), pp. 102–17. D.R. Howlett, 'Old English *ondgienvan, ongienvan, ungienvan*', *Anglia* CXVI (1998), pp. 223–6.

9 S. Cruden, *The Early Christian and Pictish Monuments of Scotland* (Edinburgh: HMSO, 1964).

10 Donnchadh Ó Corráin, 'The Vikings in Scotland and Ireland in the ninth century', *Peritia* XII (1998), pp. 296–339.

twelfth-century author. Considering the sophisticated use of Isidore's *Etymologiae* in both *Cronica de Origine Antiquorum Pictorum* and *Vita Sancti Reguli*, and intelligent quotation from Geoffrey of Monmouth's *Historia Regum Britannie* in both *De Situ Albanie* and *Vita Sancti Reguli*, and the 777–word text of the 'Chronicle of the Kings of Alba' and the 777–word text of the *Vita Sancti Reguli*, and the description of William as *Rufus* in both *De Situ Albanie* and *Cronica Regum Scottorum*, and the seven parts of *De Situ Albanie* and the seventy lines of the 'Chronicle of the Kings of Alba' and the seventy-seven lines of *Cronica Regum Scottorum*, we may infer a single idea underlying, if not a single mind unifying, the entire collection, written between 1175 and 1189.

From the shared features of forty lines and 276 words and play on the number 52 and the alphanumeric values of names in the Prologues of *Vita Sancti Seruani* and *Vita Sancti Kentigerni*, with Kentigern presented as the pupil of Serf, we might infer that a single author composed these two Lives and name him Symeon of Glasgow Archdeacon of Teviotdale. If he were identical with the Simeon who wrote the *Versus in Sanctum Columbam* we might reckon the church in Glasgow as a centre for composition of hagiography in both prose and verse, as well as composition of the occasional historical verse about Sumerled. But the verse about Columba was composed probably in 1112 and the prose about 1147 x 1164, the prose writer describing himself as an immigrant to Scotland and complaining about the lack of Scottish hagiography. As the poet infixed in his work a numerical value of 71 for the name Simeon, and the hagiographer infixed in his work a numerical value of 84 for the name Symeon, we may safely infer the existence of two distinct writers.

We may see further close links with these texts in the use of Isidore in the *Vita Sancti Seruani*, quotation of Geoffrey of Monmouth in the *Vitae Sanctorum Kentigerni et Waltheui* by Jocelin, in play on the numbers 40 and 276 by the author of the *Vita Sancti Reguli* and Adam of Dryburgh.

Here from a period little more than one hundred years long, before which nothing has survived, are seven authors already named, Turgot of Durham, Simeon, William of Glasgow, Jocelin of Furness, John of Kelso, Adam of Dryburgh, and Ralph of Melrose, to whom we add an eighth, Symeon of Glasgow. They offer clear indications of having read, marked, learned, and inwardly digested important texts of earlier Romano-British, Cambro-Latin, Hiberno-Latin, and Anglo-Latin writers, and widely separated as they may have been in a sparsely populated country, they read each others' works. No other explanation can account for the intimate lexical, structural, and thematic connections between the prose and verse accounts of Saint Margaret's Gospel Book, among all the texts of the Poppleton manuscript, *De Situ Albanie*, *Cronica de Origine Antiquorum Pictorum*, the 'Chronicle of the Kings of Alba', *Cronica Regum Scottorum*, and *Vita Sancti Reguli*, between the *Vita Sancti Seruani* and the *Vita Sancti Kentigerni*, between the works of Adam of Dryburgh and John of Kelso, and revision of Symeon of Glasgow's *Vita Sancti Kentigerni* and quotation of John of Kelso's Letter by Jocelin of Furness.

The named authors and the writers whose names are yet unknown incorporated incremental infixing of elements of composition in I.I, IIII.II, V.I, II, III, and IIII, VI.II and V, VII.II, III, and IIII, and VIIII.II.

They made words exhibit their meanings and numbers exhibit their values in III.I and III, IIII.I, II, and III, V.I, II, and IIII, and VIIII.II.

They played on *medius, mediocris*, and *mediocritas* in III.I, IIII.I, VI.II and III, on *maior* and *minor* in V.II.

They played on serial composition in II.II and V.I.

They played on the alphanumeric value of names in I.I, II.I, III.II, IIII.I and III, V.I, II, and III, VI.V, and VIII.I and II, and VIIII.I.

They incorporated calendrical play and infixed dates in II.I, III.II, IIII.I, III, and IIII, V.I, II, and III, VI.I and V, VII.II, VIII.I and II, and VIIII.I.

They played on particular numbers:

    2 in III.I, IIII.I, II, and III, V.I, II, and IIII, and VIIII.I;

    3 in III.II, IIII.II and III, V.I, II, and V, and VIIII.I;

    4 in II.I and II, IIII.II, and V.II;

    5 in III.III, IIII.II, VI.I, and VI.II.

    7 in III.II, IIII.I, II, and III, and VI.II;

    11 in II.II, III.I, and VIIII.II;

    13 in I.I, V.II, and VII.IIII;

    22 in III.I and V.I.

    33 in I.I, III.I and II, IIII.I and IIII, VI, IIII, and V, VIII.II, and VIIII.II;

    44 in III.I, IIII.II, V.I and VIIII.I;

    46 in VIII.I and II;

    52 in VII and III and VI.V;

    55 in III.I;

    66 in III.II and V.IIII;

    77 in IIII.I and IIII, VI.V, and VII.III;

    88 in VI.IIII and V;

    99 in VI and IIII;

    111 in III.I, V.IIII, VIII.II, and VIIII.I;

    144 in II.I, IIII.IIII, V.III, VII.II, and VIII.II;

    153 in VI.V;

    220 in IIII.I;

    222 in IIII.IIII, V.II and IIII;

    276 in V.I, II, and III and VIII.I;

    333 in IIII.I, III, and IIII, V.I and IIII;

    444 in V.I;

    777 in IIII.III and V.I;

    888 in I.I, II.I, and VIII. I;

    1180 in VIII.I and II.

They referred to patrons, authors, and subjects at places determined by extreme and mean ratio in III.II and III, IIII.I and II, V.V, VI.I, and VIII.I and II; by one-ninth and eight-ninths at III.I and II, V.II, III, and V, VIII.I, and VIIII.I, by sesquitertian ratio in V.III.

We can see influences tending in different directions. With the sartorial and literary and liturgical and devotional habits of the Anglo-Saxon princess Margaret came increased influence of the English language and English ways which became through her and her children the administrative practices and the social habits of the Scottish court. Through her biographer Turgot English diplomatic practice became Scottish diplomatic practice. In the earliest extant Scottish diplomatic document we see Malcolm and Margaret deliberately presenting themselves in a tradition of English royal patronage of Durham.[11] In the earliest extant Scottish charter we see a grant of property which may never have belonged to the alleged beneficiary, made by a man who claimed to be, but was not yet, King of the Scots. Duncan may have begun as he meant to go on, behaving like a charter-issuing English king, as if he were a king, but before he was one. In all the diplomatic documents of Malcolm and Margaret, Duncan, Eadgar, Alexander, and David considered in this book, as in *Sealed from Within: Self-Authenticating Insular Charters*, no single structural or stylistic feature, apart from proper names and the words *cana et coneuethe*, distinguishes Scottish charters from documents in the English tradition. Features in the neighbouring traditions developed *pari passu*. The Old Norse word *drengr*, for example, appears in English form in line 149 of the late Old English poem 'The Battle of Maldon', celebrating an event of A.D. 991, in the phrase *drenga sum*, referring to one of the Norse warriors. It recurs in the *Domesday Book* of 1086, volume I folio 269v, as *homines quos 'drenchs' uocabant*, and in a charter of Earl David of 1117,[12]

> Dauid comes Iohanni episcopo et Cospatrico et Colbano et Rodberto fratribus et omnibus suis fidelibus Tegnis et Drengis de Lodeneio et Teuegetedale salutem,

to be matched by examples in an English charter of 1128 and a Pipe Roll of 1130.[13] The high status of both Englishmen and Normans within Scottish territories is apparent in the order of address of a charter of Earl David of about 1120:[14]

> DAVID comes filius Malcolmi Regis Scotorum.
> Omnibus amicis suis Francis et Anglis. et Scottis.
> cunctisque sancte Dei ecclesie filiis salutem continuam.

---

11 Howlett, *Sealed from Within*, pp. 87–8.
12 Lawrie, *Charters*, no. XXX pp. 23–4.
13 *Dictionary of Medieval Latin from British Sources, s.v. drengus.*
14 Lawrie, *Charters*, no. XXXV pp. 26–8.

Throughout this period the Archbishops of Canterbury and York tried to assert and exercise metropolitan authority over the Scottish Church. Margaret corresponded with Lanfranc Archbishop of Canterbury,[15] as her daughter Mathilda corresponded with Anselm Archbishop of Canterbury.[16] Her son Alexander corresponded with both Anselm and Ralph Archbishops of Canterbury.[17] A clear statement of the claim to authority from the historic past survives in the little tract *De Subiectione Ecclesie Candide Case*. Among the episcopal *acta* we see in the oldest document relating to Whithorn profession to the Archbishop of York; in the oldest document relating to Saint Andrews a grant made in Roxburgh to the church of Coldingham with reference to other churches in Lothian on an English saint's day, in the presence of the Archbishop of York, the Bishop of Durham, and the Abbot of Saint Alban's; in the oldest document relating to Glasgow a grant made to the monks of Kelso; all this in the *regna Anglorum*, the English parts of the kingdom.

Adam wrote of himself in Dryburgh as *in regno Scottorum positus*, but ended his career in the English Charterhouse at Witham. Adam's correspondent John Abbot of Kelso sought postumous commemoration among the monks of Saint Cuthbert at Durham.

In the *Vita Sancti Kentigerni* Symeon of Glasgow announces his intention to do for Kentigern what his model Symeon of Durham had done for Cuthbert, and the author of the *Vita Sancte Bege* refers to Bede. The author of the *Cronica de Mailros*, sixty years after William of Malmesbury, *post Bedam uel solus uel primus*, announces his intention to begin his narrative where Bede had ended his. Both Adam of Dryburgh and John of Kelso refer to Venerable Bede the priest, *doctor Anglorum*, and Adam refers also to Andrew of Saint Victor, Abbot of Wigmore.

But against these Anglo-centripetal tendencies we see an opposing centrifugal tendency. In this respect the appearance of Englishmen on both sides of a conflict from the end of the eleventh century reminds us of an earlier time in which Angles fought on both sides in the *Gododdin*.[18]

The principal cause of the Anglo-centrifugal tendency was the Norman Conquest of England. When the commissioners made the *Domesday Book* for William the Conqueror in 1086 they did not include Durham, Northumberland, Cumberland, or Westmorland. One may readily understand the ardent desire of

15 *The Letters of Lanfranc Archbishop of Canterbury*, ed. and transl. Helen Clover and Margaret Gibson, Oxford Medieval Texts (Oxford: Clarendon Press, 1979), no. 50 pp. 160–3.

16 For their Latin correspondence see *S. Anselmi Cantuariensis Archiepiscopi Opera Omnia*, ed. F.S. Schmitt, 6 vols (Edinburgh: Thomas Nelson, 1946–61), Mathilda to Anselm *Epistolae* 242, 317, 320, 323, 384, 395, 400, and Anselm to Mathilda *Epistolae* 243, 246, 288, 296, 321, 329, 346, 347, 385, 406.

17 *Eadmeri Historia Novorum in Anglia*, ed. Martin Rule, Rolls Series LXXXI (London: Longman, 1884), pp. 279–82, 286–8.

18 *The Gododdin of Aneirin: Text and Context from Dark-Age North Britain*, ed. and transl. John Thomas Koch (Cardiff: University of Wales Press, 1997).

Northern English landowners not to be incorporated into the centralized feudal and administrative systems of Winchester- and London-based Normans, and the equally fervent desire of Northern English Churchmen not to be subjected to the centralized ecclesiastical jurisdictions of Normanized Canterbury and York, as what generally accompanied such incorporation and subjection was dispossession, if not death. Gaels and Picts north of the Forth cannot be proven to have composed any of our extant literary monuments, perhaps because they were well aware of their personal and cultural identities, which they did not suppose threatened. Because of the large numbers of Englishmen who had lived in the Lowlands since the sixth and seventh centuries and because of their wealth and their language and the advantages of long-established diplomatic and administrative practices associated with the evolution of the English state, in effect the creation by Englishmen of many of the organs of the Scottish state, there was little likelihood that Englishmen would be submerged by Picts and Gaels from the North, but there were real and present dangers from the South. As late an author as Jocelin of Furness wrote of the Conquest as *uiolenta Normannorum direptio*, hardly the words of one who admired or wished to be subject to it. The interests of Northern Englishmen, then, lay in creating from diverse ethnic groups and languages — British, Pictish, Irish, English, Norse, and Norman — a kingdom, a *Regnum Scottorum*. James Campbell, in stating memorably 'it is almost as if there are two Englands and one of them is called Scotland',[19] has hit an historical nail squarely on the head. Englishmen wrote the oldest extant copies of the phrases *Rex Scottorum* in the Memorandum of 1093, *Rex Scotiae* in Duncan's charter of 1094, *Edgarus Dei gratia Rex Scottorum omnibus per regnum suum Scottis et Anglis salutem* in a charter of *c*1098, all composed or formerly retained at Durham. English authors ensured that the kingdom would have its own historical topography, *De Situ Albanie*, its own chronicles, from the Pictish past *Cronica de Origine Antiquorum Pictorum*, from the Scottish, British, and Norse past the 'Chronicle of the Kings of Alba', and beginning where the *gloria nostrae gentis*, English Bede, ended, *Cronica de Mailros*. In this enterprise *Willelmus Rex Scottorum* was supplied in the *Cronica Regum Scottorum* with a genealogy through 150 generations right back to Adam son of the living God. The Scottish kingdom, *Scotia*, was supplied with a national apostle older than the David of the Welsh, the Patrick of the Irish, and the Alban of the English, the *primus apostolus a Xpisto Ihesu Domino nostro electus*, whose relics arrived not from Rome but from the Greek East, directly from Constantinople.[20] The most important

19 James Campbell, 'The United Kingdom of England: The Anglo-Saxon Achievement', *Uniting the Kingdom: The Making of British History*, ed. A. Grant and K.J. Stringer (1995), pp 31–47 at 47.
20 Compare the attempts by the eleventh-century Cambro-Latin authors Rhygyfarch ap Sulien, son of the Bishop of Saint David's, and Lifris of Llancarfan, son of the Bishop of Glamorgan, to present their Welsh saints David and Cadog as older than and independent of the authority of the Kings of England and the metropolitan Archbishops of Canterbury, *Cambro-Latin Compositions*, pp. 103–28.

indigenous saints were British Kentigern son of Thaney, taught by Serf, son of a king of Canaan and a daughter of a king of Arabia, and Irish Columba. All of these texts were written by Angles, who deliberately avoided any mention of Christianity from Rome or Canterbury or York.

Within the emerging Scottish tradition are clear signs of internal continuity. As the author of the *Miracula Sancte Margarite Regine Scotorum* refers in his Prologue to Turgot's *Vita Margaritae Reginae*, written between A.D. 1100 and 1107, and mentions the years 1180 in chapter IX, 14 October 1257 in chapter XLII, and the year 1260 in chapter XVI, one may suppose that knowledge of Turgot's work was continuous from the moment of publication, and that from the decision in 1180 to improve the tomb, through the canonization in 1250 by Innocent IV and the translation on 19 June 1251, to the mention of the year 1260 in chapter XVI, the cult of Margaret was continuous. The impetus to collect and publish the *Miracula* may have been associated with the translation. The prose of the *Miracula* reveals this author as fully aware of the forms of thought and composition in all the earlier monuments of the Scottish Latin tradition.

When our authors began to create Scottish Latin literature, they turned, in the absence of any local precedents, to sound models. Grounding all their texts in the Latinity of Jerome's *Biblia Vulgata*, they made other connections to Late Latin learning through Isidore of Seville in *Cronica de Origine Antiquorum Pictorum* and *Vita Sancti Reguli* and Symeon of Glasgow's *Vita Sancti Seruani*, through Sulpicius Seuerus in Symeon's *Vita Sancti Kentigerni*.

They made connections to Cambro-Latin learning through Gildas *De Excidio Britanniae* and *Historia Brittonum* and Geoffrey of Monmouth's *Historia Regum Britannie* and *Annales Cambriae* in *Cronica de Origine Antiquorum Pictorum* and *Vita Sancti Reguli* and Jocelin's *Vitae Sanctorum Kentigerni et Waldeui*.

They made connections to Hiberno-Latin learning through regnal and genealogical lists and topographical literature. The account of immersion of Margaret's Gospel Book may owe something to Adomnán's statement that manuscripts written by Saint Columba were impervious to water. There are other connections to Adomnán in Simeon's *Versus in Sanctum Columbam*, composed to adorn a manuscript of Adomnán's *Vita Sancti Columbae*, and in Symeon of Glasgow's *Vita Sancti Kentigerni*, which quotes Adomnán's *Praefatiuncula* to the same work.

There is, in accordance with both Cambro-Latin and Hiberno-Latin models, but with none other known to the present writer, synchrony of Scottish with ancient Mediterranean and specifically Roman history in *De Situ Albanie* and *Cronica Regum Scottorum*.

Our authors made connections to Anglo-Latin learning in the *Cronica de Mailros*, which refers both explicitly by name and implicitly in its numerical structure to the work of the Venerable Bede, in Symeon of Glasgow's *Vita Sancti Kentigerni*, which takes as a model Symeon of Durham's alleged treatment of Saint Cuthbert, in the anonymous *Vita Sancte Bege*, which refers to Bede, and in *De Subiectione Ecclesie Candide Case*, which cites evidence *in hystoria et ueteribus Anglorum uoluminibus*.

Symeon of Glasgow practised an artifice shared with John the Evangelist, with Æthelstan the Chaplain, author of *Beowulf*, and with Dante, in naming and referring to himself while appearing to consider others.[21]

We read praise of Margaret in the verses prefixed to her copy of the Gospels, in Turgot's *Vita Margaritae Reginae* and the *Miracula Sancte Margarite* and the *Cronica Regum Scottorum*.

We read of Melrose in the 'Chronicle of the Kings of Alba', the *Cronica Regum Scottorum*, the *Vita Sancti Waltheui* by Jocelin of Furness, the *Eulogium* by Ralph of Melrose, who also mentions Waltheof, and the *Cronica de Mailros*. Melrose may have been the centre in which a single editor revised all the texts of the Poppleton manuscript to form a coherent collection. It was certainly an eminent centre for composition of historical, hagiographic, diplomatic, and forensic oratorical prose as well as historical verse.

We read praise of Glasgow and Saint Kentigern and Bishop Herbert in William of Glasgow's *Carmen de Morte Sumerledi* and in Symeon of Glasgow's *Vita Sancti Kentigerni*. We read of another Bishop of Glasgow in the oldest of the extant Glaswegian episcopal *acta*, of another in the Prologue to the *Vita Sancti Kentigerni* addressed by Jocelin of Furness to Bishop Jocelin, who is celebrated also in the Eulogy by Ralph of Melrose.

We see also appropriation of the heroes of earlier Insular traditions. As early as the ninth century the author of the *Historia Brittonum* wrote that Palladius, the missionary to the Irish, had died among the Picts,[22]

> Et profectus est ille Palladius de Hibernia
> Et peruenit ad Brittanniam
> Et ibi defunctus est in terra Pictorum,

as if to ground in Scotland the first bishop sent to the Irish believing in Christ.

As Patrick states that his grandfather was a *presbyter* and his father a *diaconus* and a *decurio* who owned land, a *uillula*, and slaves of both sexes, in †*Bannauem Taburniae*, perhaps *Bannauenta Berniae*, he must have lived in a civilian zone of Roman Britain, probably somewhere in southeastern Wales or along the Severn estuary, where the Ordnance Survey maps show large numbers of villas, and where capture by pirates would be easier than in a northern inland or military zone with few villas and fewer civilian bureaucrats.[23] But in the period we have been considering Patrick was claimed for Strathclyde. In the *Vita Quarta Sancti Patricii*, extant in a unique manuscript, London, British Library, MS Additional 19890, written about A.D. 1000, the hagiographer tells us, *parentes eius in regionem Srato Cluade perrexerunt in qua terra conceptus est Patricius.*[24]

---

21 Howlett, *British Books in Biblical Style*, pp. 81–2, 531–40.
22 Howlett, *Cambro-Latin Compositions*, p. 75.
23 Howlett, *Liber Epistolarum Sancti Patricii Episcopi*, pp. 15, 52, 116–18.
24 *BCLL*, no. 366 p. 107. *Four Latin Lives of St. Patrick*, ed. Ludwig Bieler, *Scriptores Latini Hiberniae* VIII (Dublin Institute for Advanced Studies, 1971), pp. 47–114 at 51.

Similarly Gildas, who was ill-informed about the northern Roman walls and about the geography of southeastern England, seems to have written *De Excidio Britanniae* in A.D. 540 somewhere around what is now Wiltshire and to have attacked rulers of what is now Devon, Dyfed, and Gwynedd. But in the period we have been considering Gildas also was claimed for Strathclyde. The first sentence of *Vita Prima Sancti Gildae* names the saint as *Beatus Gildas Arecluta fertilissima regione oriundus.*[25] In the first sentence of the *Vita Sancti Gildae* by Caradog of Llancarfan *Nau fuit rex Scotie nobilissimus regum aquilonalium qui XXIIII filios habuit uictores bellicosos quorum unus nominabatur Gildas.*[26]

This, like the alienation of property from Durham, the richest and most powerful church in northern England, and its appropriation to Glasgow, suggests the importance of Glasgow during the period we have been considering, much as the Catalogue of Ships in the *Iliad* and the list of sites along the route of the Exodus include names of places that had not existed at the supposed dates of the 'historical' events, but had become important by the time of the literary accounts of them. Association of Patrick and Gildas with Strathclyde may be part of an imaginative attempt to enrich the historic antiquity of Scotland by including in it the very founders of the traditions of the British and the Irish.

All the texts we have been considering are monuments of a coherent literary culture, in which writers of prose and verse, of *belles lettres* and diplomatic instruments, of topography, history, hagiography, and theology, even those with opposing political views, spoke to each other in the same language. Even Jocelin of Furness, condescending to the defects of a supposedly inferior predecessor, revised and recast Symeon of Glasgow's *Vita Sancti Kentigerni* from within the same tradition of thought and composition, using identical structural components.[27]

Two features among many make Scottish Latin literature remarkable. One is that at the beginnings late in the eleventh century its authors, unlike the neighbouring Welsh and Irish and English, had no ancient tradition of continuous composition in both Latin and one vernacular literary language. By the end of the eleventh century Englishmen had to cope with both English and French, but no other Insular peoples had within their borders such large numbers of speakers of languages as diverse as Cumbrian Brittonic, Pictish, Gaelic, Norse, English, and French. That may be one reason for the zeal with which our

25 *BCLL*, no. 914 p. 250. *Vita Gildae Auctore Monacho Ruiensi*, ed. and transl. Hugh Williams, Cymmrodorion Record Series III (London: David Nutt, 1901), pp. 322–89 at 322.

26 *BCLL*, no. 37 p. 17. *Vita Gildae Auctore Caradoco Lancarbanensi, Ibid.*, pp. 394–413 at 394. Howlett, *Celtic Latin Tradition*, pp. 346–51.

27 For similar condescension by Giraldus Cambrensis to the work of his refined predecessor Rhygyfarch ap Sulien see Howlett, *Cambro-Latin Compositions*, pp. 138–41, and consider the strictures of Aelred of Rievaulx about the earlier hagiography of Ninian, of William of Newburgh about the prose of Gildas, *sermo admodum impolitus atque insipidus, Ibid.*, p. 55.

authors took to Latin. But even that hardly accounts for the other feature, the astonishing speed with which the literature sprang into existence, from nothing to a considerable library, in which every extant text is more than competent. In this Scottish Latin authors may resemble the authors who created Old French literature in Anglo-Norman England.[28] They may resemble authors like Godric of Finchale and Reginald of Wretham, who composed verse at the very nadir of the fortunes of English as a literary language, affirming the continuing validity of their tradition.[29] They may resemble eleventh-century Cambro-Latin authors like Rhygyfarch ap Sulien and Ieuan ap Sulien and Lifris of Llancarfan, who tried to define their culture in terms apprehensible to Welshmen and Normans alike, creating cultural defences against the invasive expansionism of Norman military and ecclesiastical rulers. The English in Scotland may have tried to define themselves as distinct from the Normanized English, to create cultural bulwarks that might help them to avoid the political and ecclesiastical fate of the English in England, of the Welsh, of the Irish, all at the hands of the Normans. In this enterprise one notes that all of the authors whose names we know were English. Among the others Symeon of Glasgow tells us explicitly that he was a newcomer to Scotland, and the author of the *Cronica de Mailros* tells us that he was an Angle. The author of *De Situ Albanie* gives the name of the Firth of Forth as English *Scottewatre*, though he says he is reporting it *Romane* 'in French', and William of Glasgow provides in his title an English soubriquet *Sumerledus site bi þe king*.

Margaret was the sister of Eadgar the Ætheling, the daughter of Eadweard the Exile, and the granddaughter of Eadmund Ironside. She and Malcolm III stipulated in a memorandum of agreement with the community of Saint Cuthbert at Durham that *Anniuersariusque eorum festiue sicut regis Ethelstani singulis annis celebretur* 'their anniversary should be celebrated festally just as King Æthelstan's in separate years'. This ends a composition that contains 894 letters and spaces between words, coincident, perhaps, with the year of Æthelstan's birth, A.D. 894,[30] a phenomenon that makes sense only if Margaret and Malcolm intended to align themselves with a tradition of English royal patronage of Durham, like Æthelstan's but from the North, a policy consistent with Malcolm's presence at the laying of the cornerstone of Durham Cathedral. Margaret's spiritual advisor and biographer was Turgot Prior of Durham, an Englishman with an English form of a Norse name *Þorgautr*. Margaret's sons Kings Eadgar and Alexander and David were half English, and they married English wives. The appeal to Earl David to confirm Eadgar's gift to the community of Saint Cuthbert at Durham came from an Englishman with a Norse name, *Thor Longus*, whose brother bore an English name *Leofwine*.

28 Howlett, *The English Origins of Old French Literature*.
29 Howlett, *British Books in Biblical Style*, pp. 589–613.
30 Howlett, *Sealed from Within*, pp. 87–8.

Let us consider our texts from another perspective, that of form and genre. In verse we have compositions in quantitative Classical hexameters and rhyming leonine hexameters and rhythmic pentadecasyllabic lines that exhibit both internal and end-rhymes, this last perhaps in imitation of the oldest extant Latin verses composed in these islands, in pentadecasyllables.[31] In prose we have both quantitative clausulae and rhythmic cursus. Among diplomatic texts we have a memorandum of agreement between Malcolm III and Margaret and the monks of Durham, and charters by royal and episcopal and lay donors, as well as royal confirmations of others' grants both ecclesiastical and lay. Among historical texts we have mytho-historical topography and distinct but related histories of the Brittonic and Pictish and Gaelic and English parts of the kingdom, as well as ecclesiastical history. Among hagiographic texts we have Lives of the first apostle and Brittonic and Gaelic and English saints, as well as royal hagiography. Among religious texts we have liturgical prayers and sermons and funeral oratory and discursive exegesis of Biblical texts. There are no duplicates. Even the Lives of Saint Kentigern are utterly distinct in focus and style. Allowing for accidents of survival, it is difficult not to infer from the extant texts that our writers undertook deliberately to supply for the new *Regnum Scottorum* a defined range of literary compositions like those that existed already among neighbouring peoples. These men created a canon of texts, calculated to include all the varied cultural traditions of the kingdom, and to give to the united whole historical depth, a semblance of antiquity not only comparable with the traditions of the Welsh and the Irish and the English, but older than any of them, as old as the foundation of the Roman Republic.

In the thirty-three texts considered above one might see, in artistic terms the creation of Scottish Latin literature, in political terms the literary definition of the Kingdom of Scotland, in both respects a direct response by Englishmen to the Norman Conquest of England. Englishmen successfully defined Scotland as a place in which to preserve their Englishness, not by exclusive English nationalism, but by inclusive statecraft, an imaginative attempt to create for the first time in Europe a *regnum* that was based upon neither a single people nor a single language.[32] Except for the Treaty of Falaise the attempt succeeded in some measure for many centuries, and the monuments of that enterprise may interest Scots who want to define themselves at the beginning of the twenty-first

---

31 'Saint Sechnall's Hymn *Audite Omnes Amantes Deum*' in Howlett, *Celtic Latin Tradition*, pp. 138–52.

32 The nearest analogue might be the Normans, but they were a Northern military elite who captured first a duchy and later a kingdom, the inhabitants of which they did not exterminate. They incorporated talented foreigners, Bretons and Flemings and Italians like Lanfranc and Anselm, into an existing elite group, and they all spoke French. This is quite different from, and less difficult than, trying to forge a kingdom from at least six distinct ethnic groups, speaking at least six different languages, and lacking any common ancient institutions. See R.H.C. Davis, *The Normans and their Myth* (London: Thames and Hudson, 1976).

century. But in another respect these literary monuments, having long outlived their original purpose, can delight and instruct by affording windows into the minds of intelligent men, separated from us by nine hundred years, but apprehensible. Perhaps some exist who can see through and behind what these men wrote to 'what actually happened'. But more accessible is the 'form' of what they wished to communicate to us. This also is 'history'. It was theirs, and it can be ours.

IMPLICATIONS

We see in all these texts, liturgical, diplomatic, poetic, historical, hagiographic, theological, epistolary, and administrative, that particular details participate in elaborate and tightly composed structures, from which they derive their meanings, sometimes partly, sometimes entirely. Many of the details cannot be understood without consideration of their structural function. Abstraction of such details, and comparison with other details similarly abstracted from their sources, is not a reliable way to construct a view of Scottish (or indeed any) history. To present snippets of 'information', filleted and diced, without their context, and above all without their original language, to say the least, misrepresents the sources. It can hardly satisfy a student interested in discovering who really did what when.

Those who live during the second half of the twentieth century know how difficult it is to discover 'the truth' about such voluminously reported events as the deaths of John Fitzgerald Kennedy, Marilyn Monroe, and Diana Princess of Wales. Discovery of 'what happened' from the ninth century to the twelfth is at this remove more difficult than that. But discovery of an author's thought as expressed in a wrought literary composition is not only possible, it is easy. The preceding analyses suggest that one can read much more in such texts than modern scholars, literary and historical alike, have yet read, and with fair certainty of recovering authorial intentions as distinct from modern readers' suppositions introduced into or otherwise imposed upon the texts. There are two principal requirements: to rid one's mind of the baggage of modern critical theory and to acquire the philological competence to deal with the texts first in their original forms and then in the forms in which they have been transmitted, in that order. *Incipiamus.*

in die Sancti Andreae
Anno Domini MCMXCVIII
Oxoniae

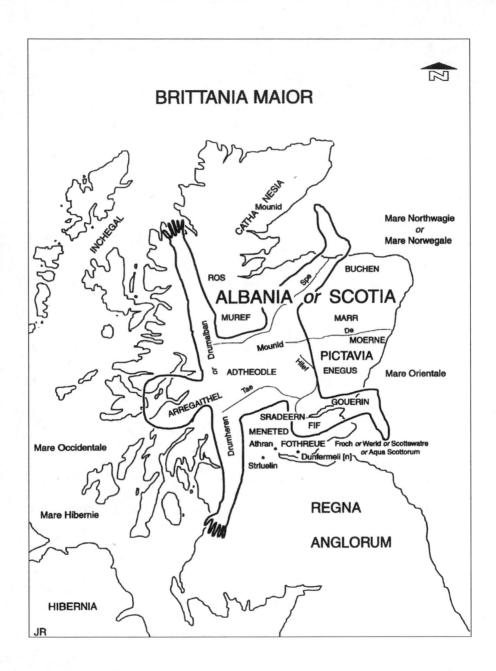

Map of Scotland with the shape of a man superimposed as envisaged in *De Situ Albanie*. Place-names and descriptions are taken from the original text. The map was created by David Howlett, drawn by J. Renny.

INDICES

I. INDEX OF MANUSCRIPTS

City	Library	Shelfmark	Page
Cambridge	Corpus Christi College	139	24–6
	University Library	Ii.6.32	1–2
Dublin	Archbishop Marsh's Library	Z.4.5.5	86–7, 116–18
Durham	Dean and Chapter	B.IV.24	174–5
		Cartularium Vetus	10–11, 13–14
		Miscellaneous Charter 554	6–7
		Miscellaneous Charter 722	12–13
Edinburgh	National Library of Scotland		
	Advocates' Manuscripts	Adv.MS.16.1.10	153–4
		Adv.MS.34.5.1	151
London	British Library	Additional 19890	197
		Additional 25014	185–6
		Cotton Claudius B.III	143–4
		Cotton Domitian A.VII	199
		Cotton Faustina B.IV	98–101
		Cotton Faustina B.IX	181
		Cotton Tiberius D.III	19–20, 107–8, 111–12
		Cotton Titus A.XIX	91–2
		Cotton Vitellius C.VIII	116–18
Madrid	Patrimonio Nacional Biblioteca	II.2097	103–4, 124–6
Oxford	Bodleian Library	Lat. Liturg. F.5	15–16
		Rawlinson G.38	131–5
Paris	Bibliothèque Nationale de France	latin 4126	29–32, 40–1, 44–7, 52–4, 64–70, 76–9

II. INDEX OF FACSIMILES

III. INDEX OF
'A BIBLIOGRAPHY OF CELTIC-LATIN
LITERATURE 400–1200'

IIII. INDEX OF
'A HANDLIST OF THE LATIN WRITERS OF GREAT
BRITAIN AND IRELAND BEFORE 1540'

V.
INDEX OF 'EARLY SCOTTISH CHARTERS'

VI. INDEX OF DATES